Lecture Notes in Computer Science 15533

The series Lecture Notes in Computer Science (LNCS), including its subseries Lecture Notes in Artificial Intelligence (LNAI) and Lecture Notes in Bioinformatics (LNBI), has established itself as a medium for the publication of new developments in computer science and information technology research, teaching, and education.

LNCS enjoys close cooperation with the computer science R & D community, the series counts many renowned academics among its volume editors and paper authors, and collaborates with prestigious societies. Its mission is to serve this international community by providing an invaluable service, mainly focused on the publication of conference and workshop proceedings and postproceedings. LNCS commenced publication in 1973.

Kamel Adi · Simon Bourdeau · Christel Durand ·
Valérie Viet Triem Tong · Alina Dulipovici ·
Yvon Kermarrec · Joaquin Garcia-Alfaro
Editors

Foundations and Practice of Security

17th International Symposium, FPS 2024
Montréal, QC, Canada, December 9–11, 2024
Revised Selected Papers, Part II

Springer

Editors
Kamel Adi
Université du Québec en Outaouais
Gatineau, QC, Canada

Simon Bourdeau
Université du Québec à Montréal
Montréal, QC, Canada

Christel Durand
Deloitte
Toronto, ON, Canada

Valérie Viet Triem Tong
CentraleSupélec
Cesson-Sévigné, France

Alina Dulipovici
HEC Montréal
Montréal, QC, Canada

Yvon Kermarrec
IMT Atlantique
Brest, France

Joaquin Garcia-Alfaro
Institut Polytechnique de Paris
Palaiseau, France

ISSN 0302-9743 ISSN 1611-3349 (electronic)
Lecture Notes in Computer Science
ISBN 978-3-031-87495-6 ISBN 978-3-031-87496-3 (eBook)
https://doi.org/10.1007/978-3-031-87496-3

This Springer imprint is published by the registered company Springer Nature Switzerland AG
The registered company address is: Gewerbestrasse 11, 6330 Cham, Switzerland

Preface

This two-volume set LNCS 15532 and LNCS 15533 constitutes the refereed proceedings of the 17th International Symposium on Foundations and Practice of Security (FPS 2024), held in Montréal, Canada, in December 9–11, 2024 and hosted by HEC Montréal.

The event brought together more than 200 researchers and practitioners from 20 countries, all working in fields such as security, privacy, cyber resilience, and related disciplines. This global gathering provided a platform for participants to share knowledge, present cutting-edge research, and discuss challenges and opportunities in these critical areas.

In today's increasingly interconnected world, protecting data and infrastructure is essential for the smooth functioning of all aspects of daily life. The growing dependence on digital systems has elevated the importance of security, privacy, and cyber resilience as distinct topics, but they are interrelated fields of scientific investigation and research. These domains are characterized by multifaceted challenges that require interdisciplinary collaboration, drawing on expertise from mathematics, computer science, information systems, management, human factors, and other related areas.

In addition to exploring technical features of cybersecurity, the 17th Symposium placed a strong emphasis on innovative behavioral research aimed at enhancing privacy and cyber resilience. This approach underscores the importance of understanding human factors and societal dynamics in designing effective solutions to cyber threats.

The 28 full papers and 11 short papers presented in these two books were carefully reviewed and selected from 75 submissions. On average, each paper was reviewed (single blind) by three program committee members, and there were several online discussions in case of divergent evaluations. The selected papers cover a range of topics such as Protection and Data Management Issues; Cybersecurity, Ethics and AI; Privacy in Complex Systems; and New Trends in Advanced Cryptographic Protocols.

The conference was complemented by two keynotes on major expected changes with the consolidation of quantum computing and new perspectives on how organization culture contributes to mitigation and innovation in cybersecurity.

The FPS (Foundations and Practice of Security) series of conferences serves as a forum for the exchange of theoretical and practical ideas addressing privacy, security, and cyber resilience issues in interconnected systems. Its objectives extend beyond academic presentations, aiming to foster scientific collaboration, establish joint research initiatives, and promote student exchanges among institutions engaged in this rapidly evolving field. By facilitating such interactions, the conference contributes to the advancement of knowledge and the development of strategies to tackle the complex challenges of the digital age.

We are also grateful to the program committee members for their careful and insightful reviews of the papers submitted. Joaquin Garcia-Alfaro and his mastery of EasyChair performed an excellent job for the collection of the final version of the papers and forging these proceedings.

Finally, we wish to express our sincere gratitude to HEC Montréal, our hosting organization, for providing exceptional facilities that greatly contributed to the success of the event. We also acknowledge the valuable contributions of the sponsors (IMC^2 - Institut Multidisciplinaire en cybersécurité et cyberrésilience, Portage Cybertech, Nymion Solutions, ISACA section de Montreal, Banque Nationale du Canada, and Cybereco), whose innovative proposals and tools in cybersecurity helped create a productive and professional atmosphere, fostering rigorous and meaningful discussions and interactions between the participants.

January 2025

Alina Dulipovici
Yvon Kermarrec
Kamel Adi
Simon Bourdeau
Christel Durand
Valérie Viet Triem Tong

Organization

General Chairs

Alina Dulipovici	HEC Montréal, Canada
Yvon Kermarrec	IMT Atlantique, France

Program Committee Chairs

Kamel Adi	University of Quebec in Outaouais, Canada
Simon Bourdeau	Université du Québec à Montréal, Canada
Christel Durand	Deloitte, Canada
Valérie Viet Triem Tong	CentraleSupélec, France

Local Organization Chair

Mickaël Ringeval	HEC Montréal, Canada

Publication Chair

Joaquin Garcia-Alfaro	Institut Polytechnique de Paris, France

Publicity Chairs

Paria Shirani	University of Ottawa, Canada
Reda Yaich	IRT SystemX, France
Raphaël Khoury	Université du Québec en Outaouais, Canada

Steering Committee

Frédéric Cuppens	Polytechnique Montréal, Canada
Nora Cuppens	Polytechnique Montréal, Canada
Mourad Debbabi	Concordia University, Canada
Joaquin Garcia-Alfaro	Institut Polytechnique de Paris, France

Evangelos Kranakis	Carleton University, Canada
Pascal Lafourcade	University of Clermont Auvergne, France
Jean-Yves Marion	Université de Lorraine, France
Rei Safavi-Naini	Calgary University, Canada
Nadia Tawbi	Laval University, Canada

Program Committee

Kamel Adi	Université du Québec en Outaouais, Canada
Esma Aïmeur	University of Montreal, Canada
Furkan Alaca	Queen's University, Canada
Abdelmalek Benzekri	Université de Toulouse, France
Simon Bertrand	Laval University, Canada
Simon Bourdeau	Université du Québec en Outaouais, Canada
Jérémy Buisson	École de l'Air et de l'Espace, France
Ana-Rosa Cavalli	Institut Polytechnique de Paris, France
Yannick Chevalier	Université de Toulouse, France
Kimberly Cornell	University at Albany, USA
Nora Cuppens	Polytechnique Montréal, Canada
Alina Dulipovici	HEC Montréal, Canada
Benoit Dupont	University of Montréal, Canada
Christel Durand	Deloitte, Canada
Jamal El Hachem	Université de Bretagne Sud, France
Sebastien Gambs	Université du Québec à Montréal, Canada
Joaquin Garcia-Alfaro	Institut Polytechnique de Paris, France
Talal Halabi	Université Laval, Canada
Sylvain Hallé	Université du Québec à Chicoutimi, Canada
Khaled Hamouid	Gustave Eiffel University, France
Daniel Hono	University at Albany, USA
Li Huang	University at Albany, USA
Abdessamad Imine	Université de Lorraine, France
Padmavathi Iyer	University at Albany, USA
Jason Jaskolka	Carleton University, Canada
Guy-Vincent Jourdan	University of Ottawa, Canada
Yvon Kermarrec	IMT Atlantique, France
Kobra Khanmohammadi	Concordia University, Canada
Raphael Khoury	Université du Québec en Outaouais, Canada
Hyoungshick Kim	Sungkyunkwan University, South Korea
Youcef Korichi	Université Laval, Canada
Hyungjoon Koo	Sungkyunkwan University, South Korea
Gildas Kouko	Université Laval, Canada

Achin Kulshrestha	Google Inc., USA
Romain Laborde	Université de Toulouse, France
Pascal Lafourcade	University of Clermont Auvergne, France
Maryline Laurent	Institut Polytechnique de Paris, France
Hyung Koo Lee	HEC Montréal, Canada
Olivier Levillain	Institut Polytechnique de Paris, France
Luigi Logrippo	Université du Québec en Outaouais, Canada
Wissam Mallouli	Montimage, France
Jean-Yves Marion	Université de Lorraine, France
Daiki Miyahara	University of Electro-Communications, Japan
Mohamed Mosbah	University of Bordeaux, France
Djedjiga Mouheb	University of Sharjah, United Arab Emirates
Paliath Narendran	University at Albany, USA
Omer Nguena Timo	Université du Québec en Outaouais, Canada
Huu Nghia Nguyen	Montimage, France
Manh-Dung Nguyen	Montimage, France
Mawloud Omar	Université Bretagne Sud, France
Isabel Praça	Instituto Superior de Engenharia do Porto, Portugal
Josue Ruiz	University at Albany, USA
Khosro Salmani	Mount Royal University, Canada
Giada Sciarretta	Fondazione Bruno Kessler, Italy
Florence Sèdes	Université de Toulouse, France
Renaud Sirdey	Commissariat à l'Energie Atomique, France
Nabil Tabbane	SupCom Tunis, Tunisia
Rania Taleb	Université du Québec à Montréal, Canada
Nadia Tawbi	Laval University, Canada
Sadegh Torabi	Concordia University, Canada
Valeria Valdés Ríos	Université Paris-Saclay, France
Valérie Viet Triem Tong	CentraleSupélec, France
Nicola Zannone	Eindhoven University of Technology, The Netherlands

Contents – Part II

New Trends of Machine Leaning and AI Applied to Cybersecurity

Contents – Part I

Cybersecurity and AI When Applied to Emerging Technologies

Cybersecurity and Ethics

Cybersecurity and Privacy in Connected and Autonomous Systems for IoT, Smart Environments, and Critical Infrastructure

Preserving Privacy and Maintaining Trust for End Users in a Complex and Numeric Cyberspace

Another Walk for Monchi

Riccardo Taiello[1(✉)], Emre Tosun[2(✉)], Alberto Ibarrondo[3(✉)], Hervé Chabanne[4(✉)], and Melek Önen[2(✉)]

[1] Inria, Sophia Antipolis, Biot, France
riccardo.taiello@eurecom.fr
[2] Eurecom, Sophia Antipolis, Biot, France
melek.onen@eurecom.fr
[3] Arcium, Zurich, Switzerland
ibarrond@eurecom.fr
[4] Idemia & Telecom Paris, Paris, France
chabanne@telecom-paristech.fr

Abstract. Monchi is a new protocol aimed at privacy-preserving biometric identification. It begins with scores computation in the encrypted domain thanks to homomorphic encryption and ends with comparisons of these scores to a given threshold with function secret sharing. We here study the integration in that context of scores computation techniques recently introduced by Bassit et al. that eliminate homomorphic multiplications by replacing them by lookup tables. First, we extend this lookup tables biometric recognition solution by adding the use of function secret sharing for the final comparison of scores. Then, we introduce a two-party computation of the scores with lookup tables which fits nicely together with the function secret sharing scores comparison. Our solutions accommodate well with the flight boarding use case introduced by Monchi.

Keywords: Privacy-Preserving biometric systems · Homomorphic Encryption · Two-Party Computation · Function Secret Sharing · MFBR schemes

1 Introduction

We investigate the use of biometric identification in an airplane boarding use case, where passengers are authorized to enter the plane only if their faces are identified with respect to an early prepared, privacy-preserving database of registered passengers' faces. Set on this scenario, Monchi [11,12] makes use of (i) a homomorphic encryption (HE) scheme and relevant packing solutions to protect both the live templates and the reference ones stored in the database and enable the computation of scalar products between them, and, inspired by Funshade [10], (ii) a Function Secret Sharing (FSS) scheme to obliviously compare the score obtained from the scalar product to a threshold. Combining these two primitives enables Monchi to only reveal the final authorization decision without disclosing the identification scores.

K. Adi et al. (Eds.): FPS 2024, LNCS 15533, pp. 3–11, 2025.
https://doi.org/10.1007/978-3-031-87496-3_1

We revisit that same goal, aiming to optimize even further the computation cost incurred by the scalar products over encrypted templates. In [3,4], authors propose a method to compute these identification scores over encrypted data through the use of lookup tables that entirely replace the multiplication operations. [4] reports a faster runtime by a factor of 2 to 3 orders of magnitude on facial features while keeping the biometric accuracy of the system. We integrate this multiplication-free scheme while making it compatible with the underlying BFV encryption scheme [1,7,8] and the FSS scheme [10].

To ensure the confidentiality of the values in the table and the computations of the scores, we also propose – in addition to HE – to study the use of two-party computation (2PC), and more specifically, additive secret sharing [16]. As no multiplications are needed, no interactions between the two parties are neither required. In the next Sect. 2, we detail how multiplication-free recognition (MFBR) biometric schemes in the encrypted domain work. Section 3 describes our first proposal, named MonchiLuts, where MFBR LUTs replace multiplications with HE. Section 4 gives our second proposal, called Monchichi, where we implement scores computation in 2PC. Section 5 is devoted to the confidentiality of live templates. Finally, Sect. 7 gives conclusive remarks.

2 Multiplication-Free Biometric Recognition (MFBR)

In biometric systems, discriminative features are extracted from images of captured biometric traits (e.g., faces, fingerprints...) and transformed into vectors called *templates* via the execution of a neural network model. Two templates are assumed belonging to the same person if they are close with respect to some distance. To check whether a person is present in a database, scores of his live template against existing reference templates are computed – in Monchi, scores for faces' templates are computed by a scalar product measuring their cosine similarity – and then compared with a given threshold which depends of the underlying biometric system (see [14] for more details).

To ease their use with cryptographic techniques, components of templates are often quantized. We denote $Y = (y_1, \ldots, y_d)$ (resp. $X = (x_1, \ldots, x_d)$) to a quantized reference (resp. live) template with d components of n bits each (Fig. 1).

The first Multiplication-Free Biometric Recognition scheme was introduced in [2] by Bassit et al. This work has then been extended in [3] and further in [4]. MFBR schemes substitute scalar products for the scores computation with well-crafted LookUp Tables (LUT) and additions. These system-dependent LUT provide, for each of the $i \in \{1, \ldots, d\}$ components, a "local" score between a live template component x_i and its corresponding reference template component y_i. The partial scores are stored in a 2D matrix T_i, accessible by indexing the desired row with the value of y_i and the column with x_i. We compute the score s as:

$$s = T_1(y_1, x_1) + \ldots + T_d(y_d, x_d) \tag{1}$$

where $T_i(y_i, x_i)$ represents the lookup (indexing) operation.

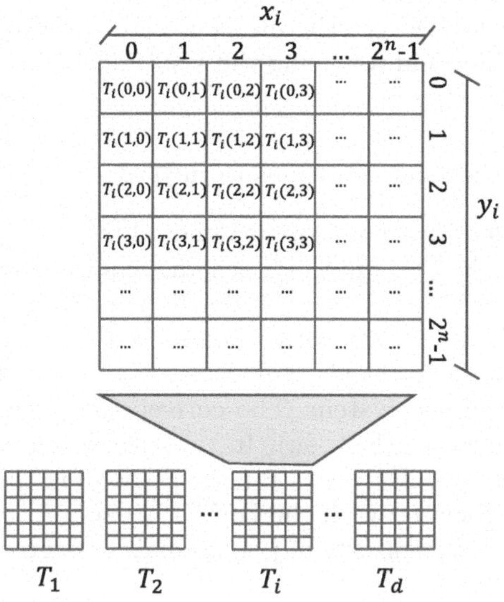

Fig. 1. Look-Up Table visualization.

Equation 1 can be easily adopted in the encrypted domain by virtue of homomorphic encryption (HE) or arithmetic secret sharing [16]. Instead of encrypting the plain reference templates directly, rows $T_i(y_i, .)$ $\forall i$ are stored in database, now returning the corresponding looked-up values encrypted or secret-shared when queried. A cleartext[1] live template $(x_1, \ldots, x_d)$ triggering a verification, leads to picking all $T_i(y_i, x_i)$ and then adding together the encrypted or secret-shared partial score. No multiplications are needed.

3 MONCHILUTS: MONCHI with MFBR LUTs

This section describes our first proposal – called MONCHILUTS – that combines the use of MFBR LUTs and function secret sharing.

Participants. Besides a trusted setup realized by a trusted key server, here are the main participants of our identification protocol (Fig 2):

- BIP (Biometric Identity Provider) holding the database containing LUTs corresponding to the reference templates and responsible for the computation of the encrypted masked scores between a freshly live template and each reference template.
- Gate, in charge of capturing the live biometric template of the users requesting access and forwarding them to the BIP, after protection, during the identification phase. Later on, Gate receives the final decision on this actual identification and allows or not the user to access the plane.

[1] Much like in [3], the use-case must support this requirement.

- P_j, (two) parties who decrypt the masked score and evaluate its comparison operation to the threshold following the FSS Funshade scheme.

Notations. We use the same notations as in [11]:

- The $n\log(d)$-bit identification score is denoted by s.
- Each evaluation of the FSS Funshade scheme requires the use of a fresh mask, which we denote by r. Let $\hat{s} = s + r$ be the masked score, i.e., the input of the FSS Interval Containment gate [5] employed for comparison.
- The encryption of the masked score is: $c_{\hat{s}} = Enc(\hat{s}, \mathrm{pk})$ where pk stands for the public key of the system. The corresponding private key is sk. The decryption is denoted as $Dec(., \mathrm{sk})$. In practice, as in MONCHI, the private key is shared among the $P_j, j = 0, 1$, each P_j holding the share $\langle \mathrm{sk} \rangle_j$.
- The parameters associated with the BFV scheme are:
  - The plaintext space consists of polynomials of degree at most $N - 1$ with coefficients in $\mathbb{Z}_t$.
  - The ciphertext modulus $R_q = \mathbb{Z}_q[X]/(X^N + 1)$ is set based on the security parameter q.
  - $e_i \leftarrow \chi_{R_q}$ stands for some error term (see Appendix A of [15]).

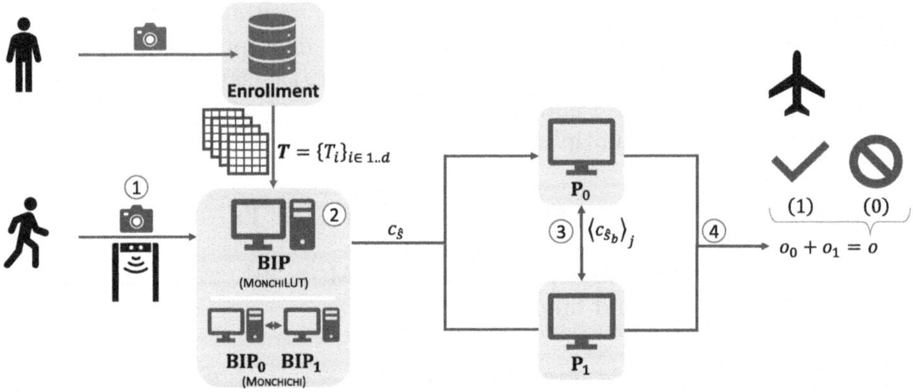

Fig. 2. Biometric access control system using MONCHICHI's protocol.

Score Evaluation by the BIP. For one reference and one live template $Y = (y_1, \dots, y_d)$ and $X = (x_1, \dots, x_d)$, BIP has to obliviously compute the encryption of a score s masked with r in $\mathbb{Z}_{2^n}$. This operation is no longer performed with multiplications as in the original MONCHI scheme but instead by using LUTs.

For each reference template, $Y = (y_1, \ldots, y_d)$, let $S_{Y,i}(.) = T_i(y_i, .) + r_i \mod 2^n, i = 1, \ldots, d$ with $r_1 + \ldots + r_d = r$. The masked score between a live template $X = (x_1, \ldots, x_d)$ and Y, $\hat{s} = s + r \mod 2^n$ can thus be computed as:

$$\hat{s} = S_{Y,1}(x_1) + \ldots + S_{Y,d}(x_d) \mod 2^n \tag{2}$$

We write $ES_{Y,i}, i = 1, \ldots, d$ to denote their encrypted counterparts, i.e. $ES_{Y,i}(x_i) = Enc(S_{Y,i}(x_i), \text{pk})$, for all the x_i's (for the sake of simplicity, mentions to mask r have been omitted).

Hence, given one live template X, for each of its d features, the BIP will look-up and retrieve the relevant cells from the corresponding LUT.

FUNSHADE [10], i.e. the FSS protocol also used in [11] to compare scores with a pre-defined threshold, requires as input the masked score which is defined in $\mathbb{Z}_{2^n}$ where n is a small integer; typically, $n = 16$.

Correctness. Our first proposal can be described as follows:

1. The Gate gets a new live quantized template $X = (x_1, \ldots, x_d)$ and sends it to the BIP.

   For each reference template:

2. The BIP computes the encrypted masked score and sends this $c_{\hat{s}}$ to the P_j's.
3. The two P_j's decrypt the result. Let $c_{\hat{s}} = (c_{\hat{s}_a}, c_{\hat{s}_b})$. Each P_j computes: $\langle c_{\hat{s}_b} \rangle_j = \langle sk \rangle_j c_{\hat{s}_b} + e_i$ with $e_i \leftarrow \chi_{R_q}$ and then sends it to the other[2]. Finally, each P_j gets the masked score as: $\hat{s} = \left[\left[\frac{t}{q} \left[(c_{\hat{s}_a} + \langle c_{\hat{s}_b} \rangle_0 + \langle c_{\hat{s}_b} \rangle_1) \right]_q \right]_t \right]_{2^n}$
4. Each P_j evaluates whether the score is under a threshold or not thanks to the FSS FUNSHADE scheme, and sends shares of this result to the Gate.

Step 4 is the same as the one in MONCHI and FUNSHADE [11]. Step 3 distributes BFV decryption [13,15] of the masked score. The correctness of our scheme thus comes from the correctness of Step 2. We know that:

$$\hat{s} = Dec(\sum_{i=1}^{d} S_{Y,i}(x_i)) \mod 2^n$$

Hence, our first proposal is correct.

4 MONCHICHI: MONCHI with Two-Party Look-Up Tables

We now describe MONCHICHI, our second proposal where the Biometric Identity Provider is implemented by 2 entities, denoted as BIP^k, $k = 0, 1$. LUTs are now secret shared among the two BIP^ks, for $k = 0, 1$, we define $S^k_{Y,i}(.)$, s.t.

$$S^0_{Y,i}(.) + S^1_{Y,i}(.) \mod 2^n = S_{Y,i}(.)$$

[2] A finer choice of noise distribution might be required to prevent certain key recovery attacks to threshold BFV schemes [6].

for all $i = 1, \ldots, d$ and all reference templates Y. Score computation (2) is implemented by each BIP^k which locally computes:

$$\hat{s}^k = S^k_{Y,1}(x_1) + \ldots + S^k_{Y,d}(x_d) \mod 2^n$$

With the introduction of the two BIPs, P_j's now receive shares of the masked scores that first need to be reconstructed by simple addition: $\hat{s} = \hat{s}^0 + \hat{s}^1 \mod 2^n$. P_j's can then launch the FSS operation and output the result of the comparison.

5 Confidentiality of Live Templates

[3,4] make use of client secret permutations to hide live template X as they are otherwise leaked by which indexes in the rows $T_i(y_i, .)$ are used. The boarding scenario of [11] cannot accommodate these permutations kept by passengers as we want them to come to cross the gates hand-free. In our scheme, LUTs are renewed at each score computation and we can implement secret permutations both at the Gate and in LUTs stored by Biometric Identity Provider(s). We thus turn the constraint to have to cope with the need to only consume single-use pre-processed data for FSS to our advantage

Permutations are not picked by clients/passengers anymore but are rather generated during the trusted setup by the system. At Step 1, Gate takes a new secret permutation for the BIP or BIP^k and applies it to the live template before sending the permuted live template to the BIP or BIP^k's. The Gate and the BIP or BIP^k's have to be synchronized as the LUTs held by BIP^k's have to take into account these permutations.

6 Performance Evaluation

We implement MonchiLuts and Monchichi in Golang like the Monchi solution [11]. Similar to Monchi, these implementations use: (i) the Lattigo implementation [13] of the (2, 2) threshold-variant of BFV, the LUT implementation from [4] the FunShade library [10] and a native Golang implementation for additive secret sharing. The code can be found in https://github.com/emretosn/another-walk-for-monchi. The performance of both solutions is evaluated through experiments executed on a single core machine with an Intel(R) Core(TM) i7-7800X CPU @ 3.50GHz and 126 GB of RAM.

For MonchiLuts, BFV parameters are set to: polynomial degree $N = 2^{11}$, ciphertext modulus size $q = 183$ bits, and plaintext modulus $t = 32$ bits, with default values for noise distributions[3]. For Monchichi, the two-party secret-sharing is executed in $Z_{2^{16}}$. Regarding the implementation of LUTs, we use the same parameters as in [4], specifically the quantization factor is set to 3 bits for LUT creation, reference, and live template. Finally, for the FSS instantiation, we also use 16-bit modular arithmetic.

[3] The final choices of noise distributions for both smudging and fresh encryption require extra care to avoid recently highlighted pitfalls [6].

To study and evaluate the performance of our protocols in the context of the airport use case ($\leq$ 1000 IDs), we use the publicly available Labeled Faces in the Wild (LFW) dataset [9], which includes 13,233 facial images of 5,749 individuals. The same pre-processing steps proposed by [11] are applied, obtaining templates of $d = 128$ features per face.

Table 1. Benchmark between MONCHILUTS and MONCHICHI protocols in terms of execution time (LUTs/FSS/Total) and communication overhead for varying dataset sizes T.

DB Size (T)	MONCHILUTS				MONCHICHI			
	Time (ms)			Comm.	Time (ms)			Comm.
	LUT	FSS	Total	(Bytes)	LUT	FSS	Total	(Bytes)
1	8.86	0.12	8.98	196730	<0.00	0.12	0.12	<10
200	1772	24	1796	196730	<0.01	24	24.01	<10
1024	9072.64	122.88	9195.52	196730	0.5	122.93	122.88	<10

Table 1 presents the execution time (in ms) and the communication overhead (in bytes) of the BIP for the different steps of an identification operation of one fresh template in MONCHILUTS and MONCHICHI. The measurements are the result of an average across 20 executions (Table 2).

Table 2. Performance metrics for multiplication, rotation, and addition.

Multiplication Time (μs)	Rotation Time (ms)	Addition Time (μs)
415.81 ± 15.38	6.89 ± 0.40	98.96 ± 5.89

Regarding the bandwidth cost, MONCHICHI only requires the transmission of a secret-shared masked score (a single value in $\mathbb{Z}_{2^{16}}$) and the final masked score, which is again a scalar value. Although as opposed to MONCHICHI, MONCHILUTS involves a single BIP, the latter sends two encrypted values to the P_i's which results in a non-negligible overhead compared to MONCHICHI.

In the flight boarding scenario with a database with 1,000 faces, MONCHICHI (with 1-core machine) outperforms the original MONCHI scheme (with 4-core machine) by 60% leveraging the comparatively lightweight look-up operations over secret shares (no HE rotations). On the other hand, MONCHILUTS exhibits significant overhead compared to MONCHI.

7 Conclusion

This work introduces two new protocols:

- MonchiLuts which is an extension of the work by Bassit et al. [3,4] to handle secure scores comparison to a threshold;
- Monchichi a full 2PC biometric identification solution combining MFBR LUTs and FSS.

These two schemes enable us to integrate at a system level the permutations needed to protect the confidentiality of live templates. These permutations were originally given to the users which forbids the hand-free boarding plane scenario introduced by Monchi. Our experiments confirm the practicability of both MonchiLuts and Monchichi for this use case.

Acknowledgements. We thank Amina Bassit for her assistance by sharing her expertise in the topic, as well as the reviewers' constructive remarks. Hervé Chabanne has been partially supported for this work by Horizon Europe project ATHENA (Grant agreement ID: 101139941).

References

1. Bajard, J.-C., Eynard, J., Hasan, M.A., Zucca, V.: A full RNS variant of FV like somewhat homomorphic encryption schemes. In: Avanzi, R., Heys, H. (eds.) SAC 2016. LNCS, vol. 10532, pp. 423–442. Springer, Cham (2017). https://doi.org/10.1007/978-3-319-69453-5_23
2. Bassit, A., Hahn, F., Peeters, J., Kevenaar, T., Veldhuis, R.N.J., Peter, A.: Fast and accurate likelihood ratio-based biometric verification secure against malicious adversaries. IEEE Trans. Inf. Forensics Secur. **16** (2021)
3. Bassit, A., Hahn, F., Veldhuis, R.N.J., Peter, A.: Multiplication-free biometric recognition for faster processing under encryption. In: IJCB. IEEE (2022)
4. Bassit, A., Hahn, F., Veldhuis, R.N.J., Peter, A.: Improved multiplication-free biometric recognition under encryption. IEEE Trans. Biom. Behav. Identity Sci. (2023). https://doi.org/10.1109/TBIOM.2023.3340306
5. Boyle, E., et al.: Function secret sharing for mixed-mode and fixed-point secure computation. In: Canteaut, A., Standaert, F.-X. (eds.) EUROCRYPT 2021. LNCS, vol. 12697, pp. 871–900. Springer, Cham (2021). https://doi.org/10.1007/978-3-030-77886-6_30
6. Checri, M., Sirdey, R., Boudguiga, A., Bultel, J.-P.: On the practical CPA D security of "exact" and threshold FHE schemes and libraries. In: Annual International Cryptology Conference, pp. 3–33. Springer, Cham (2024)
7. Fan, J., Vercauteren, F.: Somewhat practical fully homomorphic encryption. IACR Cryptol. ePrint Arch. (2012)
8. Halevi, S., Polyakov, Y., Shoup, V.: An improved RNS variant of the BFV homomorphic encryption scheme. In: Matsui, M. (ed.) CT-RSA 2019. LNCS, vol. 11405, pp. 83–105. Springer, Cham (2019). https://doi.org/10.1007/978-3-030-12612-4_5
9. Huang, G.B., Ramesh, M., Berg, T., Learned-Miller, E.: Labeled faces in the wild: a database for studying face recognition in unconstrained environments. Technical report 07-49, University of Massachusetts, Amherst (2007)

10. Ibarrondo, A., Chabanne, H., Önen, M.: Funshade: function secret sharing for two-party secure thresholded distance evaluation. Proc. Priv. Enhancing Technol. **2023**, 4 (2023)
11. Ibarrondo, A., Kerenciler, I., Chabanne, H., Despiegel, V., Önen, M.: Monchi: multi-scheme optimization for collaborative homomorphic identification. In: IH&MMSec. ACM (2024)
12. Ibarrondo, A., Kerenciler, I., Chabanne, H., Despiegel, V., Önen, M.: Monchi: multi-scheme optimization for collaborative homomorphic identification. In: IACR Cryptol. ePrint Arch. (2024)
13. Insight, T.: Lattigo v5. EPFL-LDS, Tune Insight SA (2023). https://github.com/tuneinsight/lattigo
14. Jain, A.K., Flynn, P., Ross, A.A.: Handbook of Biometrics. Springer (2007)
15. Mouchet, C., Troncoso-Pastoriza, J.R., Bossuat, J., Hubaux, J.: Multiparty homomorphic encryption from ring-learning-with-errors. Proc. Priv. Enhancing Technol. **2021**, 4 (2021)
16. Shamir, A.: How to share a secret. Commun. ACM **22**, 11 (1979)

An Innovative DSSE Framework: Ensuring Data Privacy and Query Verification in Untrusted Cloud Environments

Khosro Salmani(✉)

Mount Royal University, 4825 Mt Royal Gate SW, Calgary, AB T3E 6K6, Canada
ksalmani@mtroyal.ca

Abstract. Dynamic Searchable Symmetric Encryption (DSSE) empowers cloud servers to execute search queries on encrypted user documents while maintaining the encryption of both queries and documents. This technology also supports efficient updates to the document set by the user. However, most current DSSE approaches rely on the "honest-but-curious" server model, where the cloud server is expected to follow the protocol without deviation. Given that cloud servers are not always fully trustworthy, this assumption can be problematic in real-world scenarios. In our paper, we introduce a new forward-private DSSE scheme that includes efficient result verification. To achieve this, the server must provide a "verification token" with the search results to confirm the integrity of the data returned. We enhance retrieval efficiency by using a customized B^+ tree to store verification token values and a tailored linked-list data structure. Our cost-effective scheme supports both document updates and searches. Security proofs and performance evaluations demonstrate the scheme's practicality, efficiency, and robust security.

Keywords: Data Privacy · Verifiable DSSE · Forward Privacy

1 Introduction

Cloud computing provides unlimited storage and computing power, which benefits users with limited resources by allowing them to store data on cloud servers. However, this convenience comes with risks. Outsourcing data means users lose full control, raising security and privacy concerns. A data breach by a cloud provider could expose sensitive information, leading to potential identity theft or unauthorized access [1–3].

To protect outsourced data privacy, users can encrypt their data before transferring it to the cloud. However, this hampers efficient search queries. Searchable Symmetric Encryption (SSE) schemes [4–7] address this by allowing searches on encrypted data while keeping it protected. Early SSE schemes only supported static data, making updates difficult [4,8]. Later, Dynamic SSE (DSSE) approaches [9–14] improved the efficiency of modifying outsourced data.

K. Adi et al. (Eds.): FPS 2024, LNCS 15533, pp. 12–28, 2025.
https://doi.org/10.1007/978-3-031-87496-3_2

However, most SSE and DSSE methods compromise sensitive information for efficiency. For example, DSSE schemes let the cloud link new documents to past queries, potentially revealing information about previously searched keywords. To counter this, *forward privacy* was introduced [9] to keep new documents private relative to past queries. Forward-private DSSE schemes use ephemeral search tokens [10,11,13,14] that change after each use, preventing the server from identifying repeated queries and reducing data leakage.

Nevertheless, most DSSE approaches assume servers are honest-but-curious, meaning they follow protocols but may collect user data. However, this is often unrealistic due to the potential for server malfeasance. To address this, verifiable DSSE schemes were developed [15–20] to handle potentially malicious servers. These schemes allow users to verify the correctness, completeness, and freshness of results. Efficiency remains a key challenge, and verifying results can conflict with other DSSE requirements like forward privacy [19].

This paper introduces a forward-private DSSE scheme that efficiently ensures result verifiability. The server provides a "verification token" with search results to confirm integrity of them. Our lightweight index structure supports both resource-constrained and powerful devices. Our main contributions are:

1. We tackle result verification in forward-private DSSE schemes by developing an efficient, verifiable scheme that supports search, update (add and delete) operations, and parallelism for improved efficiency [11].
2. We provide a proof of security against adaptive adversaries, demonstrating the security and privacy of our scheme.
3. We implement our forward-private DSSE scheme and demonstrate its practical efficiency using real-world datasets.

2 Related Work

Searchable Symmetric Encryption (SSE) allows servers to perform search queries on encrypted data. Song et al. [4] introduced the concept with a two-layer encryption scheme for each word. Goh et al. [5] later improved search times using a secure index structure, and Curtmola et al. [21] enhanced security and privacy to protect against adaptive adversaries. Despite Oblivious RAM [22] achieving full privacy without leaking information, its high computation costs make it impractical for real-life applications. As efficiency is crucial in searchable encryption, several approaches [4,5,7,8,21] have been designed to selectively leak information, trading a small amount of leakage for improved efficiency.

Dynamic SSE (DSSE) schemes enable operations such as adding, deleting, and updating outsourced data [13]. Kamara et al. [23] proposed a DSSE scheme that is secure against adaptive chosen keyword attacks. Additionally, Naveed et al. [24] developed a DSSE scheme known as "Blind Storage," which prevents the leakage of the number of stored files and their sizes.

DSSE methods, due to their interactive protocols, tend to leak more information about the outsourced data, particularly during file additions, which can reveal relationships between new files and previous search results. To address this, Stefanov et al. [9] introduced forward privacy and developed a forward-private DSSE construction. Bost et al. [10] improved efficiency with their forward-private method, but it required a sequential scan, making parallelization impossible. Etemad et al. [11] overcame this by creating a forward-private DSSE scheme that supports parallelism. Recently, Salmani et al. [14] advanced the concept by introducing full-forward privacy, which maintains forward privacy even after numerous searches.

Ensuring the search results' integrity is the main focus of the verifiable DSSE schemes. Kurosawa *et al.* [15] formulated the security of verifiable SSE schemes against active adversaries by using the notion of privacy and reliability and proposed a scheme that satisfies their security definitions. Cheng *et al.* [25] adopted indistinguishability obfuscation to design a SSE scheme with searching functionalities. Liu *et al.* [12] proposed verifiable searchable symmetric encryption schemes that can detect a malicious server. Zhu *et al.* [16] also presented a verifiable SSE scheme which leverage from Merkle Tree structure. Soleimanian *et al.* [18] improved the efficiency of the verifiable SSE schemes by employing common security primitives such as pseudo-random functions. Zhang *et al.* [17] then proposed a verifiable SSE scheme based on the multi-set hash functions. Salmani *et al.* [20] also constructed a new forward-private DSSE scheme that achieves result verifiability using a customized data structure that they designed.

3 Problem Formulation

3.1 Preliminaries

For a finite set X, $x \leftarrow X$ indicates that x is sampled uniformly from the set X. The symbol λ represent the security parameter, and $||$ denotes concatenation. A function $\mathsf{neg}(k) : \mathbb{N} \rightarrow [0,1]$ is negligible if, for every positive polynomial p, there exists a constant c such that: $\forall\ k > c,\ neg(k) < 1/p(k)$ [8,11,13,20].

Definition 1. *(Symmetric-key Encryption). A symmetric encryption scheme consists of three probabilistic polynomial time (PPT) algorithms demoted as* $\mathsf{SE} = (\mathsf{Gen}, \mathsf{Enc}, \mathsf{Dec})$. *The algorithm* Gen *takes an unary security parameter* λ *and generates a secret key* k. *The algorithm* Enc *takes a key* k *and* n*-bit message* m *and returns a ciphertext* c. *The algorithm* Dec *takes in a key* k *and a ciphertext* c, *and returns* m *if* k *was the key used to generate* c. *The* SE *is required to be secure against chosen plaintext attack (CPA) [21].*

Definition 2. *(Pseudorandom function). Consider a deterministic function* $F : \{0,1\}^\lambda \times \{0,1\}^l \rightarrow \{0,1\}^{l'}$ *which maps* l*-bit strings to* l'*-bit strings. We define* $F_s(x) = F(s,x)$ *as a pseudorandom function* (PRF) *if:* $\forall$ *PPT distinguishers* $\mathcal{D}$: $|Pr[\mathcal{D}^{F_s(.)}(1^\lambda) = 1] - Pr[\mathcal{D}^{f(.)(1^\lambda)} = 1]| \leq neg(\lambda)$, *where* $f(.)$ *is a truly random function, and* λ *is the security parameter.*

In Definition 3, the notation $(c_{out}, s_{out}) \leftarrow \mathsf{protocol}(c_{in}, s_{in})$ [13,20] denotes a client-server interaction where c_{in} and s_{in} are inputs from the client and server, respectively, and c_{out} and s_{out} are their outputs after executing the protocol.

Definition 3. *(VDSSE Scheme). Let $D = \{D_1, \ldots, D_n\}$ be a collection of n documents, a Verifiable Dynamic Searchable Symmetric Encryption (VDSSE) is composed of six PPT algorithms:*

- *$(sk, \perp) \leftarrow \mathsf{GenKey}(1^\lambda, 1^\lambda)$: In this algorithm, the data owner (client) generates a secret key sk based on the security parameter λ.*
- *$(\mathcal{I}_c, \mathcal{I}_s) \leftarrow \mathsf{BuildIndex}((sk, D), \perp)$: In this algorithm the client's secret key sk and document collection D are used to generate a client-index $\mathcal{I}_c$, and server outputs index $\mathcal{I}_s$.)*
- *$(\perp, C) \leftarrow \mathsf{Encryption}((sk, D), \perp$: The client inputs secret key sk, and document collection D, and outputs the encrypted corpus $C = \{C_1, \ldots, C_n\}$.*
- *$((\mathcal{I}'_c, D_w), \mathcal{I}'_s) \leftarrow \mathsf{Search}((sk, \mathcal{I}_c, w), (\mathcal{I}_s, C))$: In this algorithm the client inputs the secret key sk, index $\mathcal{I}_c$, and query w; and outputs the updated index $\mathcal{I}_c$, along with the resultant documents D_w. Note that D_w includes both the verification token and the resultant documents. The server also, inputs the index I_s, and the encrypted document collection C and outputs the updated index $\mathcal{I}'_s$.*
- *$(\mathcal{I}'_c, (\mathcal{I}'_s, C')) \leftarrow \mathsf{Update}((sk, \mathcal{I}_c, \mathsf{op}, , in), (\mathcal{I}_s, C))$: In this algorithm the client inputs the secret key sk, index $\mathcal{I}_c$, and an operation op = add or op = del, and an input "in", which is parsed as a set of keywords $\boldsymbol{w}_{in}$ and a document identifier id_{in}. The client then outputs the updated index $\mathcal{I}'_c$. The server inputs the index $\mathcal{I}_s$, and the encrypted document collection C, and outputs the updated index $\mathcal{I}'_s$ and updated encrypted document collection C'.*
- *$(V, \perp) \leftarrow \mathsf{Verify}(sk, P)$: The client inputs secret key sk, while the server inputs the "Verification Token", P. The client then verifies the verification token and outputs $V \in \{yes, no\}$.*

*We refer to the first three protocols (*GenKey, BuildIndex, Encryption*) as the* ***Setup phase.***

3.2 System Model

Our system model involves two parties, as depicted in Fig. 1: a data owner (user-client) and a cloud (server). The data owner creates an inverted index that maps each keyword to the file identifiers (documents) containing that keyword. This index, along with the files, is then encrypted and stored on the server. When the server receives a search query, it executes the query on the index and returns the relevant documents along with a Verification Token (VT). The data owner, upon receiving the VT, verifies the results (detailed in Sect. 4) to confirm their integrity. Since both the index and files are encrypted, the cloud does not have access to the contents of the files or the searched keywords.

3.3 Threat Model

In our model, we consider a semi-honest-but-curious cloud server, as described in previous works [9–11, 20]. This server follows the protocol but may also act maliciously by deviating from it. We also assume that the cloud server is aware of the encryption scheme being used, as well as having access to the encrypted documents, index, and queries, but it does not possess the encryption key.

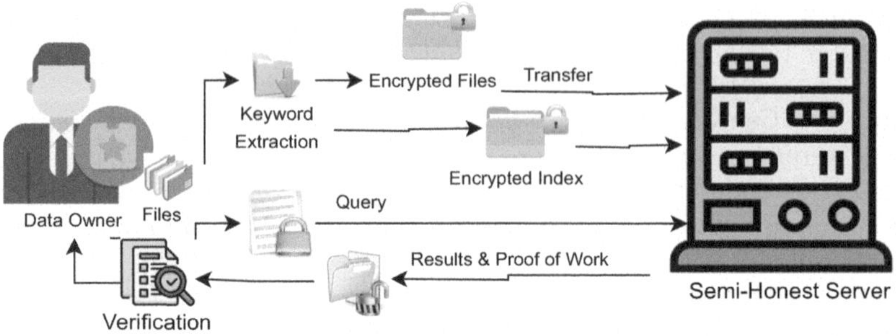

Fig. 1. The system model.

3.4 Approach Overview

Before sending documents $D = \{D_1, \ldots, D_n\}$ to an external server, the client extracts keywords $\Delta = \{w_1, \ldots, w_m\}$ and creates an inverted index with entries (id_i, L), where id_i links to keyword w_i and L lists document identifiers containing w_i. For result verification, a B^+ tree node is created for each list, including a verification token and the header's id (see Sect. 4). The client stores some information $\mathcal{I}_c$ (see Sect. 4.3) and then encrypts the documents $C = \{C_1, \ldots, C_n\}$ and index entries before sending them to the server.

The server stores the encrypted entries $\mathcal{I}_s$, builds the B^+ tree, and holds the encrypted corpus C. Each query, $\mathbf{q} = \{q_1, \ldots, q_k\}$, include sub-queries with added noise to obscure access patterns. The server processes the queries, returns results with verification tokens (VTs), and the client uses these VTs to verify the results. Finally, the client updates and encrypts index entries with new keys and ids for keywords in $\mathbf{q}$, sending them back to the server.

3.5 Security Definitions

Existing SSE methods deliberately sacrifice some information, like document identifiers (*ids*) and the number of keywords, to improve efficiency [7–9,13,14, 20,21]. Additionally, each client query discloses extra information to the server. In this context, we first define the leakage functions to specify the information revealed to the server by each query.

Definition 4. *(Search pattern). Let* $Q = (\boldsymbol{q}_1, \boldsymbol{q}_2, \ldots, \boldsymbol{q}_t)$ *represent the list of queries over* t *queries. The search pattern for the query list* Q *is defined as a tuple,* $\mathsf{SP} = (\hat{w}_1, \hat{w}_2, \ldots, \hat{w}_t)$*, where* $\hat{w}_i$*,* $1 < i < t$*, is the encrypted keyword (or its hash) in the* i*-th query.*

Definition 5. *(Access pattern). The access pattern for a query list* Q *is defined as a set* $\mathsf{AP} = (R(\boldsymbol{q}_1), R(\boldsymbol{q}_2), \ldots, R(\boldsymbol{q}_t))$ *over* t *queries, where* $R(\boldsymbol{q}_i)$*,* $1 < i < t$*, represents the resultant document identifiers (result set) for the* i*-th query.*

To illustrate the information leaked to the server, we use the leakage function $\mathcal{L}^{\mathsf{op}}$, which indicates the information exposed to the adversary after executing the operation op. We begin by defining $\mathcal{L}^{\mathsf{Setup}}$ and $\mathcal{L}^{\mathsf{Search}}$, and then we demonstrate the information leakage during Update through Definition 6.

- $\mathcal{L}^{\mathsf{Setup}}(D) = \{N, M, n, (id(D_i), |D_i|, C_i)_{1 \leq i \leq n}\}$, where N is the number of server index entries,M is the number of tree nodes, $\mathcal{I}_s$; n is the number of documents, $id(D_i)$ is the document D_i's identifier, $|D_i|$ is the size of document D_i, and C_i is the encrypted corpus.
- $\mathcal{L}^{\mathsf{Search}}(\mathbf{q}_i) = \{R(\mathbf{q}_i), |R(\mathbf{q}_i)|, C_{\mathbf{q}_i}\}$ where $\mathbf{q}_i$ is a client's query, and $R(\mathbf{q}_i)$ is the resultant document identifiers, and $C_{\mathbf{q}_i}$ is the encrypted resultant documents.

Definition 6. *(Forward privacy). A SSE scheme is forward private if the update leakage function* $\mathcal{L}^{\mathsf{Update}}$ *is restricted to:* $\mathcal{L}^{\mathsf{Update}}(in, D_i, \mathsf{op}) = \{id_{in}(D_i), |\boldsymbol{w}_{in}|, |D_i|, \mathsf{op}\}$.

To define the security of the VDSSE scheme, we use the standard simulation model, which involves a real-ideal simulation [9,11,13,14,20]:

Definition 7. *(DSSE Security). Let* VDSSE = (GenKey, BuildIndex, Encryption, Search, Update, Verify) *be a VDSSE scheme. Let* $\mathcal{A}$ *be an adversary (server), and the* $\mathcal{L}^{\mathsf{Setup}}$, $\mathcal{L}^{\mathsf{Search}}$, *and* $\mathcal{L}^{\mathsf{update}}$ *be the leakage functions. The following describes the real and ideal world:*

- $\mathbf{Ideal}^{\mathsf{VDSSE}}_{\mathcal{F},\mathcal{S},\mathcal{Z}}(\lambda)$*: An environment* $\mathcal{Z}$ *provides the client with a set of documents* D *for outsourcing. The client sends these documents to the ideal functionality* $\mathcal{F}$*. A simulator* $\mathcal{S}$ *receives* $\mathcal{L}^{\mathsf{Setup}}$*. Later,* $\mathcal{Z}$ *instructs the client to perform an* Update *or* Search *operation by providing the necessary details. For a search request,* $\mathcal{Z}$ *includes a keyword* w*. For an update request,* $\mathcal{Z}$ *selects an operation from* $\{add, del\}$*. Add requests include a new document, while delete requests specify a document identifier. The client prepares and sends the appropriate request to the ideal functionality* $\mathcal{F}$*. Based on* $\mathcal{L}^{\mathsf{Update}}$ *and* $\mathcal{L}^{\mathsf{Search}}$, $\mathcal{F}$ *informs* $\mathcal{S}$ *of any leakage.* $\mathcal{S}$ *then decides whether to* abort *or* continue*. The ideal functionality* $\mathcal{F}$ *responds to the client with either* abort *or success for* Update, *or with the set of matching document identifiers for* Search*. Finally, the environment* $\mathcal{Z}$ *outputs a bit as the result of the experiment.*
- $\mathbf{Real}^{\mathsf{DSSE}}_{\Pi_F,\mathcal{A},\mathcal{Z}(\lambda)}$*: An environment* $\mathcal{Z}$ *sends the client a set of documents* D *to be outsourced. Then, the client executes the* GenKey(1^λ) *to generate the key* sk *and starts the* BuildIndex *and* Encryption *protocols with the real world adversary* $\mathcal{A}$*. Later, the environment* $\mathcal{Z}$ *provides the required information and asks the client to run a* Search *or an* Update *request. The search request contains a keyword* w *to search for.* $\mathcal{Z}$ *picks an operation from* $\{add, del\}$ *for an update request. Add requests are accompanied with a new document and del requests contain a document identifier. The client then executes the real-world protocols with the server on the inputs that are selected by* $\mathcal{Z}$*. The client outputs either* abort *or "success" for* Update, *or a set of matching document ids for* Search. $\mathcal{Z}$ *observes the output. Finally, outputs a bit* b *as the output of the experiment.*

We say that a VDSSE *scheme* (Π_F) *emulates the ideal functionality* $\mathcal{F}$ *in a semi-honest model, if for all PPT real world adversaries* $\mathcal{A}$*, there exists a PPT simulator* $\mathcal{S}$ *such that for all polynomial-time environments* $\mathcal{Z}$*, there exists a negligible function* $\mathsf{negl}(\lambda)$ *on the security parameter* λ *such that [13]:*

$$|Pr[\mathbf{Real}^{\mathsf{VDSSE}}_{\Pi_F,\mathcal{A},\mathcal{Z}(\lambda)} = 1] - Pr[\mathbf{Ideal}^{\mathsf{VDSSE}}_{\mathcal{F},\mathcal{A},\mathcal{Z}}(\lambda) = 1]| \leq \mathsf{negl}(\lambda).$$

4 Construction

In this section, we propose an efficient forward-private VDSSE scheme. The user creates an inverted index linking keywords to document identifiers and constructs a B^+ tree where each node contains a verification token and the id of the linked list's header for result verification. To obscure search and access patterns, each query $\mathbf{q}_i$ includes multiple sub-queries $\mathbf{q}_i = \{q_{i1}, q_{i2}, \ldots, q_{ik}\}$, with only one being genuine and the rest as decoys. These sub-queries also support secure *add* operations (see Sect. 4.3). Our scheme utilizes a linked list and B^+ tree structure, detailed in the following sections.

4.1 Our Linked-List Structure

In our customized linked list, each node is a 3-tuple $(id, \mathbf{data}, \mathbf{next})$, where id is the node identifier, **data** is a document identifier, and **next** points to the next node. The bold elements are encrypted with an ephemeral key, shared with the server during a keyword query to retrieve results. The *id* field remains in plaintext. If there's no next node, **next** is set to *null*. The linked list operates using the following algorithms:

- $\mathsf{AddNode}(\mathbb{L}, k, id, data)$: This algorithm encrypts a node using the key k and data, then appends it to the end of the linked list $\mathbb{L}$.
- $\mathsf{RetrieveList}(k, id_h)$: This algorithm restores a linked list starting from node id_h, decrypting the **data** and **next** fields with the key k. It follows the **next** value to each subsequent node until reaching the last node ($\mathbf{next} = null$).

4.2 Our B^+ Tree Data Structure

To efficiently manage verification tokens, we designed a customized B^+ tree for quick retrieval of VTs and the linked-list header's *id* for each subquery. Its balanced structure and logarithmic search complexity significantly improve search efficiency. The B^+ tree also simplifies add operations by updating the VT directly, without modifying the entire linked list, as noted in Salmani *et al.* [20]. Our approach, as shown in Sect. 5.2, outperforms Salmani's method.

In our customized B^+ tree, each node is a 5-tuple $(LLink, id, \boldsymbol{VT}, \boldsymbol{id_h}, RLink)$, where $LLink$ and $RLink$ link to child nodes, id is the node identifier, $\boldsymbol{VT}$ is the verification token, and $\boldsymbol{id_h}$ is a linked list header node's identifier. The **bold** elements are encrypted: $\boldsymbol{id_h}$ with an ephemeral key, and $\boldsymbol{VT}$ with the client's private key. The server retrieves the node using the ephemeral key, while only the client can decrypt $\boldsymbol{VT}$ for verification.

During updates, the client only updates the respective tree node without sharing the ephemeral key, making our approach more efficient than similar methods [20], as it avoids modifying the entire linked list. Other fields remain in plaintext, and links are set to *null* if no children exist. The B^+ tree supports the following algorithms:

- $\mathsf{CreateNode}(k(k_e, k_p), id, VT, id_h)$: It generates an encrypted B^+ tree node using the key k (composed of an ephemeral key k_e and the client's private key k_p), the verification token (VT), and the linked list header identifier (id_h).
- $\mathsf{RetrieveNode}(k_e, id)$: This algorithm retrieves a node from the B^+ tree using its identifier, decrypts $\boldsymbol{id_h}$, and uses it to call $\mathsf{RetrieveList}(k, id_h)$ to access the linked list during query processing.
- $\mathsf{RestoreNode}(id)$: This algorithm retrieves a node from the B^+ tree using its identifier, deletes it, and sends the verification token (VT) and $\boldsymbol{id_h}$ back to the client. The server does not receive the ephemeral key (k_e) and cannot decrypt $\boldsymbol{id_h}$. The client generates a new VT, creates a new node, and sends it to the server to update the tree. Unlike previous methods (e.g., Salmani et al. [20]), our approach avoids retrieving the entire linked list or regenerating keys for operations such as *add*, reducing system costs and improving efficiency.

We build the secure index using linked lists and B^+ tree nodes containing a Verification Token (VT). The VT is a pseudo-random number generated by the client using a Pseudo-Random Function (PRF), $G_v(.)$, which takes a secret key k and a number δ, computed by XORing the node identifiers of a linked list. For example, for the inverted index $(w_3, \{D_2, D_5, D_7\})$, the client creates three linked list nodes and a B^+ tree node $(null, id, \mathbf{VT}, \boldsymbol{id_{D2}}, null)$, where $VT = G_v(k, \delta)$ and $\delta = id_{D2} \oplus id_{D5} \oplus id_{D7}$. The node identifiers are ephemeral and encrypted, preventing adversaries from linking them.

4.3 Our Scheme

In this section, we describe our approach and explain how each algorithm in Definition 3 operates.

- GenKey: let $\mathsf{SE} = (\mathsf{Gen}, \mathsf{Enc}, \mathsf{Dec})$ be a CPA-secure symmetric encryption scheme. Let $G_k(.)$, $G_{id}(.)$ and $G_v(.)$ be three PRFs and $\mathsf{GenPK}(1^\lambda)$ be a key generator function. The following describes $(sk, \perp) \leftarrow \mathsf{GenKey}(1^\lambda, 1^\lambda)$:

  1: $k_{SE} = \mathsf{SE.GEN}(1^\lambda)$
  2: $k_G \leftarrow \mathsf{GenPK}(1^\lambda)$
  3: *return* $sk = (k_{SE}, k_G)$

  The secret key sk consists of a two-part tuple, where k_{SE} is used for document encryption, and k_G is applied in the functions $G_n(.)$, $G_{id}(.)$, and $G_w(.)$.
- $\mathsf{BuildIndex}$. The algorithm begins by extracting the keywords $\Delta = \{w_1, \ldots, w_m\}$ (see Algorithm 1) and assigning an *id* (label) to each document. Next, the client index $\mathcal{I}_c$ is generated, and a corresponding linked list

is created for each keyword. For future operations, especially the Search function, the user must maintain an $m \times 2$ lookup table, $\mathcal{I}_c$, which stores a counter cnt_i for each keyword w_i, as well as length of a linked list, $\#len$. All elements in $\mathcal{I}_c$ are initialized to zero. Finally, the index entries are sent to the server. The Rand() function generates a random number to assign to each document. Algorithm 2 outlines the process for generating the plaintext inverted index PI, and in lines 4–9, we add nodes to their respective lists.

Next, we generate a linked list for each keyword (see Algorithm 3) along with B+ tree nodes containing the Verification Tokens (VTs). When the client generates the tree nodes, the left and right child pointers are initially set to *null*. The server receives these tree nodes in a random order and inserts them into a B+ tree based on their node *ids* (generated in line 10). Additionally, the algorithm generates a unique, ephemeral node identifier for each linked list's node, $id_n = G_{id}(k_G, w_i || cnt)$ (line 15), where cnt is the node counter for the keyword w_i (stored in $\mathcal{I}_c[i][0]$).

To encrypt the content of each node, we generate an ephemeral key for each list, $k_h = G_k(k_G, id_{VT})$ (line 11). This key is used to encrypt all nodes in the current list, as well as the corresponding B+ tree node, except for the Verification Token (VT), which is encrypted using the user's private key. In line 16, we compute the XOR of all node IDs within the same linked list. Subsequently, in line 21, we use this value to generate the VTs.
After generating the necessary nodes, including both linked list nodes and tree nodes, the client sends them to the server. The server only sees a collection of encrypted nodes and cannot link them, particularly the linked list nodes, as they are encrypted. Once the server receives the tree index entries, it constructs the B+ tree using the node *ids* and stores the linked list nodes in the corresponding index, $\mathcal{I}_s$.

Algorithm 1. $(\mathcal{I}_c, \mathcal{I}_s) \leftarrow$ BuildIndex$((sk, D), \perp)$

<u>Client</u>
1: $\Delta =$ ExtractKeywords(D)
2: $D' = \{\}$
3: **while** $D \neq empty$ **do**
4: $lbl_{next} =$ Rand()
5: D_{cur} = randomly choose one doc and assign lbl_{next} to it
6: $D' \cup D_{cur}$
7: **end while**
8: $PI =$ BuildPlainIndex(Δ, D')
9: Create $\mathcal{I}_c$ initialize all elements to zero
10: $\mathbb{L} =$ GenLinkedList(sk, PI)
11: Send $\mathbb{L}$ to server
<u>Server</u>
12: Generate $\mathcal{I}_s$ using $\mathbb{L}$

Algorithm 2. BuildPlainIndex

1: **procedure** BuildPlainIndex(Δ, D')
2: $PI = \{\}$
3: for all w_i in Δ creates an empty L_i
4: **for all** D_j **in** D' **do**
5: **for all** w_i **in** Δ **do**
6: **if** $w_i \in D_j$ **then**
7: $L_i \cup \{lbl(D_j)\}$
8: **end if**
9: **end for**
10: **end for**
11: Shuffle and Add all (w_i, L_i) to PI
12: **return** PI
13: **end procedure**

– Encryption. The user encrypts all the files in the corpus with the secret key k_{SE} and sends them to the server, each paired with its unique document id.

Algorithm 3. GenLinkedList

```
procedure GenLinkedList(sk, I_c, PI)
    L_l = {}
    L_t = {}
    for all e ∈ PI do
        w_i = e.w_i
        L = e.L_i
        len = 0
        checkSum = 0
        cnt = I_c[i][0]
        id_VT = G_id(k_G, w_i||cnt)
        k_h = G_k(k_G, id_VT)
        L_s = {}
        cnt + +
        for all lbl_doc ∈ L do
            id_n = G_id(k_G, w_i||cnt)
            checkSum ⊕ = id_n
            AddNode(L_s, k_h, id_n, lbl_doc)
            len + +
            cnt + +
        end for
        VT = G_v(k_G, checkSum)
        I_c[i][1] = len
        L_t ∪ CreateNode(k(k_h, k_SE), id_VT, VT, id_h)
        L_l ∪ L_s
    end for
    return L_t and L_l
end procedure
```

Algorithm 4. $((\mathcal{I}_c'), (\mathcal{I}_s', C')) \leftarrow$ Update$((sk, \mathcal{I}_c, add, \text{in}), (\mathcal{I}_s, C))$

```
Client
Δ_D = ExtractKeywords(D_{n+1})
L = {}
for all w_i ∈ Δ_D do
    L_s = {}
    cnt = I_c[i][0]
    len = I_c[i][1]
    id_VT = G_id(k_G, w_i||cnt − len)
    k_h = G_k(k_G, id_VT)
    id_newNode = G_id(k_G, w_i||cnt
    AddNode(L_s, k_h, id_newNode, lbl_doc)
    I_c[i][1] + +
    checkSum = decrypt (RetrieveNode(⊥, id_VT))
    VT = G_v(k_G, checkSum ⊕ id_newNode)
    L ∪ VT
    I_c[i][0] + +
    L ∪ L_s
end for
C_{n+1} = Enc(k_SE, D_{n+1})
Send L, C_{n+1} to server
Server
C ∪ C_{n+1}
Update I_s and tree using L
```

Algorithm 5. $((\mathcal{I}_c', D_w), (\mathcal{I}_s')) \leftarrow$ Search$((sk, \mathcal{I}_c, w, \nu), (\mathcal{I}_s, C))$

```
Client
counter = 0;
Δ_q = {w}
while counter < ν do
    w_i = GenRandom()
    if w_i ∉ Δ_q then
        Δ_q ∪ w_i
        counter + +
    end if
end while
q = {}
for all w_i in Δ_q do
    cnt = I_c[i][0]
    len = I_c[i][1]
    id_VT = G_id(k_G, w_i||cnt − len)
    k_h = G_k(k_G, id_VT)
    q ∪ (id_VT, k_h)
end for
Shuffle(q)
Send q to server
Server
bag = {}
VTs = {}
for all q_i in q do
    checkSum_i = 0
    VT_node =Find the node with id_VT in the tree
    Decrypt VT_node and retrieve id_h and VT_i
    node_id = id_h
    while node ≠ lastNode do
        checkSum_i ⊕ = node_id
        Decrypt the node using k_h in q_i
        Add lbl to R(q_i)
        node_id = next node
    end while
    Add files corresponds to R(q_i) to bag
    Add VT_i and checkSum_i to VTs
end for
Send (R(q_1), . . . , R(q_k), bag, VTs) to client
Client
Decrypt results R
for all VT_i in VTs do
    V = Verify(k_SE, VT_i, checkSum)
    if V == no then
        Show an Alarm message
    end if
end for
PI = {}
for all w_i in Δ_q do
    L = All doc-ids contain w_i in R
    PI ∪ (w_i, L)
end for
L = GenLinkedList(sk, I_c, PI)
Send L to server
Delete noise results
Consume real results
Server
Update I_s and the tree using L
```

– Search. To conceal and obscure the search pattern, each query $\mathbf{q}_i$ consists of a finite set of sub-queries $\mathbf{q}_i = \{q_{i1}, q_{i2}, \ldots, q_{ik}\}$. Each sub-query q_{ij} targets a specific linked list and is represented as a tuple (id_{VT}, k_h), where id_{VT} is the identifier of the VT node in the tree, and k_h is the corresponding ephemeral key. The client is able to regenerate id_{VT} and k_h using $\mathcal{I}_c$ and k_G.
To further obfuscate the query $\mathbf{q}_i$, the client adds random sub-queries as noise. A random generator function GenRandom() is used to select random

keywords for these noise sub-queries. The number of noise queries, ν, can be chosen arbitrarily. The algorithm then randomly shuffles the sub-queries within $\mathbf{q}_i$ before sending it to the server. Algorithm 5 outlines how the query for keyword w is generated. Our approach accommodates clients with varying resources. As a result, parameters like ν are user-defined based on available resources, such as computational power.

Upon receiving the query $\mathbf{q}_i$, the server processes each sub-query $q_{ij} = (id_{VT}, k_h)$ by locating id_{VT} in the tree and as a result, it finds the corresponding linked-list using $\mathcal{I}_s$. The server then removes the corresponding entries from $\mathcal{I}_s$, decrypts them using k_h, and adds the decrypted document *ids* and Verification Tokens (VTs) to the result set. Although the server can retain the accessed entries, they no longer provide new information, as they have already been revealed. Finally, the server returns a tuple $(R(q_{i1}), \ldots, R(q_{ik}), \text{bag}, \text{VTs})$, where $R(q_{ij}), 1 \leq j \leq k$, represents the document *ids* from sub-query q_{ij}, the bag contains the encrypted documents from $\mathbf{q}_i$, and VTs for all sub-queries.

After obtaining the results for $\mathbf{q}_i$, the user, who is aware of the real sub-query's position, filters out the noise and retrieves and decrypts the actual results from the *bag*. Additionally, in lines 38–43, the user verifies the results. For the searched keywords in $\mathbf{q}_i$, new entries are randomly generated. This process utilizes the GenLinkedList algorithm to construct the linked lists.

Random noise queries and non-deterministic search tokens ensure forward privacy. After updating $\mathcal{I}_c$, the user generates new secret keys and node *ids* for each linked list and VT token. The changing *cnt* value leads to new node *ids* and keys k_h. The client then sends the newly encrypted nodes to the server, where they are stored in different positions within $\mathcal{I}_s$ and the tree. Although the server knows new entries relate to the last search, it cannot distinguish real keywords from noise. Non-deterministic search tokens and ephemeral id_{VT} values prevent the server from inferring the search pattern, preserving confidentiality and forward privacy (see Algorithm 5).

- Update. This algorithm includes two operations, *add* and *del*, as follows:
  - *add*. To add a new document D_{n+1}, the algorithm extracts its keywords and regenerates k_h and id_{VT} for each keyword using $\mathcal{I}_c$. New nodes are added to the end of the relevant linked lists, and the corresponding VT_{node} is updated. This update does not require exposing the ephemeral key; the server uses id_{VT} to locate and return the VT value to the user. The user decrypts, updates, and sends the new VT value, along with the new nodes, back to the server. This approach is efficient as it avoids regenerating entire linked lists or ephemeral keys, outperforming methods like those in [11,20] (see Algorithm 4). The server updates $\mathcal{I}_s$ and the tree upon receiving the Update request.
  - *del*. To delete a document D_k, the client sends an Update request containing the identifier of D_k and the *del* operation. Upon receiving this request, the server deletes the document itself but cannot immediately remove the related index entries, as it lacks the necessary keys to identify the associated nodes. However, the server will gradually remove these

index entries as it processes future client queries, deleting any nodes that reference the deleted document or no longer reference any documents. In the context of Algorithm 5, line 33, the server first checks if the document corresponding to the node's data still exists. If it does, the server adds the document *id* to $R(q_i)$; otherwise, the client will refrain from generating new index entries for nodes linked to deleted documents.

5 Complexity Analysis and Experimental Results

In this section, we compare the complexity of our approach with the similar schemes by Stefanov et al. [9], Bost et al. [10], Etemad et al. [11], and Salmani et al. [20], followed by our experimental results on real-world datasets.

5.1 Complexity Analysis

Client and Server Storage. In our approach, the client maintains a local index, $\mathcal{I}_c$, which is an $O(m \times 2) \approx O(m)$ dictionary (m is number of keywords). The client index requires minimal memory space. For instance, if the corpus contains 1 million keywords, with an average size of 10 bytes per keyword and each integer using 4 bytes, the client index would require approximately 18 MB of space (1M $\times(10 + 4 + 4) \approx$ 18MB). This size is manageable even for devices with limited processing power and memory, such as smartphones. Alternatively, the client index can be outsourced using the method proposed by Etemad *et al.* [11]. In terms of storage requirements, Sophos [10] needs $O(m)$, Stefanov *et al.* [9] requires $O(\sqrt{N})$, Etemad *et al.* [11] demands $O(m+N)$, where N is the number of $(keyword, doc\ id)$ pairs and n is the number of files, and Salmani *et al.* [20] requires $O(m)$. The server index is of size $O(N)$ in all of these DSSE schemes except for Salmani *et al.* [20], which uses $O(N+m)$. Similarly, our approach also requires $O(N + m)$, as we generate an additional node to store the VTs.

Parallelism. Parallelism is a key feature supported only by Etemad *et al.* [11] and Salmani *et al.* [20] among similar schemes. In our approach, the server's index entries are independent, and node *ids* are generated using a pseudorandom function. This design enables the distribution of sub-queries across multiple processors, allowing for parallel execution and reducing search and update costs.

5.2 Experimental Results

We performed an extensive experimental evaluation of our scheme using a prototype implemented in Java (JDK-17). For cryptographic operations, we utilized the Security and Crypto packages. The experiment involved a client and server communicating via a TCP connection, both running on Mac machines equipped with Intel Core i7 (Quad-Core) CPUs at 2.3 GHz and 16 GB of RAM. Each result in the experiment represents the average of 10 trials, with variances too small to be significant. We used the Enron email dataset [26] for testing. To evaluate system performance with and without parallelism, we ran the queries both sequentially (single-threaded) and in parallel using four cores (multi-threaded). The results show that the system incurs reasonable and acceptable costs, making it feasible for clients to use the service even on devices with limited resources.

Setup Time. In the first experiment, we measured the setup time for varying numbers of documents. The setup time encompasses the creation of the plain index, encrypted linked lists, B^+ tree nodes, and the encryption process. Our results indicate that setting up the scheme for 50,000 documents takes about than four and half minutes, while setting up for 20,000 documents takes approximately one minute. This setup is a one-time operation that occurs at the start of the protocol. Additionally, we assessed the number of server index entries for each corpus. The server holds fewer than 4.5×10^6 entries for 50,000 files and 1.57×10^6 entries for 20,000 files (Table 1 and Fig. 2).

Table 1. # of server index entries.

#Docs	#server entries
10000	821965
20000	1694478
30000	2591619
40000	3671208
50000	4492797

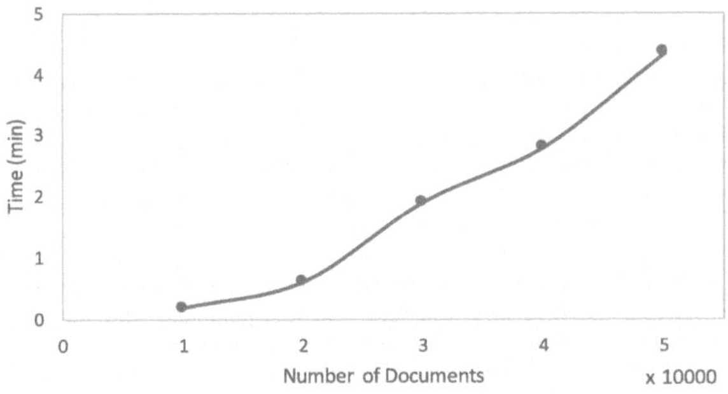

Fig. 2. Client setup time.

Generating a Query. The client generates a query to search for a specific keyword, with each query consisting of a finite number of sub-queries. Each sub-query includes a node identifier (the *id* of the corresponding node in the tree) and a key. In our tests, we searched for the same keyword, varying the number of noise keywords included. Our results show that generating a query takes approximately 0.0028 ms with no noise keywords and 1.07 ms with 50 noise keywords. These tests were conducted on a corpus containing 50,000 documents.

Search Time. When the server receives a search query, it identifies and returns all documents matching the query. The number of documents retrieved significantly impacts search time. Our experiment shows that for a keyword found in 195 documents within the corpus, the single-threaded algorithm (with noise = 3) takes approximately 32.4 ms. The multi-threaded algorithm reduces the search time by about 43% in the same scenario. In this assessment, we compared our search time with the method used by Salmani *et al.*, finding that our approach is around 19% faster. This improvement is primarily due to our use of a B+ tree to store verification tokens, whereas their method relies on a list structure, which increases search time.

Update Requests. An update request can include either an add or delete operation. To delete a document, the client sends its identifier to the server. Generating a delete request is quick (0.55 ms) since the user only needs to set the operation mode (in this case, *del*) and include the document identifier. For adding a new document, the client extracts the keywords, creates plain index entries, generates the encrypted linked-list, encrypts the document, and sends it to the server along with the index and tree entries. Upon receiving the add request, the server stores the document and updates its indexes. Since all index entries are encrypted, the server remains unaware of any relationship between the newly added document and previous queries, ensuring forward privacy. We tested this by adding a file containing 93 keywords and 338 words (excluding stop words) from the Enron dataset, and the process took approximately 1.07 ms on the client side-8% faster than the method used by Salmani *et al.*.

6 Security Proof

In this section, we prove that the proposed DSSE scheme (Sect. 4.3) ensures security as defined in Definition 7.

Theorem 1. *Let* $\mathsf{SE} = (\mathsf{Gen}, \mathsf{Enc}, \mathsf{Dec})$ *be a CPA- secure symmetric encryption scheme, and* G_n*,* G_{id}*, and* G_w *be three pseudorandom functions, our DSSE scheme in Sect. 4.3 is secure under Definition 7.*

Proof. To prove the security of our DSSE scheme, we show that no PPT distinguisher can distinguish between the real and ideal worlds. We define a probabilistic polynomial-time simulator $\mathcal{S}$, using the leakage functions, that simulates client behavior indistinguishably from a real client. The following explains how $\mathcal{S}$ adaptively simulates encrypted indexes, queries, and documents:

Setup. In this phase, the simulator $\mathcal{S}$ generates a secret key k_{SE}, simulates an encrypted document set C, and creates N index entries for $\mathcal{I}_s$ and M entries for the tree. Using the leakage function output $\mathcal{L}^{\mathsf{Setup}}(D) = \{N, M, n, (id(D_i), |D_i|)_{1 \leq i \leq n}\}$, the required data is generated. All documents in C, as well as entries in $\mathcal{I}_s$ and the tree, are encrypted, so $\mathcal{S}$ simulates them by encrypting strings of size $|D_i|$ filled with zeros. The CPA security of the symmetric encryption ensures no adversary can distinguish this process. To handle Search and Update requests, the simulator maintains two local dictionaries: *keyDict* (storing keywords, node IDs, node counts, and keys) and Δ_s (storing simulated keywords). After simulating C, $\mathcal{S}$ generates keywords, linked-lists, and tree nodes as random values, updating *keyDict* and Δ_s to ensure consistent search and update tokens.

Add. $\mathcal{S}$ uses the update leakage $\mathcal{L}^{\mathsf{Update}}(in, D_i, \mathsf{op}) = \{id_{in}(D_i), |\mathbf{w}_{in}|, |D_i|, \mathsf{op}\}$ to add a new document. It generates an encrypted document C_i and assigns $|\mathbf{w}_{in}|$

random keywords from Δ_s based on the same keyword distribution. Finally, $\mathcal{S}$ creates the corresponding linked lists and tree nodes, updating the dictionaries as needed.

Search. The simulator uses the $\mathcal{L}^{\mathsf{Search}}$ leakage function to simulate search operations. Based on this, it selects random keywords from Δ_s and generates sub-queries using the *keyDict* dictionary, retrieving node identifiers and keys for each keyword. After obtaining the results, $\mathcal{S}$ creates new index entries for the tree and linked lists and updates the *keyDict* accordingly. Since search tokens are one-time use and non-deterministic, tracking the search pattern is not possible.

Hence, we designed a simulator and defined leakage functions to execute our scheme. All operations and queries are polynomial-time, making it indistinguishable to the server from the real client's output, except with negligible probability $neg(\lambda)$ or by breaking the encryption or pseudorandom functions.

7 Conclusions

In this paper, we tackle the issue of result verification in forward-private DSSE schemes. We propose a new parallelizable and efficient scheme that ensures forward privacy. Along with the search results, the server provides a "Verification Token" that allows the user to verify the results' accuracy. Our scheme supports search, add, and delete operations. In our model, a data owner interacts with a semi-trusted cloud server. To obfuscate search patterns, each query contains multiple sub-queries, with only one being real, while the rest are fake (noise). We also prove the scheme's security using a standard simulation model. Performance analysis of our prototype demonstrates reasonable and acceptable system costs.

References

1. Linkedin massive data leak expose. https://fortune.com/2021/06/30/linkedin-data-theft-700-million-users-personal-information-cybersecurity/. Accessed 17 July 2024
2. Hacker selling data of 538 million weibo users. https://www.zdnet.com/article/hacker-selling-data-of-538-million-weibo-users/. Accessed 17 July 2024
3. Cloud misconfiguration causes massive data breach at toyota motor. https://www.cybersecurity-review.com/cloud-misconfiguration-causes-massive-data-breach-at-toyota-motor/. Accessed 17 July 2024
4. Song, D.X., Wagner, D., Perrig, A.: Practical techniques for searches on encrypted data. In: Proceedings of 2000 IEEE Symposium on Security and Privacy, S&P 2000, pp. 44–55. IEEE (2000)
5. Goh, E.-J., et al.: Secure indexes. IACR Cryptology ePrint Archive, 2003:216 (2003)
6. Chang, Y.-C., Mitzenmacher, M.: Privacy preserving keyword searches on remote encrypted data. In: Ioannidis, J., Keromytis, A., Yung, M. (eds.) ACNS 2005. LNCS, vol. 3531, pp. 442–455. Springer, Heidelberg (2005). https://doi.org/10.1007/11496137_30

7. Cao, N., Wang, C., Li, M., Ren, K., Lou, W.: Privacy-preserving multi-keyword ranked search over encrypted cloud data. IEEE Trans. Parallel Distrib. Syst. **25**(1), 222–233 (2014)
8. Salmani, K., Barker, K.: Leakless privacy-preserving multi-keyword ranked search over encrypted cloud data. J. Surveill. Secur. Saf. (2020)
9. Stefanov, E., Papamanthou, C., Shi, E.: Practical dynamic searchable encryption with small leakage. In: NDSS, vol. 71, pp. 72–75 (2014)
10. Bost, R.: Forward secure searchable encryption. In: Proceedings of the 2016 ACM SIGSAC Conference on Computer and Communications Security, pp. 1143–1154. ACM (2016)
11. Etemad, M., Küpçü, A., Papamanthou, C., Evans, D.: Efficient dynamic searchable encryption with forward privacy. Proc. Priv. Enhancing Technol. **2018**(1), 5–20 (2018)
12. Liu, X., Yang, G., Mu, Y., Deng, R.: Multi-user verifiable searchable symmetric encryption for cloud storage. IEEE Trans. Dependable Secure Comput. (2018)
13. Salmani, K., Barker, K.: Don't fool yourself with forward privacy, your queries still belong to us! In: Proceedings of the Eleventh ACM Conference on Data and Application Security and Privacy, CODASPY 2021, pp. 131–142. Association for Computing Machinery, New York (2021)
14. Salmani, K., Barker, K.: Dynamic searchable symmetric encryption with full forward privacy. In: 2020 IEEE 5th International Conference on Signal and Image Processing (ICSIP), pp. 985–995 (2020)
15. Kurosawa, K., Ohtaki, Y.: UC-secure searchable symmetric encryption. In: Keromytis, A.D. (ed.) FC 2012. LNCS, vol. 7397, pp. 285–298. Springer, Heidelberg (2012). https://doi.org/10.1007/978-3-642-32946-3_21
16. Zhu, J., Li, Q., Wang, C., Yuan, X., Wang, Q., Ren, K.: Enabling generic, verifiable, and secure data search in cloud services. IEEE Trans. Parallel Distrib. Syst. **29**(8), 1721–1735 (2018)
17. Zhang, Z., Wang, J., Wang, Y., Su, Y., Chen, X.: Towards efficient verifiable forward secure searchable symmetric encryption. In: Sako, K., Schneider, S., Ryan, P.Y.A. (eds.) ESORICS 2019. LNCS, vol. 11736, pp. 304–321. Springer, Cham (2019). https://doi.org/10.1007/978-3-030-29962-0_15
18. Soleimanian, A., Khazaei, S.: Publicly verifiable searchable symmetric encryption based on efficient cryptographic components. Des. Codes Crypt. **87**(1), 123–147 (2019)
19. Guo, Y., Zhang, C., Jia, X.: Verifiable and forward-secure encrypted search using blockchain techniques. In: ICC 2020 - 2020 IEEE International Conference on Communications (ICC), pp. 1–7 (2020)
20. Salmani, K.: An efficient, verifiable, and dynamic searchable symmetric encryption with forward privacy. In: 2022 19th Annual International Conference on Privacy, Security & Trust (PST), pp. 1–10. IEEE (2022)
21. Curtmola, R., Garay, J., Kamara, S., Ostrovsky, R.: Searchable symmetric encryption: improved definitions and efficient constructions. J. Comput. Secur. **19**(5), 895–934 (2011)
22. Goldreich, O., Ostrovsky, R.: Software protection and simulation on oblivious rams. J. ACM (JACM) **43**(3), 431–473 (1996)
23. Kamara, S., Papamanthou, C., Roeder, T.: Dynamic searchable symmetric encryption. In: Proceedings of the 2012 ACM Conference on Computer and Communications Security, CCS 2012, pp. 965–976. ACM, New York (2012)

24. Naveed, M., Prabhakaran, M., Gunter, C.A.: Dynamic searchable encryption via blind storage. In: 2014 IEEE Symposium on Security and Privacy, pp. 639–654 (2014)
25. Cheng, R., Yan, J., Guan, C., Zhang, F., Ren, K.: Verifiable searchable symmetric encryption from indistinguishability obfuscation. In: Proceedings of the 10th ACM Symposium on Information, Computer and Communications Security, ASIA CCS 2015, pp. 621–626. Association for Computing Machinery, New York (2015)
26. Gutenberg publication. https://www.cs.cmu.edu/~enron/. Accessed 06 Nov 2024

Privacy-Preserving Machine Learning Inference for Intrusion Detection

Manigandan Ramadasan[1(✉)], Omar Tahmi[2], Hakima Ould-Slimane[3], Chamseddine Talhi[2], and G. Suganya[1]

[1] School of Computer Science and Engineering, Vellore Institute of Technology, Chennai, India
manigandan582002@gmail.com, suganya.g@vit.ac.in

[2] Department of Software and IT Engineering, École de technologie supérieure (ÉTS), Montréal, QC, Canada
omar.tahmi.1@ens.etsmtl.ca, chamseddine.talhi@etsmtl.ca

[3] Department of Mathematics and Computer Science, Université du Québec à Trois-Rivières (UQTR), Trois-Rivières, Canada
hakima.ould-slimane@uqtr.ca

Abstract. Cyber-attacks are becoming increasingly sophisticated, prompting more interest in Anomaly-based Intrusion Detection Systems for their ability to detect zero-day threats. As networks expand, outsourcing detection services to third parties raises concerns about data security demanding a need for privacy preservation techniques. Homomorphic Encryption (HE) offers a solution, enabling privacy-preserving anomaly detection by allowing computations without compromising privacy. Our work focuses on developing Private classifiers using Cheon-Kim-Kim-Song (CKKS) scheme of HE for intrusion detection. Experiments on the CICIDS2017 dataset using five Machine Learning (ML) classifiers reveal that private Deep Learning (DL) methods achieve performance levels comparable to traditional classifiers. Among these, the Convolutional Neural Network (CNN) strikes a balance between classification speed and detection performance, making it the preferred choice for privacy-preserving intrusion detection.

Keywords: Cybersecurity · Intrusion Detection · Privacy-Preserving Machine Learning (PPML) · Fully Homomorphic Encryption (FHE) · Cheon-Kim-Kim-Song (CKKS) Scheme

1 Introduction

Nowadays, the importance of Intrusion Detection Systems (IDS) has significantly grown due to the escalating number of attacks. Network-based Intrusion Detection Systems (NIDS) monitor and analyze networks to identify various cyber threats [11]. NIDS are generally categorized into Signature-based Intrusion Detection Systems (SIDS) and Anomaly-based Intrusion Detection Systems (AIDS) [12]. SIDS contain patterns (a.k.a rules or signatures) to detect known

K. Adi et al. (Eds.): FPS 2024, LNCS 15533, pp. 29–42, 2025.
https://doi.org/10.1007/978-3-031-87496-3_3

attacks. The drawback of SIDS is its inability to detect unknown attacks. By contrast, an AIDS identifies unusual behaviors by utilizing ML techniques to learn normal traffic patterns and differentiate them from any deviations, which are then identified as malicious activities. Hence, it can detect zero-day attacks.

As cloud services evolve, companies have begun outsourcing their anomaly detection services. This transformation introduces new challenges in terms of security and privacy, particularly as enterprise data traffic is redirected through potentially untrusted environments [18]. To address these issues, new cryptographic solutions are being proposed, such as Searchable Encryption (SE) and Homomorphic Encryption (HE), which allow for search and computation, respectively, over encrypted data. This opens the door to privacy-preserving applications of the computational techniques behind SIDS and AIDS, such as pattern matching for deep packet inspection (DPI) and ML training/classification, respectively.

In this work, we employ HE to build private classifiers. Our main objective is to investigate the efficacy of the CKKS HE scheme for privacy-preserving ML inference. Our aim is to show that this method can achieve performance levels comparable to those obtained using traditional classifiers, while also ensuring efficient evaluation time. Our experiments were conducted using the CICIDS2017 dataset, employing five ML classifiers.

2 Related Work

Several works in the literature employ the use of SE and HE for the task of privacy-preserving intrusion detection. Starting with the use of SE for intrusion detection. SE is a cryptographic technique designed to protect users' sensitive data while preserving searchability on the server side. Starting from BlindBox [16], a line of works, such as [3,13], utilizes SE to construct privacy-preserving SIDS.

Switching to the use of ML for intrusion detection. A method for classifying malware traffic using a 2D-CNN is proposed in [21]. The main problem with this work is that it works only for unencrypted data (raw traffic data). However, nowadays, encrypted communications have become a challenge for traditional traffic classification methods. End-to-end encrypted traffic classification method is proposed in [20]. However, their focus is on encrypted traffic characterization (associating traffic with a specific type of application e.g., chat or streaming). In our work, we specifically concentrate on the classification of encrypted traffic for intrusion detection, distinguishing between benign and malicious activities. Sharafaldin et al. [15] introduced two powerful datasets, CICIDS2017 and CSE-CICIDS2018, designed to be representative of real-world data and scenarios for the task of intrusion detection. 78 statistical features, defining network flow, were extracted using the CICFlowMeter software [1]. The datasets include various types of cyber attacks, such as DoS, DDoS, Brute Force, XSS, SQL Injection, Infiltration, Port Scans, and Botnets. CSE-CICIDS2018 is an extended version dataset of CICIDS2017, derived from a much larger network. In 2020, Kaur et al. [11] introduced a deep image learning method for classifying attacks. Results showed high accuracy using the two datasets. However, the model struggled with classifying infiltration instances accurately, primarily due to their similarity to benign traffic, particularly when relying solely on statistical features.

When it comes to the application of ML on homomorphically encrypted data, a.k.a Privacy Preserving Machine Learning (PPML) for private training and inference. In this study, we focus on the latter. CryptoNets [9], was the first Neural Network (NN) developed for privacy preserving inference which used leveled HE scheme. The core idea is to combine simplifications of the NN with HE to achieve both confidentiality of the manipulated data and efficiency of the processing. CryptoNets are NNs quantized to integers, with the activation function approximated using a square function. While efficiency and accuracy are demonstrated when the number of non-linear layers is small, CryptoNets unfortunately become ineffective for deeper NNs. In [5], a method for performing comparison operations, argmax, sign determination, and dot product over homomorphically encrypted data at the bit-level was developed. In [17], an improved HE scheme was proposed, incorporating efficient noise controlling techniques. Surveys [14,22] provided an overview of HE and its applications, including privacy-preserving techniques in machine learning (ML). Another work [2] analyzed the impact of Fully Homomorphic Encryption over the Torus (TFHE) scheme [8] on the performance of NNs for DDoS attack detection. The findings indicate that TFHE restrictions have a minor impact on NNs' performance, achieving performance metrics comparable to plaintext-based NNs.

This review highlights the importance of SE, HE, and ML in intrusion detection. To the best of our knowledge, we are the first work to employ HE for PPML inference in intrusion detection, subsequent to the work in [2], which was limited to DDoS attacks only. Furthermore, this work serves as the baseline for our next study, CryptoKANs for Intrusion Detection, which builds upon our recent work, CryptoKANs-Kolmogorov-Arnold Networks over Encrypted Data-a novel approach enabling neural networks to operate on encrypted data [19].

3 Proposed Methodology

HE has been widely utilized in various studies to enable the private classification of encrypted data, employing ML classifiers trained on unencrypted data. In this work, we adopt this approach, referred to as PPML inference. Typically, the classification of an encrypted data point can be performed using either encrypted or unencrypted trained model parameters. When using unencrypted parameters, a client encrypts a data point and transmits the encrypted result to the model owner. Subsequently, the latter applies their unencrypted model to this encrypted data. Another scenario where both the model parameters and input data are encrypted becomes pertinent when all computational tasks are outsourced to an external service [22]. In this work, our focus is on conducting private classification using unencrypted trained model parameters. That is, we are only considering the privacy of the data during the classification process.

The proposed architecture is depicted in Fig. 1, where the network traffic from the Internet, destined for the enterprise network, passes through the gateway for feature extraction and homomorphic encryption of the extracted features. After the encryption process is completed, the encrypted features are sent to the model owner (cloud server) for outsourced anomaly detection. The latter utilizes the model's weights and biases to perform computations on the encrypted data (encrypted evaluation). The results are then sent back and decrypted. If any anomalous behavior is detected, necessary actions are taken. The privacy of sensitive network data is maintained through the use of HE. Although the server can perform computations on the data for anomaly detection, it cannot access the actual content due to the encryption. Thus, even if the server attempts to derive sensitive information, it would only be analyzing encrypted data, rendering any extracted information meaningless without the secret key. We could further enhance security by encrypting the model parameters. However, we have only considered the privacy of the data in this work.

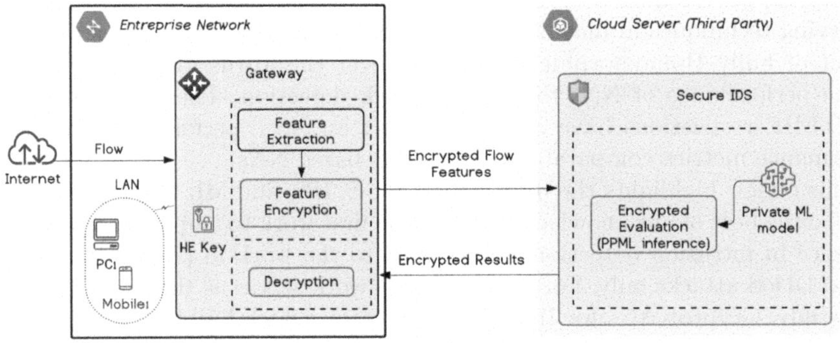

Fig. 1. Architecture of the proposed model (HE operations in red) (Color figure online)

HE is a form of encryption that enables computations to be executed on encrypted data for maintaining privacy in computations and ensuring the security of outsourced data. During the encryption process, noise a.k.a. error e is introduced for security purposes. However, after each operation performed on the ciphertext, the level of noise increases. If the noise surpasses a certain threshold, it can lead to incorrect results upon decryption. FHE is a variant of HE that enables the execution of an unlimited number of operations on encrypted data. However, it is computationally expensive. Another type of HE is Leveled FHE, where the number of operations that can be performed on the encrypted data is predetermined and limited by a parameter set during the encryption process. This type of encryption is selected for this work because the number of operations is known in advance. CKKS scheme [6], is a specific HE scheme designed for performing operations on both real and complex numbers. The main idea is to consider the noise as part of the message m we want to encrypt. The message and the noise are combined to generate the plaintext $(m + e)$ that we encrypt. Similar to other FHE schemes, in CKKS, as we compute on ciphertexts, the plaintext magnitude grows. However, at the heart of the CKKS scheme is a mechanism, called RESCALE, that is used to reduce the magnitude of the plaintext [10]. CKKS decryption generates an approximate value of the message m with adequate precision. This approach is only effective if the magnitude of the error is significantly smaller than that of the message. This is generally the case when the scheme is wisely parameterized. Given the nature of our dataset, which consists of floating-point numbers, we opted for the CKKS scheme to perform HE operations. We will now delve into the details of the CKSS scheme as elaborated in the work of Inferati [10].

The plaintext and ciphertext spaces include elements of the polynomial ring $R_q = \mathbb{Z}_q[x]/f(x)$, where q is the coefficient modulus, should be large enough to support the desired multiplicative depth of the computed circuit, and $f(x)$ is the polynomial modulus, typically chosen as $f(x) = x^n + 1$ with n (or N) represents the ring dimension and the size of ciphertexts produced. It is determined to ensure a sufficient level of security. The CKKS scheme includes a codec method that maps a vector of complex numbers into a single plaintext object and vice versa. CKKS scales the message by a parameter, known as the Scale Factor (SF), denoted as Δ. For encoding, given a $\frac{n}{2}$-vector of complex numbers z in $\mathbb{C}^{n/2}$, the method returns a single plaintext element a in R. Decoding performs the reverse operation.

For encryption, SK represents the secret key and PK is the public key composed of a pair of polynomials $(PK_1 = [-a \cdot SK + e]_{q_l}, PK_2 = a)$. q_l is the coefficient modulus at the level l. a is a random polynomial, and e is a random error polynomial. The notation $[\cdot]_{q_l}$ indicates that polynomial arithmetic is performed modulo q_l. The encryption of a plaintext message M in R generates a ciphertext C formed as a pair in $R_{q_l}^2$ as follows:

$$(C_1 = [PK_1 \cdot u + e_1 + M]_{q_l}, \quad C_2 = [PK_2 \cdot u + e_2]_{q_l})$$

u is a random polynomial and e_1 and e_2 are random error polynomials. Decryption is performed by evaluating the input ciphertext in level l on the secret key SK as follows: $\check{M} = [C_1 + C_2 \cdot SK]_{q_l}$.

We used ciphertext-plaintext operations to accelerate the process since they are substantially faster than ciphertext-ciphertext operations. This involves taking unencrypted parameters and computing them with encrypted features.

$$C_{\text{AddPlain}} = (C_1 + \tilde{M}, C_2)$$
$$C_{\text{MultPlain}} = (\tilde{M} \cdot C_1, \tilde{M} \cdot C_2)$$

where $\tilde{M}$ represents a plaintext message.

Rescaling procedure is applied to scale down a ciphertext C in $R^2_{q_l}$ by a factor of Δ, resulting in an equivalent ciphertext $\hat{C}$ in $R^2_{q_{l-1}}$.

$$\text{RESCALE}(C, \Delta) = \frac{1}{\Delta} \cdot [C_1, C_2]_{q_l} = [\hat{C}]_{q_{l-1}}$$

For the CKKS implementation, we used TenSEAL [4], a Python library specifically designed for performing HE operations on tensors. Choosing the right parameters is crucial for ensuring correctness and efficiency in encryption. In TenSEAL, the parameter q is a list of numbers that indicates the multiplicative depth. It represents the bit length of the prime numbers generated for rescaling after each multiplication operation. The sum of all numbers in the list should have an upper bound with respect to the parameter N to maintain 128-bit security. The scaling factor determines the precision of the floating-point numbers. The subtraction of the first and second elements represents the bit precision of the integer part.

During pre-processing of the dataset, null, infinity values, duplicate instances were removed. All malicious samples were consolidated into a single class. Subsequently, features with zero variance and those highly correlated were removed, resulting in 30 key features. The importance of these features was confirmed using the feature importance scores derived from the Random Forest model. We selected 30 features to minimize overhead and reduce the model's complexity, as we are dealing with encrypted data. We have concentrated on utilizing five ML/DL classifiers, which are: Logistic Regression (LR), Support Vector Machine (SVM), Artificial Neural Network (ANN), CNN, and Decision Tree (DT). Standard Scaling was applied to the data for all models except DT model where Min-Max Scaling was applied. These models were developed using PyTorch, except for DT, which was developed using scikit-learn. All training details are presented in Table 1.

LR model requires one multiplication operation followed by a sigmoid activation function. Since HE operations support only linear operations, there is no direct way to implement the sigmoid function. This challenge can be addressed by using a polynomial approximation, or by pursuing the application of the sigmoid operation on the client side. We are adopting the latter approach. SVM model was implemented with a linear kernel. ANN has 4 layers: an input layer with 30 features, two hidden layers with 16 and 8 neurons, and an output layer with 1 neuron. We follow CryptoNets' approach, replacing the ReLU activation function with a square function in the input and hidden layers. For the output layer, we employ the sigmoid function. CNN consists of one convolutional layer and two dense linear layers, with a square activation function after every layer and sigmoid for the last one. In order to perform convolution in HE, we use image-to-column convolution (im2col), which translates 2D convolution into a single matrix multiplication operation. However, this operation prevents further operations such as pooling/convolutions. Only linear dense layers can be added to the network. DT model, implemented in this work, is a binary DT classifier. However it requires the comparison operation. HE does not offer a straightforward means to evaluate comparison operations directly. Cheon et al. [7] proposed a new method for the comparison of two word-wise homomorphically encrypted data, which has been adopted in this research. The main idea is that the comparison of two numbers x and y can be evaluated as $f(x-y)$ which was approximated, as follows:

$$\mathrm{comp}(x, y) \approx \frac{x^k}{x^k + y^k}$$

The inverse operation is implemented using Goldschmidt's division algorithm [7]. We constructed the DT using data scaled to the range $\left[\frac{1}{2}, \frac{3}{2}\right)$. To mitigate overfitting, we conducted K-Fold Cross Validation with $K = 3$. The log loss criterion was employed to determine the best splits. For classification, we extract all the rules and form them into if-else statements. The rules, along with the input data which will be encrypted and sent to the server, where the comparison operation is performed, and the results are sent back to the client to be decrypted and converted to boolean values, which are passed as arguments to the function containing the if-else statements to obtain final results. This process is necessary because the comparison results must be decrypted at the client side again. The evaluation of the if-else function is performed at the client side to reduce client-server interaction. We did not consider hiding the tree structure.

Table 1. Model Training Details

Model	Optimizer	Loss	Epochs	Learning Rate
LR	LBFGS	BCE	300	0.001
SVM	SGD	Hinge	10	0.0007 (C = 0.001)
ANN	Adam	BCE	1000	0.013
CNN	Adam	BCEWithLogits	30 (Batch of 64)	0.001

4 Experimental Results

Table 2 provides an overview of the experimental environment. Initially, the models were trained on unencrypted data. Subsequently, the weights and biases of all layers were extracted and stored on the server. Following this, encrypted features and unencrypted model parameters were used for secure inference. The resulting encrypted data was sent back to the client or gateway, where it was decrypted, and the last non-linear function was applied to obtain the final prediction result. This process is applicable to all models except for the DT model.

One way to evaluate anomaly detection models is to use Precision, Recall and F1-Score. Low Recall indicates the model misclassifies many malicious flows, risking network damage, while high Recall indicates rare misclassification of malicious activity, crucial for an effective IDS. In essence, a lower Recall implies a terrible IDS. Low Precision indicates that the model is incorrectly classifying

Table 2. Experimental Setup

Specification	Details
Operating System	Windows 10, 64-bit
RAM	32.0 GB
Processor	Intel® Core™ i9-9880H (2.3GHz)
Frameworks	TenSEAL (for CKKS), PyTorch, scikit-learn (for DT)

more legitimate packets/flows as malicious. Conversely, high Precision indicates that the model accurately identifies true anomalies. This is crucial for minimizing false alarms and reducing the likelihood of misclassifying legitimate traffic. While it may be less critical than Recall, it still requires attention because it necessitates additional verification procedures. In simple terms, lower Precision implies an inefficient IDS. The F1-Score takes both Precision and Recall into account, offering a more holistic measure of a model's performance.

Figure 2 demonstrates the differences in various metrics for different models when applied to unencrypted and encrypted data using the best FHE parameters. We initially evaluate the methods in their unencrypted form to identify models that perform well for detection. Subsequently, we compare both the unencrypted and encrypted versions to determine which of the selected models performs better in the encrypted version, aiming to minimize differences from the unencrypted version. Starting with the unencrypted evaluation comparison, we can clearly see that ANN gives the best result for all metrics when evaluated with unencrypted data. CNN and LR interchangeably hold the second place. LR performs a little better in comparison to CNN in terms of Recall, while CNN outperforms LR in Precision, giving it an advantage in F1-Score. DT comes in third place because of the limited depth of the tree. The depth of the DT had to be limited to reduce the probability of error caused by the noise growth because of comparison operation. SVM provides the worst results, ruling it out of consideration.

For encrypted evaluation, selecting the optimal FHE parameters can be a challenging task. There is no direct method to determine this other than testing each model with various parameter sets to find the optimal configuration. Table 3 presents the results of our experiments. Starting with LR and SVM models, we observe that, beginning from $N = 8192$ and $q = [40, 31, 40]$ with a scaling factor of 31, the models start to perform at their best, achieving results similar to those obtained when testing with unencrypted data. Reducing the value of q below this threshold leads to a loss in precision, which degrades the performance due to a non-negligible number of incorrect results (FP and FN). Increasing N beyond this point does not yield any improvements; in fact, it only adds complexity to the models by increasing the ciphertext size. This, in turn, increases the time of evaluations, making the models inefficient. However, we decided to make a slight adjustment by increasing both q and SF to $q = [60, 40, 60]$ and $SF = 40$, respectively. These adjustments are made to maintain a precision of 40 bits for

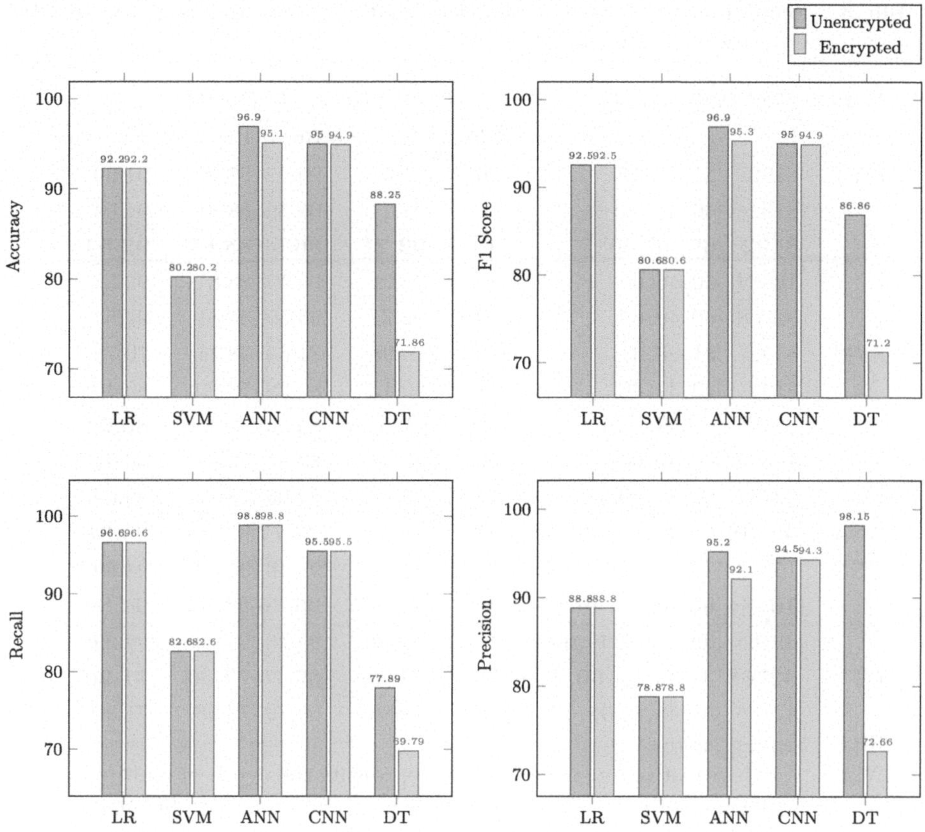

Fig. 2. Comparison Between Various Models in terms of metrics (Unencrypted vs. Encrypted Evaluation)

the fractional part and 20 bits for the integer part. This is necessary to sufficiently accommodate all unseen values extracted from real-time network traffic. The problem with the LR model is its limited Precision which necessitates a double-checking process. While SVM shows poor performances for all metrics.

Switching to DL models, starting with the ANN model, we can observe that when $N = 32768$ and $q = [60, 40, \ldots, 40, 60]_7$ with $SF = 40$, the model yields the best results compared to other sets of parameters. In contrast to LR and SVM, we observe a slight degradation in performance due to the increased depth of multiplication, which introduces more noise that is not fully controlled, leading to the loss of some precision bits with the highest parameters that can be used. Increasing q to add some bits of precision requires increasing N, to maintain a 128-bit security level, which would make predictions too slow and inefficient. Nevertheless, ANN model produces the best metric values compared to other models, except for Precision, where CNN has a slight advantage over ANN. Particularly notable is its higher Recall of 98.8%, making it the most suitable model

Table 3. Comparison of encrypted model evaluations using different sets of FHE parameters in terms of Evaluation Metrics.

Method	FHE Parameters			Evaluation Metrics (%)			
	N	q	SF(Δ)	Accuracy	Recall	Precision	F1-Score
LR	8192	$[31, 26, 31]$	26	91.31	96.42	87.25	91.60
	8192	$[40, 31, 40]$	31	92.21	96.59	88.81	92.54
	8192	$\mathbf{[60, 40, 60]}$	**40**	**92.21**	**96.59**	**88.81**	**92.54**
	16384	$[60, 40, 60]$	40	92.21	96.59	88.81	92.54
	32768	$[60, 40, 60]$	40	92.21	96.59	88.81	92.54
SVM	8192	$[31, 26, 31]$	26	79.98	81.53	78.11	79.78
	8192	$[40, 31, 40]$	31	80.12	82.29	78.60	80.40
	8192	$\mathbf{[60, 40, 60]}$	**40**	**80.18**	**82.56**	**78.81**	**80.64**
	16384	$[60, 40, 60]$	40	80.18	82.56	78.81	80.64
	32768	$[60, 40, 60]$	40	80.18	82.56	78.81	80.64
ANN	**32768**	$\mathbf{[60, 40, ..., 40, 60]_7}$	**40**	**95.13**	**98.77**	**92.08**	**95.31**
CNN	16384	$[40, 31, ..., 31, 40]_8$	31	94.86	95.46	94.33	94.89
	16384	$\mathbf{[60, 46, ..., 46, 60]_8}$	**46**	**94.86**	**95.46**	**94.33**	**94.89**
	32768	$[60, 46, ..., 46, 60]_8$	46	94.86	95.46	94.33	94.89
DT	**32768**	$\mathbf{[31, 60, ..., 60, 31]_{14}}$	**60**	**71.86**	**69.79**	**72.66**	**71.20**
	32768	$[31, 48, ..., 48, 31]_{19}$	48	71.86	69.79	72.66	71.20

SF(Δ): Scaling Factor.
$[X, Y, \ldots, Y, X]_l$: List of l elements, which represents the depth of multiplications, starting and ending with X (bits), with Y's (bits) duplicated in between.

for intrusion detection in terms of detection. CNN provides the best results with only $N = 16384$ and $[60, 46, \ldots, 46, 60]_8$ with $SF = 46$. CNN achieves the highest Precision value, indicating fewer FP, which is advantageous when additional double-checking algorithms are not desired. Despite a slight degradation in performance compared to evaluating the model on unencrypted data, DL models yield the best metric values (with LR having a slight advantage over CNN in terms of Recall). The performance of the DT algorithm is not impressive. This is due to the homomorphic comparison operation which has a high multiplicative depth (12) that generates more noise, resulting in noise accumulation that cannot be adequately controlled even with the highest parameters that was used. In addition to reduced performance, DT has a high inference time of 4.4 s on encrypted data due to the HE parameters required to control noise growth. Even though DT has good performance over plaintext data, its performance on encrypted data is limited by the noise growth. Reducing the feature space is one of the potential solutions to address these limitations which we plan to explore in future work. As conclusion, DT algorithm performs relatively poor when evaluated on encrypted data which includes very long inference time, ruling it out of consideration and comparison. LR, SVM, and CNN methods yield almost identical results for all metrics when comparing their unencrypted and encrypted evaluations; however, we are no longer interested in SVM as it gives poor results. In the case of the ANN method, slight degradations were observed, while it maintained the same high Recall. It yields the best results on encrypted data compared to other methods in all metrics, except for Precision where CNN performs slightly better, which can reduce the need for extensive double-checking.

We can also see from the confusion matrices (Fig. 3) that NN models produce the least number of FN and FP that makes them suitable for intrusion detection tasks.

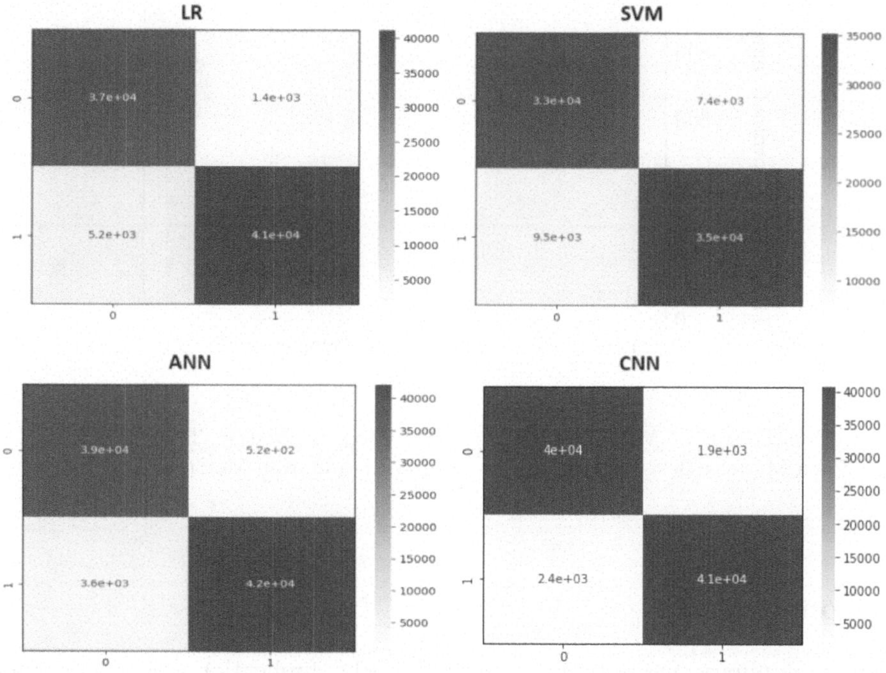

Fig. 3. Confusion Matrix for Various Encrypted Models

Another crucial aspect of IDS is prediction time, especially when handling real-time flows or packets. Delays in prediction can lead to significant network damage. Figure 4 illustrates the evaluation time (in ms) per instance, using the FHE parameters. The recorded times were 16.67 ms, 17.61 ms, 702 ms, and 1162 ms for LR, SVM, CNN, and ANN respectively. We can clearly observe that NN models require much more evaluation time. While the ANN method delivered the most accurate results on encrypted data, however, the time taken to evaluate one instance was approximately 1.162 s due to the high chosen value of N that allows achieving the best performance. This duration can be considered excessive for a real-time scenario. On the other hand, CNN showed excellent performance on encrypted evaluation. It also achieved a balanced trade-off between metrics and evaluation time, taking only 0.702 s per instance. This makes CNN a more efficient alternative to ANN, maintaining both satisfactory performance metrics and prediction time. This makes it our preferred choice for privacy-preserving intrusion detection.

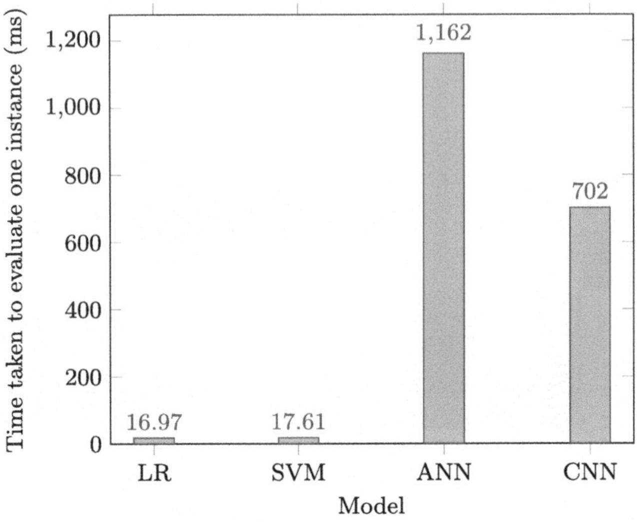

Fig. 4. Comparison of Models Based on Encrypted Evaluation Time per Instance, Using Each Model's Best Parameters for Optimal Evaluation Metrics

5 Conclusions

In this preliminary investigation, we explored the application of Homomorphic Encryption for privacy-preserving machine learning inference in intrusion detection systems. Our experiments demonstrated that using a Convolutional Neural Network model, we achieved results comparable to those obtained with unencrypted intrusion detection, while maintaining an acceptable execution time. However, relying solely on statistical features may not fully leverage the potential of HE. Our future research will focus on applying HE to various types of extracted features from the payload, which is expected to improve the precision of traffic classification, particularly for attack types that are prone to higher false positive rates when using only statistical features. The critical nature of these new features underscores the importance of preserving them through HE.

In subsequent work, we plan to explore the use of our novel privacy-preserving machine learning model, called CryptoKANs, for the task of privacy-preserving intrusion detection and compare it to this work, which will act as a baseline, with the aim of enhancing overall performance. Additionally, we will investigate the capabilities of continual learning within the context of intrusion detection with the latest dataset to further improve the generalizability of the findings and advance our approach.

References

1. CICFlowMeter (formerly known as ISCXFlowMeter), A network traffic Bi-flow generator and analyzer for anomaly detection (2023). https://github.com/ahlashkari/CICFlowMeter
2. Amorim, I., Barbosa, P., Maia, E., Praça, I.: Privacy-preserving NN for IDS: a study on the impact of TFHE restrictions. In: International Workshop on Security and Trust Management, pp. 107–125 (2023)
3. Bakhshi, T., Ghita, B.: Anomaly detection in encrypted internet traffic using hybrid deep learning. Secur. Commun. Netw. (2021)
4. Benaissa, A., Retiat, B., Cebere, B., Belfedhal, A.E.: Tenseal: a library for encrypted tensor operations using homomorphic encryption. arXiv preprint arXiv:2104.03152 (2021)
5. Bost, R., Popa, R.A., Tu, S., Goldwasser, S.: Machine learning classification over encrypted data. Cryptology ePrint Archive (2014)
6. Cheon, J.H., Kim, A., Kim, M., Song, Y.: Homomorphic encryption for arithmetic of approximate numbers. In: Takagi, T., Peyrin, T. (eds.) ASIACRYPT 2017. LNCS, vol. 10624, pp. 409–437. Springer, Cham (2017). https://doi.org/10.1007/978-3-319-70694-8_15
7. Cheon, J.H., Kim, D., Kim, D., Lee, H.H., Lee, K.: Numerical method for comparison on homomorphically encrypted numbers. In: International Conference on the Theory and Application of Cryptology and Information Security, pp. 415–445 (2019)
8. Chillotti, I., Gama, N., Georgieva, M., Izabachène, M.: Faster fully homomorphic encryption: bootstrapping in less than 0.1 seconds. In: Cheon, J.H., Takagi, T. (eds.) ASIACRYPT 2016. LNCS, vol. 10031, pp. 3–33. Springer, Heidelberg (2016). https://doi.org/10.1007/978-3-662-53887-6_1
9. Gilad-Bachrach, R., Dowlin, N., Laine, K., Lauter, K., Naehrig, M., Wernsing, J.: Cryptonets: applying neural networks to encrypted data with high throughput and accuracy. In: International Conference on Machine Learning, pp. 201–210 (2016)
10. Inferati Inc.: Introduction to the CKKS/HEAAN FHE Scheme (2022). https://www.inferati.com/blog/fhe-schemes-ckks
11. Kaur, G., Lashkari, A.H., Rahali, A.: Intrusion traffic detection and characterization using deep image learning. In: 2020 IEEE International Conference on Dependable, Autonomic and Secure Computing, International Conference on Pervasive Intelligence and Computing, International Conference on Cloud and Big Data Computing, International Conference on Cyber Science and Technology Congress, pp. 55–62 (2020)
12. Khraisat, A., Gondal, I., Vamplew, P., Kamruzzaman, J.: Survey of intrusion detection systems: techniques, datasets and challenges. Cybersecurity **2**(1), 1–22 (2019). https://doi.org/10.1186/s42400-019-0038-7
13. Lai, S., et al.: Practical encrypted network traffic pattern matching for secure middleboxes. IEEE Trans. Dependable Secure Comput. **19**(4), 2609–2621 (2021)

14. Pulido-Gaytan, L.B., Tchernykh, A., Cortés-Mendoza, J.M., Babenko, M., Radchenko, G.: A survey on privacy-preserving machine learning with fully homomorphic encryption. In: High Performance Computing: 7th Latin American Conference, CARLA 2020, Cuenca, Ecuador, 2–4 September 2020, Revised Selected Papers 7, pp. 115–129 (2021)
15. Sharafaldin, I., Lashkari, A.H., Ghorbani, A.A.: Toward generating a new intrusion detection dataset and intrusion traffic characterization. ICISSp **1**, 108–116 (2018)
16. Sherry, J., Lan, C., Popa, R.A., Ratnasamy, S.: Blindbox: deep packet inspection over encrypted traffic. In: Proceedings of the 2015 ACM Conference on Special Interest Group on Data Communication, pp. 213–226 (2015)
17. Sun, X., Zhang, P., Liu, J.K., Yu, J., Xie, W.: Private machine learning classification based on fully homomorphic encryption. IEEE Trans. Emerg. Top. Comput. **8**(2), 352–364 (2018)
18. Tahmi, O., Talhi, C., Challal, Y.: Two-layer architecture for signature-based attacks detection over encrypted network traffic. In: International Symposium on Foundations and Practice of Security, pp. 423–440 (2022)
19. Tahmi, O., Talhi, C., Ould-Slimane, H.: Cryptokans: enhancing privacy-preserving machine learning in IoT environments using kolmogorov-arnold networks over encrypted data (2024)
20. Wang, W., Zhu, M., Wang, J., Zeng, X., Yang, Z.: End-to-end encrypted traffic classification with one-dimensional convolution neural networks. In: 2017 IEEE International Conference on Intelligence and Security Informatics (ISI), pp. 43–48 (2017)
21. Wang, W., Zhu, M., Zeng, X., Ye, X., Sheng, Y.: Malware traffic classification using convolutional neural network for representation learning. In: 2017 International Conference on Information Networking (ICOIN), pp. 712–717 (2017)
22. Wood, A., Najarian, K., Kahrobaei, D.: Homomorphic encryption for machine learning in medicine and bioinformatics. ACM Comput. Surv. (CSUR) **53**(4), 1–35 (2020)

Priv-IoT: Privacy-Preserving Machine Learning in IoT Utilizing TEE and Lightweight Ciphers

Arash Kariznovi(✉) and Kalikinkar Mandal

Faculty of Computer Science, University of New Brunswick, Fredericton, NB E3B 5A3, Canada
{arash.k,kmandal}@unb.ca

Abstract. The need for lightweight cryptographic primitives is greater than ever due to the rapid advancements in the Internet of Things (IoT) and the increasing presence of resource-constrained devices. In response to this, the NIST has standardized the ASCON lightweight authenticated encryption with associated data (AEAD) and hash algorithm as a standard for lightweight cryptography (LWC). Besides protected IoT data communications, IoT data analytics is crucial for operational efficiency, data-driven innovation, improved decision-making, and predictive maintenance. We consider a real-world scenario of Cloud-IoT where an IoT application is connected to a (potentially untrusted) cloud. In this paper, we propose Priv-IoT, a privacy-preserving machine learning (PPML) system, using it, an IoT application owner can securely transport IoT data to the cloud and enable secure machine learning (ML) on the IoT data. Our secure IoT data transport protocol is based on a lightweight AEAD scheme and a standard security protocol (e.g., TLS) to resist against various external and internal attacks. We enable secure ML analytics using a trusted execution environment (e.g., Intel-SGX) in the bring-your-own-encryption paradigm. We prototype and evaluate our proposed system using a list of LWC algorithms and fundamental regression algorithms in SGX, and present extensive experimental results on real-world datasets.

Keywords: IoT · Machine Learning · Trusted Execution Environment · Lightweight Cryptography

1 Introduction

With technological advancements such as IoT and smart grids, the demand for resource-constrained devices like smart meters, smart cards, RFIDs, and low-power wireless devices is increasing rapidly. Due to the constrained nature of these devices, providing security and privacy is a significant concern and it is not possible to use the conventional cryptography standards that are used for high-speed powered processors like servers and desktops. The devices mentioned

K. Adi et al. (Eds.): FPS 2024, LNCS 15533, pp. 43–59, 2025.
https://doi.org/10.1007/978-3-031-87496-3_4

use hardware or software implementation to perform the cryptography computations. RFIDs are embedded with FPGAs and ASICs and smart meters use 16-bit, 8-bit, or sometimes 4-bit microcontrollers. When designing a cryptographic primitive, there is always a trade-off between resource and efficiency for a constant security level. In lightweight cryptography, it is much harder since the researchers are limited in using resources and they have to meet a certain security level at the same time. The resources for software include RAM, ROM, and registers, while the resources for hardware implementation are gate equivalents and gate area. Latency, power and energy consumption, and throughput are the key metrics to evaluate the performance of these primitives. Over the past more than a decade, several cryptographic primitives have been proposed including block ciphers, stream ciphers, message authentication code, and hash functions. In the case of block ciphers, DESL [29] has been proposed by reducing the S-box rounds from eight to one round and, Present [10], was designed as a dedicated algorithm. Moreover, Simon and Speck [5], RC5 [36], TEA [39] and XTEA [32] are proposed for efficient performance on resource constrained devices. Lightweight hash functions including PHOTON [22], Quark [1], SPONGNET [9] and Lesamnta-LW [24] are developed that have smaller state size and lower energy consumption. Chaskey [31], TuLP [20], and LightMAC [30] are some of the examples of lightweight MAC algorithms developed on hardware applications. The growth in IoT and smart grid, has led to the initiation of many communications between many of previously unconnected nodes in the network and thereby introducing new security and privacy challenges. The data from smaller nodes are transmitted to the more powerful nodes to be processed, aggregated or stored but data owners are sensitive about the privacy of their data. For instance, there are many sensors in a smart home, these sensors collects the data from different appliances and transmit it to the utility providers server for further analysis. With accessing this data, adversaries can understand about the pattern of the residences and extract important information. In the smart grid, thousands of smart meters send the metering data to the data aggregator, or as another example, hospitals send their patient health information to the third-party cloud provider to be processed. The adversary can be an attacker far away in another continent or an insider that is working in the utility provider company. The data must be protected against all types of misuse. A solid solution to this challenge is using Trusted Execution Environments (TEEs). TEE uses the enclaves as a protected area in the memory suitable for maintaining the sensitive information, the data residing in this area is encrypted and is only decrypted when it is being processed by CPU. By using this technology, confidentiality and integrity of the private data is guaranteed and even the OS and system administrator do not have access to its data and code. Finally, if data is encrypted using the mentioned lightweight ciphers in the resource-constrained devices, they need to be decrypted using the same lightweight algorithm before being used in the cloud or data aggregator. This shows that the resource-constrained devices are not the only devices in which lightweight primitives are performed and assessing their performance in the powerful processors is required and important equally. Although TEE is a beneficial tool and many benchmarks performed on NIST finalists, to the best of our knowledge no research has evaluated the performance of those lightweight algorithms on Trusted Execution Environments.

Our Contributions. Motivated by the deployment of Cloud-IoT system in the real-world and the need for secure IoT data processing, we propose Priv-IoT, a privacy-preserving system for secure collection and processing of IoT in the cloud. Our contributions in this paper are summarized as follows:

- **Privacy-preserving ML system for Cloud-IoT:** We present a privacy-preserving machine learning system tailored for Cloud-IoT systems. The Priv-IoT system has three main entities namely an IoT application, the owner of the application and a cloud. We leverage well-analyzed/understood cryptographic schemes and security protocols to design our secure system. Our Priv-IoT system is built upon four fundamental building blocks namely a lightweight AEAD scheme, a TEE realized by SGX, the TLS security protocol, and a key-exchange protocol for enclave. Our choice of cryptograhic primitives and protocols for IoT devices is done so that it meets the lightweight requirement. We prove the security of our proposed system against semi-honest adversaries.
- **Evaluating NIST LWC finalists in SGX.** As an independent contribution, we evaluate and benchmark the execution of the encryption and decryption algorithms of ten (finalists) AEAD algorithms from the NIST LWC competition. Our experimental shows that the overhead of running encryption/decryption algorithms inside SGX, compared to the cleartext computation, lies in the range of 1.06 and 2.23. To the best of our knowledge, our work is the first to perform such analysis of lightweight ciphers.
- **Experimental evaluation.** To capture the real-world Cloud-IoT scenario, we develop a testbed using a `Raspberry Pi Pico` (IoT device), `Raspberry Pi 4B` (IoT gateway) and the Microsoft Azure cloud. We implement our privacy-preserving ML system on IoT devices and the Azure cloud. We consider linear and logistic regression algorithms and evaluate the performances on 11 different real-world datasets from the UCI ML repository. We present experimental results for different regression training.

2 Preliminaries

2.1 Security and Privacy in IoT

Security must be lightweight due to IoT's resource limitations. It involves securing devices across layers: the perception layer against attacks, the network layer for secure routing, and the application layer with authentication and access control. The fundamental security properties of IoT data and systems include authentication, confidentiality, integrity, and availability. Moreover, privacy is critical due to an autonomous data transmission of IoT devices. Even fragmented data can reveal sensitive information when combined. Users should control their data dissemination [12].

2.2 Lightweight Cryptography

Despite all available algorithms, the National Institute of Standards and Technology was planning to develop a family of algorithms that are more fast and lightweight, and still secure in resource-constrained devices. In 2018, the NIST published a call for algorithms to describe the requirements, selection process, and evaluation criteria [34]. After two rounds of the NIST standardization process, the final rounds began by selecting ten algorithms namely, ASCON [16], Elephant [8], GIFT-COFB [3], Grain- 128AEAD [23], ISAP [15], PHOTON-Beetle [4], Romulus [25], SPARKLE [6], TinyJAMBU [40], and Xoodyak [14]. The final round ended with the selection of the ASCON family as the NIST lightweight cryptography standard in February 2023.

2.3 Trusted Execution Environments

A Trusted Execution Environment is a secure processing environment that isolates sensitive operations, data, and computations from the normal rich execution environment (REE) where typical operating systems and applications run. TEEs enhance security by ensuring confidentiality and integrity, allowing REE applications to securely partition sensitive tasks into the TEE.

Software Guard Extension. Intel Software Guard Extension (SGX) is a set of instructions added to some of Intel CPUs that ensures the confidentiality, integrity of the code and data by creating a trusted execution environment called an enclave. SGX reserves a memory region called Processor Reserved Memory (PRM). CPU protection keeps the PRM safe from non-enclave memory accesses, including kernel, hypervisor, and SMM accesses, and DMA accesses from peripherals. The PRM manages the Enclave Page Cache (EPC) with 4 KB pages housing enclave code and data. Untrusted system software assigns EPC pages to enclaves, tracked by the CPU in the Enclave Page Cache Metadata (EPCM). Initially, the system software loads code and data into enclaves from unprotected memory, establishing the initial enclave state. Once all pages are loaded, the enclave is marked as initialized, allowing application code execution inside. Enclave execution occurs in protected mode, with CPU-enforced isolation. Interruptions during enclave execution trigger an Asynchronous Enclave Exit (AEX) to handle them securely. OS or hypervisor manages EPC page allocation, using cryptographic protections for evictions to untrusted memory.

Attestation plays a vital role in SGX usage and comes in two forms: remote attestation and local attestation. Remote attestation is employed when an external client seeks to connect to the enclave. Before key exchange, the client must verify the SGX enclave. This involves requesting the enclave to generate a report, which is then passed to a platform service to produce a credential known as a quote, reflecting the enclave and platform state. The client receives the quote and employs the Intel Attestation Service to verify the enclave, enabling trust based on the IAS response for key exchange. On the other hand, local attestation is used when two enclaves within a platform wish to communicate. Each enclave sends a report to the other enclave, allowing both sides to verify each other using this report and a symmetric key (GETKEY).

2.4 Transport Layer Security

Transport Layer Security (TLS) is a cryptographic protocol ensuring secure communication over networks, most notably securing HTTPS. It provides privacy, integrity, and authenticity using techniques like certificates. TLS evolved from SSL and is currently at version 1.3 (defined in 2018). Operating at the presentation layer, it has two main components:

- **TLS Handshake**: Establishes a secure communication channel by exchanging messages between a client and server. The process involves agreeing on cryptographic parameters, authenticating identities, and generating session keys. In TLS 1.3, the handshake includes a client hello message, a server hello message, and key exchange to finalize secure communication.
- **TLS Record Protocol**: Secures data transmission after the handshake by ensuring confidentiality, integrity, and authenticity. It segments, compresses (optional), authenticates, and encrypts outgoing data, while performing the reverse on incoming data. Encrypted data is then passed to the TCP layer for transport.

3 Related Work

Lightweight Cryptography. While we could not find any studies to evaluate the NIST ten finalists performance on trusted execution environments, there are several benchmarks available for software and hardware implementations. These implementations evaluate the performance of NIST finalists on FPGAs, microcontrollers and desktops and servers bringing a wide range of insights about their efficiency on different devices from resource-constrained devices in the edge to powerful servers on the cloud. The NIST team compared AEAD finalists to AES-GCM and SHA-256 on 8-bit and 32-bit microcontrollers, with ASCON, TinyJAMBU, and GIFT-COFB performing best [33]. Weatherley [38] optimized finalists on AVR, ESP32, and Cortex-M3, with ASCON, GIFT-COFB, SPARKLE, and Xoodyak outperforming ChaChaPoly on AEAD benchmarks. SPARKLE was fastest overall. eBACS [7] showed ASCON and Xoodyak outperforming AES-GCM without AES-NI and on ARM Cortex-A7. Both were competitive with SHA-256. Renner et al. [35] benchmarked AEAD finalists on five microcontrollers, with ASCON leading in speed, code size, and RAM usage.

Privacy-Preserving ML Using TEE/SGX. The IoT has various applications of regression analysis. In general, privacy-preserving regression analysis received considerable attention. There are various ways to realize a privacy-preserving regression system such as homomorphic encryption (e.g., [11,19,27]), secret sharing (e.g., [13,17,18]), and garbled circuit (e.g., [2]). However, we focus on designing private regression systems based on TEE. Several frameworks have been developed to perform secure computations using Intel SGX. PRIVADO [21] ensures secure DNN inference in SGX by eliminating input-dependent access patterns, reducing leakage while maintaining low performance overheads across various models. SecureLR [26] proposes a hybrid cryptographic framework that combines homomorphic encryption and Intel SGX to enable secure logistic regression on biomedical data in public clouds without compromising data security or efficiency. VC3 [37] secures distributed MapReduce by isolating memory regions using SGX, achieving minimal overhead while ensuring confidentiality and integrity even if large components like the OS are compromised. EnclaveDB secures databases by placing sensitive data within SGX enclaves, ensuring confidentiality, integrity, and freshness with low overhead. Lastly, SGX-PySpark [28] integrates SGX with PySpark to secure distributed data analytics in cloud environments.

4 The Cloud-IoT System Model

In this section, we describe the Cloud-IoT system model, its adversarial model, and present a privacy-preserving machine learning system for IoT ML analytics.

4.1 Our System and Trust Model

We consider a real-world Cloud-IoT system consisting of three key entities, namely a set of IoT devices, a gateway, and a cloud server. The IoT devices are connected to the cloud via a gateway and transmit IoT data to the cloud. We assume that all the devices belong to a single owner who wishes to perform various tasks on IoT data such as data collection, processing, ML learning computations, and visualization. Figure 1 shows a high-level overview of the system.

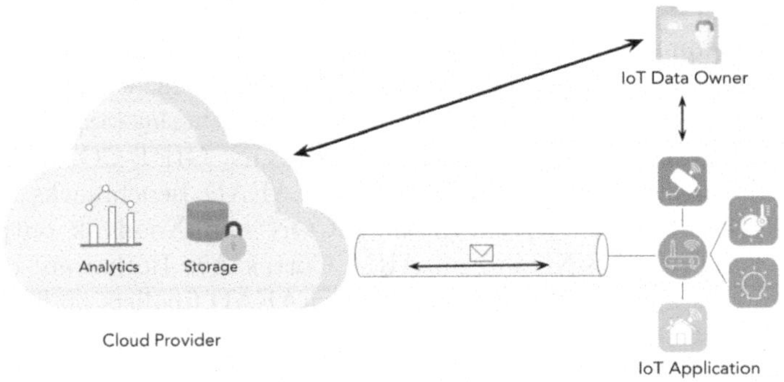

Fig. 1. A Cloud-IoT system connecting an IoT application to the cloud.

Problem Statement. Suppose the IoT devices streams high-dimensional data to the cloud. Let $\mathcal{D} = \{(\mathbf{x}, y)\}$ be a combined dataset of the same type generated by IoT devices, where $(\mathbf{x}, y)$ is a high-dimensional data point. Suppose the owner wishes to train a regression model $\boldsymbol{\theta}$, i.e., $\boldsymbol{\theta} \leftarrow \mathsf{Training}(\boldsymbol{\theta}, \mathcal{D}, f)$ where f is a linear or logistic regression algorithm. We consider the problem of *securely* transmitting data from the IoT devices to the cloud and *privately* performing training linear or logistic regression models $\boldsymbol{\theta}$ on $\mathcal{D}$ in the cloud. Our system is aimed to protect IoT data privacy and integrity when in-transit, at-rest and in-use, and ensure the fine-grain control that remains exclusively with its legitimate owner, while still allowing them to access and benefit for various purposes such as operational and automation.

Adversarial/Trust Model. Our trust model is similar to the one in [37]. In our system, we consider semi-honest adversaries where an adversary may compromise some IoT devices or the cloud applications, and observes the execution of the protocol. The goal of the adversary is to learn any unintended information about other honest IoT devices' data or the trained model. We assume that the adversary can intercept the IoT data communications including record, replay, and modify network data and can compromise the cloud software applications. We also assume that the adversary is unable to physically open and tamper the SGX-enabled processors located at the cloud. If such is possible, we claim no IoT data and ML model privacy.

5 Our Solution for Private Cloud-IoT Data Analytics

Overview. To design a secure Cloud-IoT analytics system, we take a practical approach and make use of well-understood cryptographic schemes and protocols, namely a trusted execution environment (e.g., SGX), a security protocol (e.g., TLS) and a lightweight AEAD algorithm (e.g., ASCON). In our system, fundamentally there are two tasks: 1) securely transport data from an IoT application to the cloud, and 2) privately perform an analytical algorithm in the cloud so that the cloud cannot infer any private data at-rest and in-use. Our solution takes the bring-your-own-encryption (BYOE) paradigm where the owner manages the keys of IoT devices. To achieve the IoT data security and privacy, we design a doubly-encryption mechanism by combining a lightweight AEAD with the standard TLS-like security protocol to achieve the privacy against external communication attacks and internal attacks in the cloud. We perform analytics securely in a trusted execution environment to achieve IoT data privacy against the cloud. We formalize our secure system in Definition 1. Figure 2 shows a secure version of the system.

Definition 1. *Our secure system consists of a set of four algorithms/sub-protocols involving the IoT devices, the owner, the cloud server and the TEE:*

- $\{\mathsf{K}_{\mathsf{ID}}\}_{\mathsf{ID} \in [n]} \leftarrow \mathsf{KeySetup}(1^\lambda)$*: On a security parameter* λ*, the owner runs this algorithm to generate a set of keys* $\{\mathsf{K}_{\mathsf{ID}}\}_{\mathsf{ID} \in [n]}$ *where the unique key* K_{ID}

is for each IoT device with a unique ID *and* n *is the number of IoT devices in the system. The owner securely stores and distributes the keys to the IoT devices.*

- $(c, tag, \mathsf{ID}) \leftarrow \mathsf{SecureDataTransport}(\mathsf{K}_{\mathsf{ID}}, (\boldsymbol{x}, y), \mathsf{ID})$: *The secure data transport protocol is run between an IoT device with identity* ID *and the cloud server where the IoT device gives* $\mathsf{K}_{\mathsf{ID}}, (\boldsymbol{x}, y)$ *as inputs, and the cloud receives* (c, tag, ID) *as output.*
- $(\mathsf{K}_{\mathsf{ID}}, \mathsf{ID}) \leftarrow \mathsf{SecureKeyTransport}(\mathsf{K}_{\mathsf{ID}}, \mathsf{ID})$: *The secure key transport protocol is run between the owner with identity* ID *and the TEE where the owner gives* K_{ID} *as inputs, and the TEE receives* $(\mathsf{K}_{\mathsf{ID}}, \mathsf{ID})$ *as output.*
- $\boldsymbol{\theta} \leftarrow \mathsf{SecureAnalytics}(\mathcal{D}, \{\mathsf{K}_{\mathsf{ID}}\}, f)$: *After receiving a training request from the owner for an ML training algorithm* f *and the dataset* $\mathcal{D}$*, the TEE runs this algorithm to train a model* $\boldsymbol{\theta} \leftarrow \mathsf{Training}(\boldsymbol{\theta}, \mathcal{D}, f)$ *within the trusted environment and return either an encrypted model or the cleartext model to the request party.*

5.1 Description of Components in Our Secure System

We now provide the details of the security algorithms in Definition 1.

KeySetup. Suppose there are n IoT devices in the system and each device has a unique identity (ID). Based on a security parameter λ (e.g., $\lambda = 128$-bit security), the owner randomly samples a set of symmetric-keys $\{\mathsf{K}_{\mathsf{ID}}\}_{\mathsf{ID} \in [n]}$, one key K_{ID} is for each IoT device with identity ID. These symmetric-keys will be used in an AEAD algorithm to encrypt and authenticate IoT data.

SecureDataTransport. When an IoT device with identity ID wishes to send a high-dimensional data $(\mathbf{x}, y)$, it first encrypts the data using a lightweight AEAD algorithm to produce $(c, tag) \leftarrow \mathsf{AEAD.Enc}(\mathsf{K}_{\mathsf{ID}}, (\mathbf{x}, y))$ where c is a ciphertext and tag is an authentication tag. The encrypted data (c, tag) is put in the payload of the corresponding application layer protocol. Our rationale for choosing

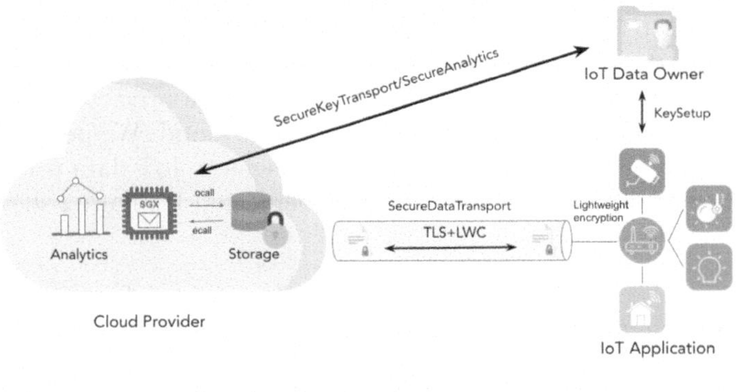

Fig. 2. Overview of Our Privacy-preserving ML System for Cloud-IoT.

a (symmetric-key) lightweight AEAD is to have a reduced computational complexity of IoT devices and less ciphertext expansion which will grately save space in the cloud.

Next, the gateway/IoT device establishes a TLS connection with the cloud and transmit the message $M := (c, tag, \mathsf{ID})$ over TLS as $(C, T) \leftarrow \mathsf{TLS.Enc}(M)$ where the TLS connection establishment includes the handshake, key establishment and record protocols. We omit these details. When the cloud receives (C, T) from the TLS, it removes the TLS layer encryption as $M \leftarrow \mathsf{TLS.Dec}(C, T)$ to obtain (c, t, ID) and stored in the database in a structured way.

SecureKeyTransport. As the owner manages the keys for the IoT devices, to decrypt an AEAD ciphertext inside the TEE/enclave, the corresponding symmetric-key has to be transported to the TEE using a security protocol and the decryption algorithm is run inside the enclave. For this purpose, the owner and the enclave first execute a key-exchange protocol, called enclave key-exchange protocol (EKEP), to establish a shared secret-key, which the owner uses to securely transport the key of the AEAD algorithm for a particular IoT device or an AEAD encrypted datasets.

SecureAnalytics. Before performing an analytics inside TEE, a necessary first step is to execute the SecureKeyTransport protocol to securely transport the key(s) to the enclave. As IoT data are stored in the encrypted form, data is transmitted to a remote attested enclave, which has received AEAD key(s) via the remote attestation. To start an analytical computation (e.g., training) within the enclave, encrypted data is decrypted first using the received key(s) and then the decrypted data/plaintext is fed into the analytics algorithms such as regression training. That is, $\boldsymbol{\theta} \leftarrow \mathsf{Training}(\boldsymbol{\theta}, \mathcal{D}, f)$ is run in the enclave. Finally, the resulting output/model $\boldsymbol{\theta}$ is encrypted or sent to the cloud without any knowledge of the fine-grained data.

Memory Optimized Training. Although our proposed system works for any ML training, we restrict ourselves to linear and logistic regression in this work. We propose two implementations of training algorithms that can be implemented as follows: 1) full enclave memory implementation – loading the entire dataset $\mathcal{D}$ in the enclave memory; and 2) low enclave memory implementation – loading a subset of $\mathcal{D}$ as needed by the training. For instance, to train a model for a linear regression model, one can build the model by solving a system of equations which will need the entire matrix associated with the dataset to be loaded in the enclave. On the other hand, training a linear model using a stochastic gradient descent (SGD) or mini-batch gradient descent requires a single or subset of data point loaded in the enclave by exploiting the tradeoff between the (secondary) storage and computation (performing the decryption of data stored in the secondary storage).

5.2 Security Discussion

In this section, we present a (semi-)formal security proof of our system. Recall that our system is built upon four fundamental secure building blocks namely a lightweight AEAD scheme, the TLS protocol, an enclave key-exchange protocol (EKEP) and a TEE realized by SGX.

Theorem 1. *Assume that the lightweight* AEAD *scheme is secure under indistinguishability under chosen plaintext attack (IND-CPA), the TLS and EKPE protocols are secure, and the TEE realized by SGX is trusted. Our proposed system is secure against semi-honest adversaries.*

Proof (Sketch). In our system, there are two types of adversaries. We use $\mathcal{A}_i$ to denote internal adversaries and $\mathcal{B}_i$ to denote external adversaries. Both adversaries may collude that can be considered as a single adversary. As the AEAD scheme is IND-CPA secure, the advantage of a (polynomial-time) adversary $\mathcal{A}_0$, denoted by $\mathsf{Adv}_{\mathcal{A}_0}^{\mathsf{IND\text{-}CPA}}$, is negligible. We consider an IND-CPA adversary $\mathcal{B}_0$ for TLS where the adversary $\mathcal{B}_0$'s goal is to distinguish encrypted messages transmitted over a TLS-secured communication. The security of TLS assures that the advantage of $\mathcal{B}_0$, denoted by $\mathsf{Adv}_{\mathcal{B}_0}^{\mathsf{TLS}}$, is negligible. The security of the EKEP, denoted by $\mathcal{B}_1$, is defined using the indistinguishability of the shared secrey-key, where there is no polynomial-time adversary that can distinguish the shared-key/session key from a random key. The security of the EKEP assures that the advantage of $\mathcal{B}_1$, denoted by $\mathsf{Adv}_{\mathcal{B}_1}^{\mathsf{EKEP}}$, is negligible. The SGX security guarantees that no adversary $\mathcal{A}_1$ can distinguish between real and simulated enclave data (analytical algorithm's code and metering data) and can break the integrity or tampering the computation with a valid output of f. The advantage of $\mathcal{A}_1$, denoted by $\mathsf{Adv}_{\mathcal{A}_1}^{\mathsf{TEE}}$ is negligible. We argue that the advantage of a (semi-honest) adversary $\mathcal{A}$ (internal or external) to break IoT data and analytical computation confidentiality with respect to IND-CPA in all phases is bounded by $\mathsf{Adv}_{\mathcal{A}}^{\mathsf{IND\text{-}CPA}} \leq 2 \cdot \mathsf{Adv}_{\mathcal{A}_0}^{\mathsf{IND\text{-}CPA}} + \mathsf{Adv}_{\mathcal{B}_0}^{\mathsf{TLS}} + \mathsf{Adv}_{\mathcal{B}_1}^{\mathsf{EKEP}} + \mathsf{Adv}_{\mathcal{A}_1}^{\mathsf{TEE}}$. We define the real system's security with the IND-CPA game where the adversary $\mathcal{A}$ interacts with the real system and aims to distinguish an IoT data at any phase. The initial game is the standard IND-CPA game between the adversary $\mathcal{A}$ and the challenger. The advantage of $\mathcal{A}$ is $\mathsf{Adv}_{\mathcal{A}}^{\mathsf{IND\text{-}CPA}}$.

- *Reduction to the AEAD security:* In this game G_1, we replace an original ciphertext $(c, tag) \leftarrow \mathsf{AEAD.Enc}(\mathsf{K}_{\mathsf{ID}}, (\mathbf{x}, y))$ with an encryption of a random plaintext $(\mathbf{r}_x, r_y)$, i.e., $(r_c, r_{tag}) \leftarrow \mathsf{AEAD.Enc}(\mathsf{K}_{\mathsf{ID}}, (\mathbf{r}_x, r_y))$. Since AEAD is IND-CPA secure, the ciphertexts c and r_c are indistinguishable. $\mathcal{A}$'s advantage in distinguishing the original game and this game is negligible. The difference between the advantages is $|\mathsf{Adv}_{\mathcal{A}}^{\mathsf{IND\text{-}CPA}} - \mathsf{Adv}_{\mathcal{A}}^{G_1}| \leq \mathsf{Adv}_{\mathcal{A}_0}^{\mathsf{IND\text{-}CPA}}$.
- *Reduction to the TLS security:* In this game G_2, we replace actual TLS encryption with a TLS encryption of a random value $M' := (r_c, r_{tag}, r_{\mathsf{ID}})$, i.e., $(C', T') \leftarrow \mathsf{TLS.Enc}(M')$ By the security of TLS, $\mathcal{A}$'s advantage in distinguishing between G_1 and G_2 is negligible, and we have $|\mathsf{Adv}_{\mathcal{A}}^{G_1} - \mathsf{Adv}_{\mathcal{A}}^{G_2}| \leq \mathsf{Adv}_{\mathcal{B}_0}^{\mathsf{TLS}}$.
- *Reduction to the EKEP security:* In this game G_3, we simulate the EKEP protocol and obtain a shared-key r_K and then use the shared-key r_K in the AEAD to encrypt K_{ID}, i.e., $\mathsf{AEAD.Enc}(r_K, \mathsf{K}_{\mathsf{ID}})$. The security of EKEP and AEAD assures that $\mathsf{AEAD.Enc}(r_K, \mathsf{K}_{\mathsf{ID}})$ and $\mathsf{AEAD.Enc}(K_s, \mathsf{K}_{\mathsf{ID}})$ are indistinguishable and the adversary's advantage is negligible. So, we have $|\mathsf{Adv}_{\mathcal{A}}^{G_2} - \mathsf{Adv}_{\mathcal{A}}^{G_3}| \leq \mathsf{Adv}_{\mathcal{B}_1}^{\mathsf{EKEP}} + \mathsf{Adv}_{\mathcal{A}_0}^{\mathsf{IND\text{-}CPA}}$.

– *Reduction to the TEE security:* In this game G_4, we replace the TEE with a simulated enclave that guarantees confidentiality and integrity of the data and computation. This game is indistinguishable from the previous one due to the security of the TEE, and A's advantage is negligible. Therefore, we have $|\mathsf{Adv}_{\mathcal{A}}^{G_4} - \mathsf{Adv}_{\mathcal{A}}^{G_4}| \leq \mathsf{Adv}_{\mathcal{A}_1}^{\mathsf{TEE}}$.

Combining all reductions, we can conclude the claimed advantage bound of the adversary $\mathcal{A}$, which is negligible. Hence, the overall system's IoT data privacy is preserved. We emphasize that the integrity against the semi-honest adversary is assured. Due to the space limit, we skip the security arguments.

6 Experimental Evaluation

In this section, we evaluate our system when instantiate by lightweight AEAD schemes from the NIST LWC competition and the TEE by Intel-SGX. We present the benchmarking results on lightweight AEAD schemes in SGX, followed by training linear and logistic regression models in SGX.

6.1 Setup

Testbed Setup. We implement our Cloud-IoT data analytics framework, ensuring privacy and security of users' sensitive data, controlled by a legitimate data owner. We simulate our system model, shown in Fig. 2, an IoT device that is a `Raspberry Pi Pico` and a gateway using `Raspberry Pi 4B`. We use a Microsoft Azure virtual machine with an `Intel Xeon (Ice Lake)` processor, 8 GB of RAM, and 4 GB of memory EPC. The Raspberry Pico is a resource-constrained device with an `ARM Cortex-M0+` processor, while the Raspberry Pi 4B, equipped with a `64-bit quad-core ARM Cortex-A7` processor, functions as a more powerful gateway. The Raspberry Pi 4B is connected to both the Microsoft Azure cloud and the Raspberry Pico. We program the Pico device so that data is set at a regular time interval and transmitted via the gateway to the Microsoft Azure cloud. Figure 3 shows a snapshot of our Cloud-IoT system implementation in our lab environment.

We prototype our system in `C/C++`. We realize a secure channel between the Raspberry Pi 4B and the cloud using the `OpenSSL` library, while the Raspberry Pi Pico uses `mbedTLS`, a lighter version of TLS, to connect to the Raspberry Pi 4B. Before performing the TLS, we use the NIST lightweight AEAD to encrypt the IoT data in the application layer where we put the AEAD ciphertext and tag in the payload. The second layer of security is enable by the standard TLS protocol before it is transmitted to the Azure cloud using the TCP/IP protocol.

Fig. 3. An Overview of Our Testbed Setup using the Azure cloud, Raspberry Pi Pico and Raspberry Pi 4B Devices.

6.2 Results on Lightweight Ciphers in SGX

AEAD Implementation Details in SGX. We use a lightweight AEAD as a symmetric-key encryption and integrity protection algorithm as it is suitable for the IoT devices. We instantiate the AEAD algorithm by ten finalists, mentioned in Sect. 2.2, from the NIST LWC competition. We use the source code implementations of these ciphers from the NIST LWC competition website [34].

We evaluate the performance of each AEAD encryption/decryption inside the SGX by counting the number of clock cycles. We also obtain the execution time outside of SGX to compare the overhead introduced by the security operations of SGX. In our experiment, we use 128-bit plaintext data and an empty associated data for both encryption and decryption operations.

In our experiment, encryption and decryption functions are performed five times for each AEAD scheme, and the average clock cycles are computed for both inside and outside the enclave. To implement an SGX version of each AEAD scheme, we create an `E-call` that triggers the encryption/decryption function and add this `E-call` to the `Enclave.edl` file. The AEAD scheme code and headers are included in the trusted part of the program, and the headers are added in the `Enclave.cpp` file. The corresponding function is run inside the `E-call` function in `Enclave.cpp`. To compare performance with the untrusted version, we measure the `E-call` clock cycles for all algorithms five times and compute the average time similarly.

Benchmark Results. Table 1 shows the number of clock cycles for the encryption operation for both trusted and untrusted execution of ten NIST finalists. Despite ASCON being in the NIST LWC standard and demonstrating a robust performance, TinyJambu exhibits a better performance, achieving the shortest encryption and decryption times in both environments. In contrast, Grain128 and Photon-Beetle exhibit the longest processing time, particularly in SGX. Table 1 also shows the overhead introduced by the SGX operations for the encryption of each AEAD algorithm. The cipher Romulus has the highest overhead that is 2.23×, and ISAP has the lowest overhead which is 1.06× (Figs. 4 and 5).

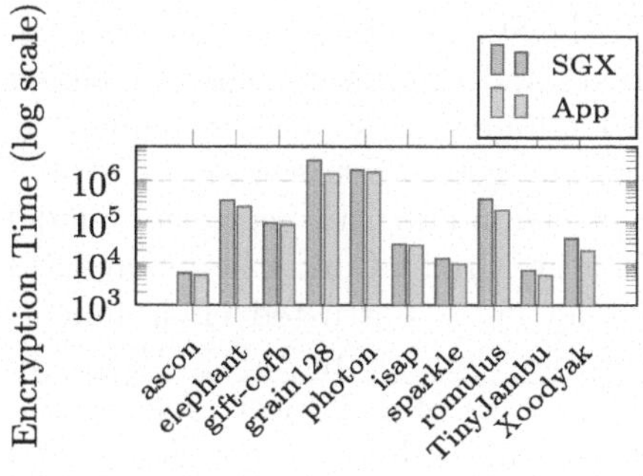

Fig. 4. Encryption Time in SGX and App.

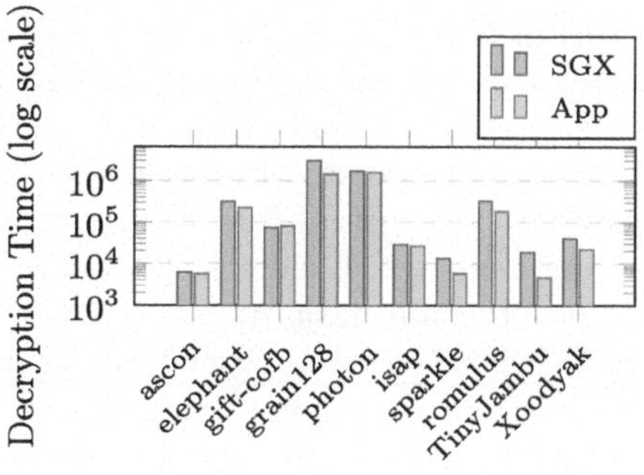

Fig. 5. Decryption Time in SGX and App.

Table 1. Encryption Performance Comparison: SGX vs App

AEAD Cipher	SGX Encryption (clock cycle)	App Encryption (clock cycle)	Overhead (×)
Ascon	5,708	5,122	1.11
Elephant	331,888	212,682	1.56
GIFT-COFB	90,864	72,918	1.25
Grain128	2,972,530	1,373,994	2.16
ISAP	28,020	26,520	1.06
Photon-Beetle	1,764,714	1,554,082	1.14
Romulus	350,980	157,296	2.23
TinyJambu	6,486	5,544	1.17
Sparkle	12,748	5,656	2.25
Xoodyak	38,764	19,818	1.95

6.3 Results on Regression Analysis in SGX

Training Implementation Details in SGX. We assume that the IoT devices already streamed their data to the cloud. To protect data privacy at-rest against the cloud provider, we store ML data to be trained in the encrypted form using a lightweight AEAD algorithm and fetch within an enclave when the training is performed. Before we perform training, we first decrypt the ciphertext inside the enclave. Our implementation design of training linear and logistic models in SGX are similar to the one in Sect. 6.2. For an SGX-memory optimized implementation of training, we perform a stochastic gradient descent (SGD)-based training where we do not require to load all training data inside the enclave simultaneously.

In our experiment, we implemented two types of regression models, namely linear regression and logistic regression and train them on 11 different datasets, mentioned in Sect. 6.1, in both the SGX environment and an untrusted environment. We measured the training duration for all models 5 times.

Timing Results. As the training time inside the SGX environment includes the timings of the decryption of AEAD ciphertexts and the linear/logistic training time. However, to better understand the only training time, we do not include the time taken the decryption and report the training time. First section in Table 2 shows the execution time in millisecond (ms) to train a logistic regression model on the Diabetes, Credit Approval, Breast Cancer, Credit Card Clients, and US Census Income datasets. Compared to training in an untrusted environment, the overhead of training the model in SGX varies from 32 ms to 15,319 ms. In Table 2, n and d denote the dimension and the size of a dataset. The second section of Table 2 shows the execution time to train a linear regression model on the Auto MPG, Boston Housing, Energy Efficiency, Wine Quality, Parkinson's Telemonitoring, and Bike Sharing datasets. Compared to training in an untrusted environment, the overhead of training a linear model in SGX varies from 15 ms to 2,471 ms. Larger datasets and those with more features generally experience a greater increase in training time in the secure environment.

Table 2. Processing times and dataset details for regression models.

Model Type	Name	n	d	Untrusted (ms)	SGX (ms)	Overhead (×)
Logistic Regression	Diabetes	9	768	83	115	1.387
	Credit Approval	14	652	96	145	1.515
	Breast Cancer	32	454	162	247	1.523
	Credit Card Clients	24	30,000	26,972	33,245	1.231
	US Census Income	20	48,842	60,276	75,595	1.255
Linear Regression	Auto MPG	8	392	53	68	1.283
	Boston Housing	14	506	104	147	1.415
	Energy Efficiency	9	768	115	138	1.217
	Wine Quality	12	1,599	323	425	1.316
	Parkinson	22	5,875	2,489	3,392	1.362
	Bike Sharing	12	17,379	9,777	12,248	1.251

7 Conclusion and Future Work

In this paper, we presented a privacy-preserving ML system for Cloud-IoT that enables secure collection and training of ML models on fine-grained IoT data. By employing a lightweight AEAD scheme for encryption and leveraging TEE for in-use data protection, our system ensures data confidentiality and integrity. We validated its practicality by encrypting IoT testbed data, securely transmitting it to the cloud, and training logistic and linear regression models on real-world datasets. As a future work, we have been continuing to implement application-specific deep learning algorithms in our testbed.

Acknowledgment. This work was supported by an NBIF RAI 2024 award and the NSERC Discovery grant.

References

1. Aumasson, J.P., Henzen, L., Meier, W., Naya-Plasencia, M.: Quark: a lightweight hash. J. Cryptol. **26**, 313–339 (2013)
2. Ball, M., Carmer, B., Malkin, T., Rosulek, M., Schimanski, N.: Garbled neural networks are practical. Cryptology ePrint Archive (2019)
3. Banik, S.: Gift-cofb v1.0. NIST, Gaithersburg, MD, USA (2024)
4. Bao, Z.: Photon-beetle authenticated encryption and hash family. NIST (2021). https://csrc.nist.gov/CSRC/media/Projects/lightweight-cryptography/documents/round-2/spec-doc-rnd2/photon-beetle-spec-round2.pdf. Accessed 3 July 2024
5. Beaulieu, R., Shors, D., Smith, J., Treatman-Clark, S., Weeks, B., Wingers, L.: The simon and speck lightweight block ciphers. In: Proceedings of the 52nd Annual Design Automation Conference, pp. 1–6 (2015)
6. Beierle, C.: Schwaemm and esch: Lightweight authenticated encryption and hashing using the sparkle permutation family. NIST (2021). https://csrc.nist.gov/CSRC/media/Projects/lightweight-cryptography/documents/round-2/spec-doc-rnd2/sparkle-spec-round2.pdf. Accessed 3 July 2024
7. Bernstein, D., Lange, T.: ebacs: Ecrypt benchmarking of cryptographic systems (2024). https://bench.cr.yp.to/. Accessed 3 Sept 2024
8. Beyne, T., Chen, Y.L., Dobraunig, C., Mennink, B.: Elephant v1.1. NIST (2021). Accessed 3 July 2024
9. Bogdanov, A., Knežević, M., Leander, G., Toz, D., Varıcı, K., Verbauwhede, I.: SPONGENT: a lightweight hash function. In: Preneel, B., Takagi, T. (eds.) CHES 2011. LNCS, vol. 6917, pp. 312–325. Springer, Heidelberg (2011). https://doi.org/10.1007/978-3-642-23951-9_21
10. Bogdanov, A., et al.: PRESENT: an ultra-lightweight block cipher. In: Paillier, P., Verbauwhede, I. (eds.) CHES 2007. LNCS, vol. 4727, pp. 450–466. Springer, Heidelberg (2007). https://doi.org/10.1007/978-3-540-74735-2_31
11. Bonte, C., Vercauteren, F.: Privacy-preserving logistic regression training. BMC Med. Genomics **11**, 13–21 (2018)
12. Chanal, P.M., Kakkasageri, M.S.: Security and privacy in IoT: a survey. Wireless Pers. Commun. **115**(2), 1667–1693 (2020)
13. Chen, C., Zhou, J., Wang, L., Wu, X.: When homomorphic encryption marries secret sharing: secure large-scale sparse logistic regression and applications in risk control. In: Proceedings of the 27th ACM SIGKDD Conference on Knowledge Discovery & Data Mining, pp. 2652–2662 (2021)
14. Daemen, J., Hoffert, S., Peeters, M., Assche, G.V., Keer, R.V.: Xoodyak, a lightweight cryptographic scheme. NIST (2021). https://csrc.nist.gov/CSRC/media/Projects/lightweight-cryptography/documents/round-2/spec-doc-rnd2/Xoodyak-spec-round2.pdf. Accessed 3 July 2024
15. Dobraunig, C.: Isap v2.0. NIST (2021). https://csrc.nist.gov/CSRC/media/Projects/lightweight-cryptography/documents/round-2/spec-doc-rnd2/isap-spec-round2.pdf. Accessed 3 July 2024
16. Dobraunig, C., Eichlseder, M., Mendel, F., Schläffer, M.: Ascon v1. 2: lightweight authenticated encryption and hashing. J. Cryptol. **34**, 1–42 (2021)

17. Dong, Y., Chen, X., Shen, L., Wang, D.: Privacy-preserving distributed machine learning based on secret sharing. In: Information and Communications Security: 21st International Conference, pp. 684–702. Springer (2020)
18. Ghavamipour, A.R., Turkmen, F., Jiang, X.: Privacy-preserving logistic regression with secret sharing. BMC Med. Inform. Decis. Mak. **22**(1), 89 (2022)
19. Giacomelli, I., Jha, S., Joye, M., Page, C.D., Yoon, K.: Privacy-preserving ridge regression with only linearly-homomorphic encryption. In: Preneel, B., Vercauteren, F. (eds.) ACNS 2018. LNCS, vol. 10892, pp. 243–261. Springer, Cham (2018). https://doi.org/10.1007/978-3-319-93387-0_13
20. Gong, Z., Hartel, P., Nikova, S., Tang, S.H., Zhu, B.: Tulp: a family of lightweight message authentication codes for body sensor networks. J. Comput. Sci. Technol. **29**, 53–68 (2014)
21. Grover, K., Tople, S., Shinde, S., Bhagwan, R., Ramjee, R.: Privado: practical and secure DNN inference with enclaves. arXiv preprint arXiv:1810.00602 (2018)
22. Guo, J., Peyrin, T., Poschmann, A.: The PHOTON family of lightweight hash functions. In: Rogaway, P. (ed.) CRYPTO 2011. LNCS, vol. 6841, pp. 222–239. Springer, Heidelberg (2011). https://doi.org/10.1007/978-3-642-22792-9_13
23. Hell, M., Johansson, T., Meier, W., Sönnerup, J., Yoshida, H.: Grain-128AEAD—a lightweight AEAD stream cipher. NIST (2021). Accessed 3 July 2024
24. Hirose, S., Ideguchi, K., Kuwakado, H., Owada, T., Preneel, B., Yoshida, H.: A lightweight 256-bit hash function for hardware and low-end devices: Lesamnta-lw. In: Information Security and Cryptology-ICISC 2010: 13th International Conference, Seoul, Korea, 1–3 December 2010, Revised Selected Papers 13, pp. 151–168. Springer (2011)
25. Iwata, T., Khairallah, M., Minematsu, K., Peyrin, T.: Romulus v1.2. NIST (2021). https://csrc.nist.gov/CSRC/media/Projects/lightweightcryptography/documents/round-2/spec-doc-rnd2/Romulus-specround2.pdf. Accessed 3 July 2024
26. Jiang, Y., et al.: Securelr: secure logistic regression model via a hybrid cryptographic protocol. IEEE/ACM Trans. Comput. Biol. Bioinf. **16**(1), 113–123 (2018)
27. Kim, M., Song, Y., Wang, S., Xia, Y., Jiang, X., et al.: Secure logistic regression based on homomorphic encryption: design and evaluation. JMIR Med. Inform. **6**(2), e8805 (2018)
28. Le Quoc, D., Gregor, F., Singh, J., Fetzer, C.: Sgx-pyspark: secure distributed data analytics. In: The World Wide Web Conference, pp. 3564–3563 (2019)
29. Leander, G., Paar, C., Poschmann, A., Schramm, K.: New lightweight DES variants. In: Biryukov, A. (ed.) FSE 2007. LNCS, vol. 4593, pp. 196–210. Springer, Heidelberg (2007). https://doi.org/10.1007/978-3-540-74619-5_13
30. Luykx, A., Preneel, B., Tischhauser, E., Yasuda, K.: A MAC mode for lightweight block ciphers. In: Peyrin, T. (ed.) FSE 2016. LNCS, vol. 9783, pp. 43–59. Springer, Heidelberg (2016). https://doi.org/10.1007/978-3-662-52993-5_3
31. Mouha, N., Mennink, B., Van Herrewege, A., Watanabe, D., Preneel, B., Verbauwhede, I.: Chaskey: an efficient MAC algorithm for 32-bit microcontrollers. In: Joux, A., Youssef, A. (eds.) SAC 2014. LNCS, vol. 8781, pp. 306–323. Springer, Cham (2014). https://doi.org/10.1007/978-3-319-13051-4_19
32. Needham, R.M., Wheeler, D.J.: Tea extensions. Report (Cambridge University, Cambridge, UK, 1997) (1997)
33. NIST: NIST lightweight cryptography (2017). https://github.com/usnistgov/Lightweight-Cryptography-Benchmarking. Accessed 02 Sept 2024
34. NIST: NIST lightweight cryptography process timeline (2017). https://csrc.nist.gov/projects/lightweight-cryptography/timeline. Accessed 02 Sept 2024

35. Renner, S., Pozzobon, E., Mottok, J.: LWC benchmark (2024), gitHub repository. https://lab.las3.de/gitlab/lwc/compare. Accessed 3 Sept 2024
36. Rivest, R.L.: The RC5 encryption algorithm. In: International Workshop on Fast Software Encryption, pp. 86–96. Springer (1994)
37. Schuster, F., et al.: VC3: trustworthy data analytics in the cloud using SGX. In: 2015 IEEE Symposium on Security and Privacy, pp. 38–54. IEEE (2015)
38. Weatherley, R.: Lightweight cryptography primitives (2024). https://rweather.github.io/lwc-finalists/index.html. Accessed 3 Sept 2024
39. Wheeler, D.J., Needham, R.M.: Tea, a tiny encryption algorithm. In: Fast Software Encryption: Second International Workshop Leuven, Belgium, 14–16 December 1994 Proceedings 2, pp. 363–366. Springer (1995)
40. Wu, H., Huang, T.: Tinyjambu: a family of lightweight authenticated encryption algorithms. NIST (2021). https://csrc.nist.gov/CSRC/media/Projects/lightweight-cryptography/documents/round-2/spec-doc-rnd2/TinyJAMBU-specround2.pdf. Accessed 3 July 2024

Intersecting Security, Privacy, and Machine Learning Techniques to Detect, Mitigate, and Prevent Threats

LocalIntel: Generating Organizational Threat Intelligence from Global and Local Cyber Knowledge

Shaswata Mitra[1(✉)], Subash Neupane[1], Trisha Chakraborty[1], Sudip Mittal[1], Aritran Piplai[2], Manas Gaur[3], and Shahram Rahimi[4]

[1] Mississippi State University, Starkville, MS, USA
{sm3843,sn922,tc2006}@msstate.edu, mittal@cse.msstate.edu
[2] The University of Texas at El Paso, El Paso, TX, USA
apiplai@utep.edu
[3] University of Maryland Baltimore County, Baltimore, MD, USA
manas@umbc.edu
[4] University of Alabama, Tuscaloosa, Alabama
srahimi1@ua.edu

Abstract. Security Operations Center (SoC) analysts gather threat reports from openly accessible *global threat repositories* and tailor the information to their organization's needs, such as developing threat intelligence and security policies. They also depend on organizational internal repositories, which act as private *local knowledge database.* These local knowledge databases store credible cyber intelligence, critical operational and infrastructure details. SoCs undertake a *manual labor-intensive* task of utilizing these global threat repositories and local knowledge databases to create both organization-specific threat intelligence and mitigation policies. Recently, Large Language Models (LLMs) have shown the capability to process diverse knowledge sources efficiently. We leverage this ability to automate this organization-specific threat intelligence generation. We present LocalIntel, a novel automated threat intelligence contextualization framework that retrieves zero-day vulnerability reports from the global threat repositories and uses its local knowledge database to determine implications and mitigation strategies to alert and assist the SoC analyst. LocalIntel comprises two key phases: *knowledge retrieval* and *contextualization.* Quantitative and qualitative assessment has shown effectiveness in generating up to 93% accurate organizational threat intelligence with 64% inter-rater agreement.

Keywords: Cybersecurity · Cyber Threat Intelligence (CTI) · Knowledge Contextualization · Generative AI · Large Language Model (LLM)

K. Adi et al. (Eds.): FPS 2024, LNCS 15533, pp. 63–78, 2025.
https://doi.org/10.1007/978-3-031-87496-3_5

1 Introduction

In 2023, there were 2,365 cyberattacks, with 29,065[1] reported Common Vulnerabilities and Exposures (CVE)[2]. Cyber analysts in the Security Operations Center (SoC) retrieve malware samples from the internet. These samples are executed in sandboxes for behavior analysis. This analysis leads to developing defensive strategies to detect and prevent cyber-attacks that use such malware. The findings are shared publicly as *generic cyber threat intelligence (CTI)* in *global threat repositories* like CVE, National Vulnerability Database (NVD) (see footnote 2), Common Weakness Enumeration (CWE) (see footnote 2) or as third-party threat reports. Security analysts of an organization manually contextualize this generic knowledge to that organization's unique operating conditions by considering factors like network, hardware & software specifics and business needs to protect from such cyber-attacks. Security measures such as policies and protocols are then deployed depending on this contextualized information to maintain secured operations. Organizations maintain this operating information and contextualized threat intelligence documented in their *local knowledge database*.

However, expeditiously developing appropriate contextualized reports is a critical challenge before deploying security policies. Manual generation not only consumes high costs but can also be erroneous and require plenty of time due to the volume and criticality of unstructured information. On the other hand, organizations must immediately integrate policies for any novel threat to safeguard operations. Failure of *timely and correct* contextualized CTI generation for policy updation can incur heavy losses. Consider a couple of scenarios where either knowledge's availability is insufficient. **Scenario 1**: An organization's internal rules detect an unknown process attempting to communicate with an external server. The Endpoint Detection and Response (EDR) team flags and blocks the process. However, without global CTI, they are unaware that this process is part of a larger ransomware campaign. Without this knowledge, the EDR team's response is inadequate, as it fails to recognize additional Indicators of Compromises (IoCs). A secondary payload may go undetected, encrypting the organization's data. **Scenario 2**: During a routine penetration test, the software and corresponding versions used by the company are identified. Based on CVE/CWE data, the testers flag many software versions due to reported vulnerabilities. However, update log reveals that the flagged software has already been patched, making the alerts unnecessary. Modern IDEs or cybersecurity tools such as Nessus[3] or Nexpose[4] can instantly notify the SoC analyst regarding the zero-day vulnerability. However, these solutions cannot suggest accurate counteractions as they cannot assume organizational status since local knowledge resides within the organizational scope. Furthermore, organizations resist granting access to this local knowledge to a third-party vendor. This situation presents a challenge for SoC analysts as they are dealing with two sets of unstruc-

[1] URLs: bit.ly/3zccFKK and bit.ly/4g8bdKk.

[2] CVE: cve.mitre.org | CWE: cwe.mitre.org | NVD: nvd.nist.gov.

[3] Nessus: tenable.com/products/nessus.

[4] Nexpose: rapid7.com/products/nexpose.

tured information. They may require more time to fully understand the context to develop the right policy before the vulnerability gets exploited in an active attack.

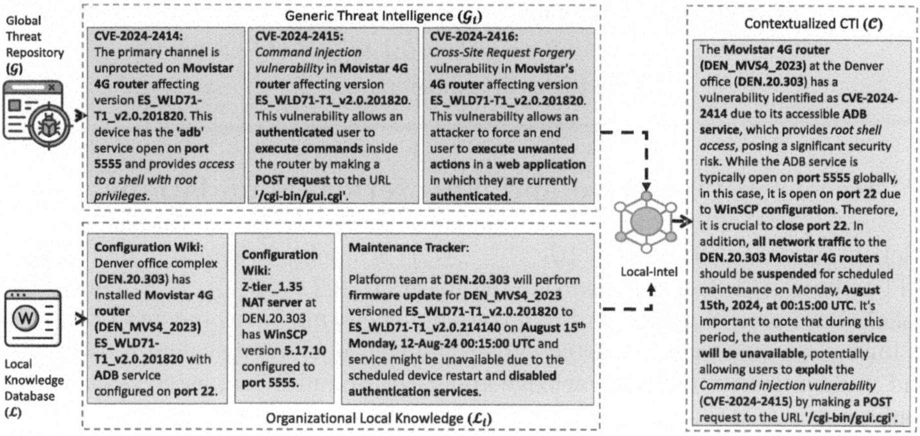

Fig. 1. Overview of our LocalIntel framework with an example use case.

To address this problem, we developed LocalIntel. Our motivation stems from the idea that an *on-premise* system capable of *automatically* generating *relevant* and *accurate* organization-specific threat intelligence, which includes *threat implications* and *counteractions*, by assimilating global and local knowledge, would empower SoC analysts to quickly understand the effects of new cyber threats on their infrastructure, thereby saving valuable time from the manual effort. Hence, SoC analysts can develop, modify, or update their cyber defense strategies in real-time, mitigating the risk of early cyber-attacks. Considering the diverse organizational infrastructure, we have designed our LocalIntel framework to be modular, meaning the framework is customizable based on the use case. To the best of our knowledge, this is the first research that contextualizes global threat intelligence adapted for an organization-specific context. Our work makes the following contributions:

- We demonstrate the feasibility of producing accurate and relevant organization-specific CTI from generic threat intelligence and its operational knowledge.
- We built a knowledge-contextualization framework that generates real-time organizational CTI from publicly available and organizational knowledge.
- We construct a prototype repository of local organizational knowledge and an evaluation dataset to assess the generation of contextualized CTI.
- Through our evaluation dataset, we illustrate LocalIntel's ability to generate precise organizational CTI using qualitative and quantitative metrics.

In Sect. 2, we discuss the problem statement and theoretical foundations. Section 3 provides a detailed description of our LocalIntel framework. The experiment and evaluation are presented in Sect. 4. Moving forward, Sect. 5 explores the related works. Concluding remarks are in Sect. 6.

Table 1. Description of Notation.

Notation	Description
$\{\mathcal{G}_i \mid \mathcal{G}_i \in \mathcal{G}\}$	Global Threat Repository
$\{\mathcal{L}_i \mid \mathcal{L}_i \in \mathcal{L}\}$	Local Organizational Database
$\mathcal{Q}$	Query to fetch global ($\mathcal{G}_i$) & local ($\mathcal{L}$) knowledge
$\mathcal{C}$	Contextualized Completion

2 Research Objective and Theoretical Foundations

Global threat repository ($\mathcal{G} = \{\mathcal{G}_1, \mathcal{G}_2, ..., \mathcal{G}_n\}$) is a publicly available set of online CTI reports ($\mathcal{G}_i$). Local knowledge database ($\mathcal{L} = \{\mathcal{L}_1, \mathcal{L}_2, ..., \mathcal{L}_n\}$) consists of policies and procedures of an organization's operating environments ($\mathcal{L}_i$), such as business requirements, trusted cyber intelligence, allowed system software list and version details, cyber knowledge about the organization, asset location and configurations, DMZ configurations, and maintenance reports.

Problem Statement

For a given set of vulnerability $\mathcal{G}_i$ in $\mathcal{G}$ and corresponding relevant organizational knowledge $\mathcal{L}_i$ in $\mathcal{L}$. The task is to generate Completion ($\mathcal{C}$), which is the contextualized knowledge of $\mathcal{G}_i$ w.r.t. $\mathcal{L}_i$. $\mathcal{C}$ can be considered as contextualization function $f(\cdot)$, that translates $\mathcal{G}_i$ to organizational context using $\mathcal{L}_i$.

$$f(\mathcal{G}_i, \mathcal{L}_i) = \mathcal{C}_i \forall \mathcal{G}_i \cap \mathcal{L}_i \neq \phi \quad (1)$$

For instance, in Fig. 1, where $\mathcal{G}_i$ is a set containing information stating vulnerability (v) through process (p). Alternatively, $\mathcal{L}_i$ contains information regarding the organization using process (p) for its operations and other relevant information. Hence, in the process of generating contextualized threat intelligence $\mathcal{C}$ considering v and p, $\mathcal{G}_i$ is being translated through $\mathcal{L}_i$, when $\mathcal{G}_i \cap \mathcal{L}_i \neq \phi$.

3 LocalIntel Framework

In this section, we explain our LocalIntel framework. We first explain our solution and each module with its functionality in detail (refer to Fig. 3). Finally, we discuss the system implementation and module interactions to generate the final contextualized threat intelligence $\mathcal{C}$.

3.1 Solution Approach

LocalIntel consists of two core phases: knowledge retrieval *(Retrieval Phase)* and generation *(Generation Phase)*. In the *retrieval phase*, knowledge from *global ($\mathcal{G}$)* and *local ($\mathcal{L}$)* sources are retrieved, and in the *generation phase*, a final contextualized threat intelligence $\mathcal{C}$ based on the retrieved knowledge $\mathcal{G}_i \cup \mathcal{L}_i$ is generated. Refer to Fig. 2 and Algorithm 1 for framework overview.

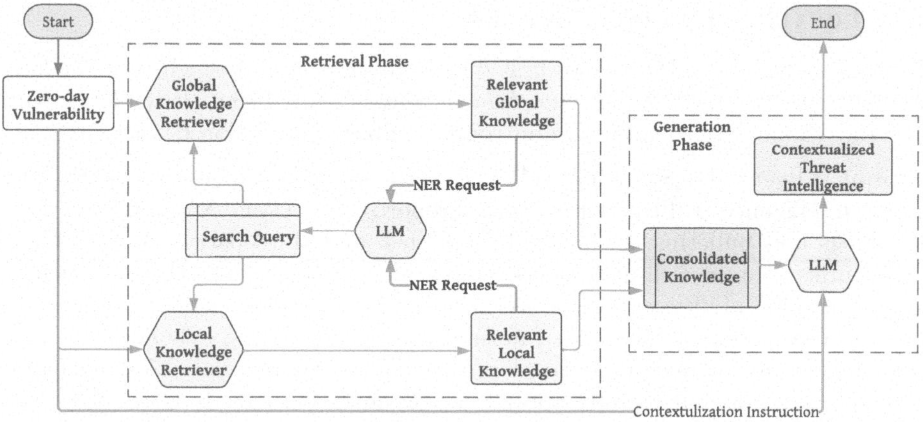

Fig. 2. LocalIntel data-flow diagram. The zero-day vulnerability triggers the system to retrieve information from global $\mathcal{G}_i$ and local $\mathcal{L}_i$ knowledge sources and then contextualizes the results, producing a final output Completion $\mathcal{C}$.

Algorithm 1: LocalIntel Pseudo-code

Input: Generic Threat Intelligence ($\mathcal{G}_i$)
Output: Contextualized Threat Intelligence ($\mathcal{C}$)
Retrieval Phase:
$\mathcal{L}_i \leftarrow execute\_local\_search(\mathcal{G}_i, \mathcal{L})$
while $\mathcal{L}_i \cap \overline{\mathcal{G}_i} \neq \phi$ **do**
  $\mathcal{Q} \leftarrow get\_search\_query(\mathcal{G}_i \cup \mathcal{L}_i)$
  forall the $\alpha \in \mathcal{Q}$ **do**
    $\mathcal{G}_i \leftarrow execute\_global\_search(\alpha, \mathcal{G})$
  $\mathcal{L}_i \leftarrow execute\_local\_search(\mathcal{G}_i, \mathcal{L})$
Generation Phase:
$\mathcal{C} \leftarrow generate\_completion(\mathcal{G}_i \cup \mathcal{L}_i)$
return $\mathcal{C}$

- In the Retrieval Phase, the system retrieves generic CTI $\mathcal{G}_i$ from $\mathcal{G}$ and relevant local knowledge $\mathcal{L}_i$ from $\mathcal{L}$ based on the relevancy. The system performs Named Entity Recognition (NER) to identify search keywords/queries $\mathcal{Q}$ over on the acquired knowledge ($\mathcal{G}_i \cup \mathcal{L}_i$). Then, it executes the search for all search queries in $\mathcal{Q}$ in the global knowledge repository $\mathcal{G}$ and local knowledge database $\mathcal{L}$ to fetch relevant threat reports and associated details. This phase continues until no additional knowledge is required ($\mathcal{L} \cap \overline{\mathcal{G}_i} \neq \phi$) to generate final contextualized threat intelligence.
- Finally, in the Generation Phase, the system generates contextualized threat intelligence $\mathcal{C}$ for the zero-day vulnerability generic threat intelligence based on the retrieved global knowledge and local knowledge ($\mathcal{G}_i \cup \mathcal{L}_i$).

3.2 LocalIntel System Modules

To implement LocalIntel, we first discuss system modules, which are *Global Threat Repository ($\mathcal{G}$), Local Knowledge Database ($\mathcal{L}$), Agent, Tools, LLM*, with zero-day threat report input $\mathcal{G}_i$ and contextualized completion $\mathcal{C}$) output.

Global Threat Repository ($\mathcal{G}$) refers to publicly available cybersecurity threat intelligence (CTI), such as threat reports from CVE, NVD, CWE, security blogs and bulletins, social media updates, and third-party reports. These repositories contain well-documented reports on cybersecurity threats, such as malware, vulnerability, cyber attacks, and many more. The primary purpose of these repositories is to facilitate information sharing among cybersecurity professionals regarding the latest developments. However, the global knowledge $\mathcal{G}_i$ is generic and may not directly apply to an organization's needs as organizations tend to customize their infrastructure depending upon the business. Moreover, the knowledge obtained from unverifiable sources is only directly usable by an organization after thorough analysis. LocalIntel is expected to be connected to these threat repositories for automated zero-day vulnerability report retrieval.

Local Knowledge Database ($\mathcal{L}$) refers to an organizations' operational information repository. Due to the generic characteristics, $\mathcal{G}$ contains a wide range of CTI, but they must be supplanted with organization-specific information to be useable. Hence, local knowledge databases or wikis are private knowledge repositories containing critical information related to organizational operations and trusted threat intelligence, such as specifics regarding the environment, operating systems, infrastructure, software, third-party systems, and processes. Confluence[5], Notion[6], are a few instances of such wiki platforms. The primary goal of these wikis is to facilitate structured development and knowledge sharing among the working professionals in an organization. Due to the unstructured nature of this information, we assume wiki platforms to be our local knowledge database. However, more structured sources like knowledge graphs can replace them with similar searching functionalities.

Agent is the main controller in our LocalIntel framework. It controls the overall flow, from receiving the input vulnerability report trigger to returning the final contextualized completion $\mathcal{C}$. Specifically, the Agent's function is to determine and regulate the sequence of actions among two phases for generating the output. The Agent actions are primarily of three types: *Query generation*, *Query execution*, and *Completion generation*. To achieve this, the Agent interacts with the other two modules: *Tool* and *LLM*, detailed following.

- *Query generation* refers to generating search queries for information retrieval from either $\mathcal{G}$ or $\mathcal{L}$. The Agent generates a search query to retrieve all the relevant information from pre-acquired knowledge ($\mathcal{G}_i \cup \mathcal{L}_i$). The Agent performs contextual embedding and keyword identification through named entity recognition (NER) to generate search queries $\mathcal{Q}$.

[5] Confluence: atlassian.com/software.

[6] Notion: notion.so/product/wikis.

- *Query execution* refers to executing search query $\mathcal{Q}$ in global threat repository $\mathcal{G}$ and local knowledge database $\mathcal{L}$ to retrieve relevant knowledge. Due to the different characteristics of $\mathcal{G}$ and $\mathcal{L}$, the retrieval process can either be a keyword search through online API calls or a semantic similarity search.
- *Text generation* can be considered an LLM inference scenario, where the Agent passes an input text to generate desired output text using LLM. Task-specific input prompts are pre-designed in the Agent.

Tool are functions that help the Agent execute some third-party actions. The actions can be diverse in type, for instance, making an online API call, performing a database search, executing custom scripts, invoking other software, and many more. However, for the scope of our research, tool functionality is limited to query generation using LLM, query execution through API calls and vector database search, and contextualized generation using LLM functionalities only. Therefore, in our LocalIntel framework, tools are responsible for executing online searches through API calls or vector database searches and parsing the results while bridging the Agent's access to different framework modules.

Large Language Model (LLM) acts as the brain of our LocalIntel framework to process diverse information and generate contextualized CTI. Besides contextualized threat intelligence generation, it acts as the parser that processes retrieved knowledge to generate queries for structured information retrieval. Depending on the task, the Agent invokes LLM with instructions and information.

Input: Zero-day threat report ($\mathcal{G}_i$) refers to publicly available CTI reports regarding any discovered vulnerability or malware. We assume that LocalIntel is connected with the global CTI repositories ($\mathcal{G}$) with active triggers to receive any newly disclosed threat reports for instant processing.

Output: Contextualized completion ($\mathcal{C}$) is the real-time generated threat intelligence specifically tailored for an organization depending on its unique operating condition. The objective of $\mathcal{C}$ is to assist SoC by providing mitigating strategies or relevant information on the specific zero-day threat ($\mathcal{G}_i$). We assume the local knowledge database ($\mathcal{L}$) contains all required organizational knowledge.

3.3 LocalIntel Implementation and Module Interactions

Previously, we have described each module in the architecture. Here, we explain the implementation phases with intermediate module interactions (refer to Fig. 3). LocalIntel initiates when a vulnerability report is received. The report can be pushed manually or via automated zero-day triggers.

Knowledge Retrieval (Phase 1): This is the first phase of our framework where the *Agent* retrieves generic threat intelligence ($\mathcal{G}_i$). It generates search queries ($\mathcal{Q}$) for relevant knowledge retrieval. The initial local knowledge search

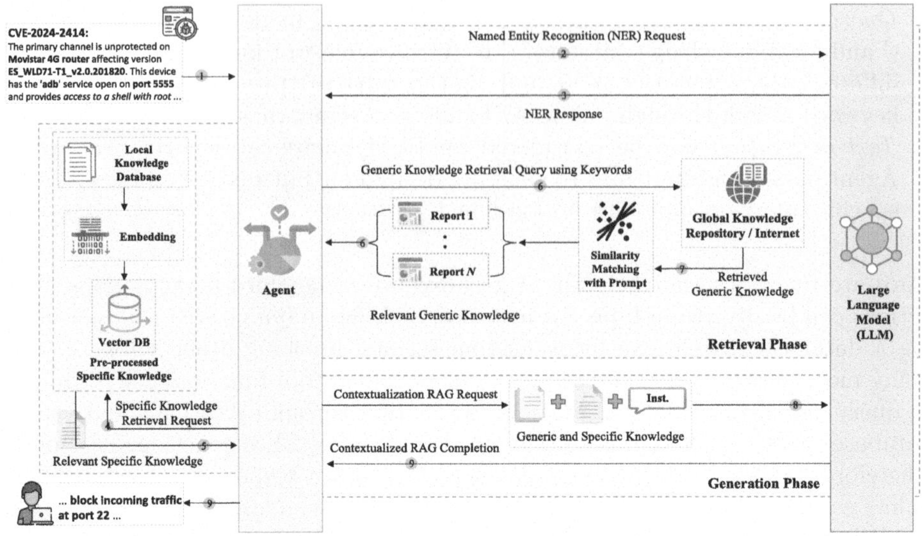

Fig. 3. LOCALINTEL framework module interaction in the two phases: knowledge retrieval, and contextualized threat intelligence generation. Processes are numbered in ascending execution order following the data-flow diagram (Fig. 2).

(refer to Algorithm 1) plays a crucial role in identifying whether the threat intelligence is relevant to the organization. If there is no overlap ($\mathcal{G}_i \cap \mathcal{L} = \phi$), then the Agent discards input $\mathcal{G}_i$, as there are no connections; hence, it cannot be contextualized. Upon overlaps discovered, it iteratively generates $\mathcal{Q}$ and executes knowledge retrieval from both global ($\mathcal{G}$) and local ($\mathcal{L}$) sources until all required knowledge needed to be considered for contextualization is retrieved. For the scope of our experiment, we implemented global knowledge retrieval from the Internet through keyword search via API endpoints of global threat repositories such as NIST, CVE, and ensemble [2] vector similarity search for local knowledge retrieval from the organizational wikis. This simplified approach efficiently fetches corresponding relevant knowledge from both sources. For instance, for the following threat intelligence, the execution is as follows:

Invoked Generic Threat Intelligence ($\mathcal{G}_i$)

CVE-2024-2414: The primary channel is unprotected on Movistar 4G router affecting E version S_WLD71-T1_v2.0.201820. This device has the 'adb' service open on port 5555 and provides access to a shell with root privileges.

Upon receiving $\mathcal{G}_i$ above, the Agent generates query embedding to perform ensemble retrieval in $\mathcal{L}$. After executing $\mathcal{Q}$ in the vector-indexed $\mathcal{L}$, the Agent identifies "Movistar 4G" to be the affecting device with following knowledge:

Phase 1: NER Query Generation ($\mathcal{Q}$)

Agent Instruction:
You are a named entity recognition (NER) tool. Given the following classes, perform NER for the provided Input text.
Classes: software, device, library, functionality, attack_vector, vulnerability ...
Input Threat Intelligence:
CVE-2024-2414: The primary channel is unprotected on Movistar 4G router affecting E version S_WLD71-T1_v2.0.201820. This device has the 'adb' service open on port 5555 and provides access to a shell with root privileges.
Output Keywords:
{"device": "Movistar 4G", "attack_vector": "port 5555", "functionality": "adb" }

The semantic search is performed through vector embedding generation and execution of similarity matching algorithms (cosine, euclidean, dot-product).

Phase 1: Retrieved Local Knowledge ($\mathcal{L}_i$) using $\mathcal{Q}_\mathcal{L}$

Configuration Wiki::
– Denver office complex (DEN.20.303) has Installed **Movistar 4G router** (DEN_MVS4_2023) **ES_WLD71-T1_v2.0.201820** with ADB service configured on port 22.
– Z-tier_1.35 NAT server at DEN.20.303 has WinSCP version 5.17.10 configured to **port 5555**.

After searching $\mathcal{L}$, the Agent performs similar query generation $\mathcal{Q}$ and execution iteratively in $\mathcal{G}$ and $\mathcal{L}$ for additional context retrieval. For this example, the additional retrieved knowledge $\mathcal{G}_i$ and $\mathcal{L}_i$ from Phase 1 is below:

Phase 1: Additional Global and Local Knowledge ($\mathcal{G}_i \cup \mathcal{L}_i$)

Global Knowledge:
– **CVE-2024-2415**: Command injection vulnerability in **Movistar 4G router** affecting version **ES_WLD71-T1_v2.0.201820**. This vulnerability allows an authenticated user to execute commands inside the router by making a POST request to the URL **'/cgi-bin/gui.cgi'**.
– **CVE-2024-2416**: Cross-Site Request Forgery vulnerability in Movistar's 4G router affecting version **ES_WLD71-T1_v2.0.201820**. This vulnerability allows an attacker to force an end user to execute unwanted actions in a web application in which they are currently authenticated.
Local Knowledge:
– **Maintenance Tracker**: Platform team at **DEN.20.303** will perform firmware update for **DEN_MVS4_2023** versioned **ES_WLD71-T1_v2.0.201820** to ES_WLD71-T1_v2.0.214140 on August 15th Monday, 12-Aug-24 00:15:00 UTC and service might be unavailable due to the scheduled device restart and disabled authentication services.

Consolidated knowledge ($\mathcal{G}_i \cup \mathcal{L}_i$) is passed for query generation. For this case, *DEN.20.303* and *DEN_MVS4_2023* used to identify related information.

Contextualized Generation (Phase 2): In this phase, upon complete retrieval of $\mathcal{G}_i \cup \mathcal{L}_i$, the Agent invokes LLM for final contextualization.

Phase 2: Contextualized Organizational Threat Intelligence ($\mathcal{C}$)

Agent Instruction:
You are an honest network security analyst. Given public threat intelligence reports fetched from trusted cybersecurity sources and organizational infrastructure and operations details. Generate a cyber threat intelligence report with all details, including the impact and mitigation strategies. Do not include any information that is not provided as additional knowledge.
Retrieved Global Knowledge ($\mathcal{G}_i$):
– **CVE-2024-2414**: The primary channel is unprotected on Movistar 4G router affecting E version S_WLD71-T1_v2.0.201820. This device has the 'adb' service open on port 5555 and provides access to a shell with root privileges.
– **CVE-2024-2415**: Command injection vulnerability in Movistar 4G router affecting version ES_WLD71-T1_v2.0.201820. This vulnerability allows an authenticated user to execute commands inside the router by making a POST request to the URL '/cgi-bin/gui.cgi'.
– **CVE-2024-2416**: Cross-Site Request Forgery vulnerability in Movistar's 4G router affecting version ES_WLD71-T1_v2.0.201820. This vulnerability allows an attacker to force an end user to execute unwanted actions in a web application in which they are currently authenticated.
Retrieved Local Knowledge ($\mathcal{L}_i$):
– **Configuration Wiki**: Denver office complex (DEN.20.303) has Installed Movistar 4G router (DEN_MVS4_2023) ES_WLD71-T1_v2.0.201820 with ADB service configured on port 22
– **Configuration Wiki**: Z-tier_1.35 NAT server at DEN.20.303 has WinSCP version 5.17.10 configured to port 5555.
– **Maintenance Tracker**: Platform team at DEN.20.303 will perform firmware update for DEN_MVS4_2023 versioned ES_WLD71-T1_v2.0.201820 to ES_WLD71-T1_v2.0.214140 on August 15th Monday, 12-Aug-24 00:15:00 UTC and service might be unavailable due to the scheduled device restart and disabled authentication services.
Contextualized Completion:
The **Movistar 4G router (DEN_MVS4_2023)** at the **Denver office (DEN.20.303)** has a vulnerability identified as **CVE-2024-2414** due to its accessible ADB service, which provides root shell access, posing a significant security risk. **While the ADB service is typically open on port 5555 globally, in this case, it is open on port 22 due to WinSCP configuration**. Therefore, it is crucial to **close port 22**. In addition, all **network traffic to the DEN.20.303 Movistar 4G routers should be suspended** for scheduled maintenance on **Monday, August 15th, 2024, at 00:15:00 UTC**. It's important to note that during this period, the **authentication service will be unavailable, potentially allowing users to exploit the Command injection vulnerability (CVE-2024-2415)** by making a POST request to the URL '/cgi-bin/gui.cgi'.

After completing both phases, we can observe that through an initial local search, the agent identified the "Movistar 4G router" as the device of interest ($\mathcal{G}_i \cap \mathcal{L}$) with additional relevant knowledge. Then, it iteratively retrieved additional threat intelligence (CVE-2024-2415 and CVE-2024-2416) for the device from $\mathcal{G}$ (we considered NVD as $\mathcal{G}$ for the experiment) and $\mathcal{L}$ (considered an organizational wiki) to obtain additional local context. The concatenation of knowledge prior to retrieval allowed the discovery of indirect relevant documents such as maintenance schedules. Without this knowledge, the mitigation strategy might become ineffective. Finally, by providing all relevant information ($\mathcal{G}_i \cup \mathcal{L}_i$) and task instruction, the Agent invokes LLM for real-time organization-specific threat intelligence generation. This relevant real-time update then equips SoC analysts with all relevant information without investing any time in manual investigation. The SoC analyst can then utilize this knowledge to take the necessary actions to safeguard the organization against imminent cyber threats.

4 Experiment and Evaluation

In this section, we discuss our experiments and the achieved evaluation results. For our evaluations, we performed experiments considering 58 publicly available threat intelligence scenarios to demonstrate the feasibility of the LocalIntel framework and assess contextualization relevancy. For the global threat repository ($\mathcal{G}$), we considered NVD-CVE data, and for the local knowledge database ($\mathcal{L}$), a curated organizational wiki (PII anonymized for confidentiality). However, as described in Sect. 3, LocalIntel[7] is modular, allowing flexibility to modify the modules depending on requirements and organization-specifics. For example, other generic threat intelligence sources can be integrated with $\mathcal{G}$, different local knowledge sources such as knowledge graphs can be incorporated, and other generative language models can be adopted for a more controlled generation. Following, we will delve into the evaluation dataset and experiment setup. Finally, we will describe our evaluation measures and findings with justifications.

4.1 Data Description and Experiment Setup

Our dataset includes (1) **58** trigger/zero-day generic threat intelligence reports ($\mathcal{G}_i$), (2) **5 organizational wikis** resembling an organizational local knowledge database source ($\mathcal{L}$), and (3) **58** subject matter expert (SME) generated (manually unbiased) ground truth ($\overline{\mathcal{C}}$). A trigger ($\mathcal{G}_i$) can be a report of any malware, vulnerability, attack vector, or security updates. For further automated relevant global knowledge retrieval, LocalIntel is connected with CVE API endpoints. The 58 trigger reports contain both positive and negative test cases. We gathered **5 organizational wikis** corresponding to 5 real-time applications and curated them (PII removed) suitable to the research. For each positive test scenario, we ensured the corresponding knowledge was present in the local knowledge database. In addition to the organizational wiki, we also collected **326** confidential organizational trusted CTI reports to allow LocalIntel to retrieve more infrastructural context and threat implications. These

[7] LocalIntel Repository: github.com/shaswata09/LocalIntel.

reports offer detailed analyses and insights from security analysts studying various global cyber attacks within the organization. For negative test scenarios, there was no intersecting knowledge present in $\mathcal{L}$ i.e. $\mathcal{G}_i \cap \mathcal{L} = \phi$. In conducting our experiments, we tested with proprietary *GPT-3.5-turbo, and GPT-4o*[8]*, and open-source meta-llama/Llama-2-7b-chat-hf, meta-llama/Meta-Llama-3.1-8B-Instruct, mistralai/Mistral-7B-Instruct-v0.2, nvidia/Mistral-NeMo-Minitron-8B-Base, Qwen/Qwen1.5-7B-Chat, AiMavenAi/AiMaven-Prometheus, senseable /WestLake-7B-v2, PetroGPT/WestSeverus-7B-DPO-v2* downloaded from *huggingface.co* as the LLM models. All models' temperatures were deliberately kept default, and instructions prompts were set the same for neutral comparison. The global knowledge was retrieved from NVD-CVE sources through search API. For local knowledge retrieval, we store the 5 organizational wikis and 326 threat reports in a vector database (Chroma[9]). We segmented and organized the data into smaller chunks to enhance processing efficiency. In our experimental setup, we opted for a *chunk size* of 1500 with a *chunk overlap* of 150. We used the *text-embedding-ada-002*[10] as our base model for embedding each chunk of data in Chroma DB and used Maximal Marginal Relevance (MMR) sorting for dense retrieval of relevant chunks. The experiment was performed over Intel i9-12900 with 24 GB GeForce RTX™ 3090Ti GPU and 128 GB of RAM.

Table 2. Evaluation results of our LocalIntel framework over following LLMs.

Model	Ragas (Sim.)	GEval (Cor.)	BertSc-F1
gpt-3.5-turbo	0.92	0.75	0.68
gpt-4o	0.91	0.75	0.66
qwen1.5-7b-chat	0.92	0.78	0.66
llama-3.1-8b-Instruct	0.85	0.46	0.53
westlake-7b-v2	0.92	0.69	0.65
llama2-7b-chat	0.91	0.69	0.65
mistral-7b-instruct-v2	0.90	0.67	0.63
prometheus-7b	0.93	0.71	0.66
westseverus-7b-dpo-v2	0.90	0.60	0.60
mistral-nemo-minitron-8b	0.84	0.56	0.55

[8] GPT Models: platform.openai.com/docs.
[9] Chroma: trychroma.com.
[10] OpenAI Embedding: platform.openai.com/docs.

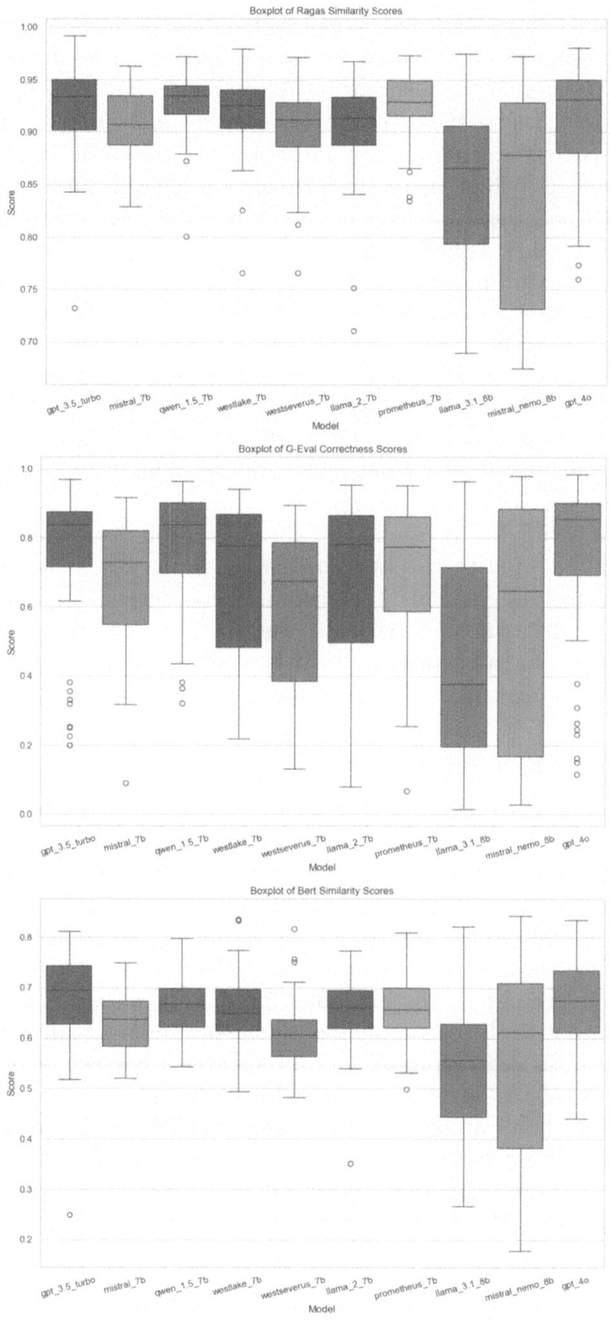

Fig. 4. Evaluation box-plot for Completion $\mathcal{C}$ with respect to ground truth.

4.2 Quantitative Evaluation

For the quantitative assessment of LocalIntel's performance in generating contextually relevant organizational threat intelligence $\mathcal{C}$, we utilize three frameworks: Retrieval Augmented Generation Assessment (RAGAs) [3], G-EVAL [6], and BertScore [15]. Using these frameworks, we evaluate two metrics, including *similarity* and *correctness*. Similarity measures the semantic similarity between ground truth and $\mathcal{C}$, while correctness measures answer correctness compared to ground truth as a combination of factuality and semantic similarity. Both metrics range from 0 to 1, with higher values indicating optimal $\mathcal{C}$. In our case, RAGAs and BertScore is used to evaluate similarity, whereas G-EVAL is used to evaluate correctness of $\mathcal{C}$. Results of our evaluation is presented in Table 2.

In our evaluation, the model *Qwen1.5-7B-Chat* performed the best, with the highest similarity score and the lowest standard deviation, as depicted in Fig. 4. On the other hand, *Mistral-NeMo-Minitron-8B-Base* was the least-performing model. We found that 'qwen' was the most stable, which is essential in critical domains such as cybersecurity. Contrarily, 'mistral-nemo' showed lower accuracy and higher variance. This can be explained through Mistral's sliding attention mechanism that struggles to retail critical information over longer contexts. We also discovered that due to the task criticality, llama 3.1 avoided suggesting a solution, indicating its cautious generation. We observed a similar trend with the 'GPT 4o' model. Another critical point to note is that we used a generic instruction prompt for all models, and it is also worth mentioning that model-specific prompt engineering techniques may lead to even better results.

4.3 Qualitative Evaluation

To justify our quantitative findings (refer to Sect. 4.2), we qualitatively evaluate the performance of LocalIntel in generating contextually relevant organizational threat intelligence through human evaluation. Given the expensive nature of human evaluation, we engage a panel of **3** Subject Matter Experts (SMEs), including *one security analyst* and *two cybersecurity researchers*. We task these SMEs to evaluate the *correctness* of generated threat intelligence based on the 58 scenarios and ground truths explained in the preceding section. The SMEs were instructed to rate the correctness of the response on a scale of **1 to 5**, where 1 represents an incorrect response, and 5 indicates a correct response. We then compare the inter-rater agreement using Fleiss Kappa [7] measure. The result of this evaluation shows an agreement score of **0.6477** with a standard error of **0.0767**, indicating that the raters' evaluations are not random and are generally aligned, and they ***substantially agree*** on the *correctness* of the threat intelligence responses generated by LocalIntel. Moreover, *qualitative results* aligns closely with the *quantitative results*, justifying the evaluation.

5 Related Works

In the last decade, within the realm of cybersecurity, NLP tasks over unstructured CTI text primarily encompass *Named Entity Recognition, text summariza-*

tion, and *analysis of semantic relationships between entities* [13], etc. Researchers have demonstrated numerous real-world applications using these techniques utilizing CTI gathered from diverse sources [8,9,11,12]. With the advancement of generative AI in this decade, the application horizon of CTI has proportionally expanded. Liu et al. [5] introduced a trigger-enhanced CTI (TriCTI) discovery system designed to identify actionable CTI automatically. They utilized a fine-tuned BERT with an intricate design to generate triggers, training the trigger vector based on sentence similarity. Similarly, in [1], the researchers employed a BERT classifier to map Tactics, Techniques, and Procedures (TTPs) to the MITRE ATT&CK framework. On the other hand, Niakanlahiji et al., [10], proposes an information retrieval system called SECCMiner utilizing various NLP techniques. With SECCMiner, unstructured APT reports can be analyzed, and critical security concepts (e.g., adversarial techniques) can be extracted. A question and answering model called LogQA that answers log-based questions in natural language form using base BERT model and large-scale unstructured log corpora is proposed by Huang et al. [4]. Recently, BERT has also been explored to generate contextualized embedding [14] in cybersecurity. Cybersecurity is a critical domain, and this specialized embedding enables language models to understand the context better. On top of the improvements mentioned, we attempt to integrate LLM to understand the problem context and generate real-time scope-specific threat intelligence while considering different factors. This work is the first attempt to generate complete CTI from diverse sources.

6 Conclusion

This paper introduced LocalIntel, a novel framework that generates contextualized CTI uniquely tailored for an organization depending on its operations. LocalIntel is a valuable tool for SoC analysts due to its unique ability to seamlessly contextualize generic global threat intelligence specific to local operations. The main benefit of this system is its ability to efficiently customize global threat intelligence for local contexts, reducing the need for manual efforts. This gives SoC analysts the necessary information to concentrate on essential tasks, such as developing defensive strategies. We employed qualitative and quantitative evaluations to evaluate LocalIntel's confidence in delivering accurate and relevant threat intelligence. The system exhibited remarkable proficiency in both evaluations, supported by human-generated ground truth responses. It achieved a remarkable RAGAs contextual similarity score of 92% and a correctness score of 78%, with a low standard deviation. This underscores the feasibility of automated CTI generation using LLMs and our LocalIntel's robust performance and ability to generate relevant CTI. In the future, we plan to perform further performance improvement measures, such as developing task-specific retrievers and connecting with cybersecurity knowledge graphs as our local knowledge database for broader evaluations. Additionally, we plan to fine-tune LLMs as part of our performance improvement measures.

Acknowledgments. This work was supported by PATENT Lab at the Department of Computer Science and Engineering, Mississippi State University. The authors would like to thank SME's for their assistance in qualitative evaluation. The views and conclusions are those of the authors.

References

1. Alves, P.M., Geraldo Filho, P., Gonçalves, V.P.: Leveraging bert's power to classify TTP from unstructured text. In: 2022 Workshop on Communication Networks and Power Systems (WCNPS), pp. 1–7. IEEE (2022)
2. Arabzadeh, N., Yan, X., Clarke, C.L.: Predicting efficiency/effectiveness trade-offs for dense vs. sparse retrieval strategy selection. In: Proceedings of the 30th ACM International Conference on Information & Knowledge Management, pp. 2862–2866 (2021)
3. Es, S., James, J., Espinosa-Anke, L., Schockaert, S.: Ragas: automated evaluation of retrieval augmented generation. arXiv preprint arXiv:2309.15217 (2023)
4. Huang, S., Liu, Y., Fung, C., Qi, J., Yang, H., Luan, Z.: Logqa: question answering in unstructured logs. arXiv preprint arXiv:2303.11715 (2023)
5. Liu, J., et al.: Tricti: an actionable cyber threat intelligence discovery system via trigger-enhanced neural network. Cybersecurity **5**(1), 8 (2022)
6. Liu, Y., Iter, D., Xu, Y., Wang, S., Xu, R., Zhu, C.: G-eval: NLG evaluation using GPT-4 with better human alignment. arXiv preprint arXiv:2303.16634 (2023)
7. McHugh, M.L.: Interrater reliability: the kappa statistic. Biochemia Medica **22**(3), 276–282 (2012)
8. Mitra, S., Piplai, A., Mittal, S., Joshi, A.: Combating fake cyber threat intelligence using provenance in cybersecurity knowledge graphs. In: 2021 IEEE International Conference on Big Data (Big Data), pp. 3316–3323. IEEE (2021)
9. Mittal, S., Das, P.K., Mulwad, V., Joshi, A., Finin, T.: Cybertwitter: using twitter to generate alerts for cybersecurity threats and vulnerabilities. In: 2016 IEEE/ACM International Conference on Advances in Social Networks Analysis and Mining (ASONAM), pp. 860–867. IEEE (2016)
10. Niakanlahiji, A., Wei, J., Chu, B.T.: A natural language processing based trend analysis of advanced persistent threat techniques. In: 2018 IEEE International Conference on Big Data (Big Data), pp. 2995–3000. IEEE (2018)
11. Pingle, A., Piplai, A., Mittal, S., Joshi, A., Holt, J., Zak, R.: Relext: relation extraction using deep learning approaches for cybersecurity knowledge graph improvement. In: Proceedings of the 2019 IEEE/ACM International Conference on Advances in Social Networks Analysis and Mining, pp. 879–886 (2019)
12. Piplai, A., Mittal, S., Joshi, A., Finin, T., Holt, J., Zak, R.: Creating cybersecurity knowledge graphs from malware after action reports. IEEE Access **8**, 211691–211703 (2020)
13. Rahman, M.R., Mahdavi-Hezaveh, R., Williams, L.: A literature review on mining cyberthreat intelligence from unstructured texts. In: 2020 International Conference on Data Mining Workshops (ICDMW), pp. 516–525. IEEE (2020)
14. Ranade, P., Piplai, A., Joshi, A., Finin, T.: Cybert: contextualized embeddings for the cybersecurity domain. In: 2021 IEEE International Conference on Big Data (Big Data), pp. 3334–3342. IEEE (2021)
15. Zhang, T., Kishore, V., Wu, F., Weinberger, K.Q., Artzi, Y.: Bertscore: evaluating text generation with bert. arXiv preprint arXiv:1904.09675 (2019)

Intelligent Green Efficiency for Intrusion Detection

Pedro Pereira(✉), Paulo Mendes, João Vitorino, Eva Maia, and Isabel Praça

Research Group on Intelligent Engineering and Computing for Advanced Innovation and Development (GECAD), School of Engineering, Polytechnic of Porto (ISEP/IPP), 4249-015 Porto, Portugal
{1211131,1211017,jpmvo,egm,icp}@isep.ipp.pt

Abstract. Artificial Intelligence (AI) has emerged in popularity recently, recording great progress in various industries. However, the environmental impact of AI is a growing concern, in terms of the energy consumption and carbon footprint of Machine Learning (ML) and Deep Learning (DL) models, making essential to investigate Green AI, an attempt to reduce the climate impact of AI systems. This paper presents an assessment of different programming languages and Feature Selection (FS) methods to improve computation performance of AI focusing on Network Intrusion Detection (NID) and cyber-attack classification tasks. Experiments were conducted using five ML models - Random Forest, XGBoost, LightGBM, Multi-Layer Perceptron, and Long Short-Term Memory - implemented in four programming languages - Python, Java, R, and Rust - along with three FS methods - Information Gain, Recursive Feature Elimination, and Chi-Square. The obtained results demonstrated that FS plays an important role enhancing the computational efficiency of AI models without compromising detection accuracy, highlighting languages like Python and R, that benefit from a rich AI libraries environment. These conclusions can be useful to design efficient and sustainable AI systems that still provide a good generalization and a reliable detection.

Keywords: Green AI · Machine Learning · Deep Learning · Programming Languages · Feature Selection · Computational Efficiency

1 Introduction

The rapid growth of Artificial Intelligence (AI) is creating remarkable advancements in many fields, but its impact on the environment is becoming an increasingly important issue [37]. A 2020 paper by Patterson et al. [24] estimated that training a large AI model, such as OpenAI's GPT-3, could consume about 1,287 MWh of energy, leading to CO2 emissions equivalent to those produced by 125 average homes in the U.S. in one year. According to an estimate from the World Economic Forum (WEF), the information and communications technology (ICT)

K. Adi et al. (Eds.): FPS 2024, LNCS 15533, pp. 79–94, 2025.
https://doi.org/10.1007/978-3-031-87496-3_6

sector, which includes AI, by 2020 was already accountable for between 1.4% to 5.9% of global greenhouse gas emissions [34]. According to another estimate from the WEF, computing is expected to account for up to 8% of global power demand by 2030 [5]. Considering these concerns and the cruciality of intrusion detection caused by the increasing threat of cyber-attacks [22], this research seeks to optimize security while minimizing environmental impact [9].

Green AI [43] highlights the importance of optimizing AI systems to minimize their energy consumption and environmental impact without compromising their performance [31]. The efficient usage of computational resources can definitely lead to achieving this goal [41], which gets affected by various factors like the choice of a programming language [25], the usage of technologies like Feature Selection (FS) [19], the hardware efficiency, the ML algorithm efficiency and renewable energy integration.

FS in ML is the process of identifying and selecting the most relevant features from a dataset for model training [19]. It can be implemented using Filter, Wrapper, and Embedded methods [21]. Filter methods evaluate features based on their statistical properties, making them efficient for high-dimensional data. Wrapper methods assess model performance with different feature sets, considering feature-model interactions, but can be computationally intensive and prone to overfitting. Embedded methods integrate FS into the model-building process, balancing accuracy and efficiency with lower computational complexity than Wrapper methods.

At the same time, the impact of FS on computational efficiency varies depending on the programming language choice. Despite being often considered, programming languages also play an essential role in impacting energy usage and computation speed [25]. This occurs because some languages have better optimized themselves to the hardware they are running on. Usually, compiled languages such as C++ take less time to execute than interpreted languages such as Python [17]. Other characteristics, such as memory handling, may also affect the performance and efficiency of the algorithms.

This paper addresses the Green AI use to improve computational efficiency in Intrusion Detection Systems (IDS), seeking to optimize security while minimizing environmental impact. It assesses the choice of programming languages and FS and their relation to computational efficiency in the Green AI context and IDS. Several experiments were performed to compare quality metrics, namely accuracy, precision, recall, and F1, and footprint metrics, namely training and prediction time, in different programming languages and FS techniques.

It aims to provide useful information to researchers and practitioners to help create environmentally sustainable AI systems. This paper includes five ML models (Random Forest (RF), XGBoost (XGB), LightGBM (LGBM), Multi-Layer Perceptron (MLP), and Long Short-Term Memory (LSTM)), four programming languages (Python, Java, R, Rust), and three FS methods (Chi-Square, Information Gain (IG), Recursive Feature Elimination (RFE)).

This paper is organized into multiple sections, including details, that might help researchers to replicate this baseline, and make comparisons with their own results. Section 2 presents related works. Section 3 details data preprocessing techniques, FS, methodology followed, and how model fine-tuning processes were carried out. Section 4 goes into detail regarding the results obtained on all datasets. Finally, Sect. 5 discusses the main conclusions that have been drawn and proposes some future research directions.

2 Related Work

The rise of Internet of Things (IoT) has spurred significant advancements in various fields, including Network Intrusion Detection (NID). AI integration with NID has yielded positive results in enhancing security and system performance [10]. Several papers have been conducted on the use of AI to improve IDS for IoT specifically. For instance, a systematic literature review conducted by Ferrag et al. explains the various ML algorithms used in IDS for IoT under three broad categories of supervised, unsupervised, and reinforcement learning [11]. This paper especially pinpoints on the benefit of FS to improve the detection accuracy as well as the computational time of these systems.

Other studies have been made on this area, Vitorino et al. [38] study the impact of applying a range of the ML methods in an IoT context targeting the intrusion detection in the IoT-23 dataset, with LGBM providing better accuracy than other candidates for binary and multi-class representations. It also showed that even the completely unsupervised methods, for example Isolation Forest (iForest), worked very well in detecting previously unobserved attack. Taken from that, Silva et al. [33] conducted an experiment to assess FS methods such as IG and RFE, the authors' understanding is that the results are satisfactory because using a smaller number of features preserves performance while shortening training time. More recently, Vitorino et al. [39] went a step further and studied adversarial robustness in IoT IDS proposing that through adversarial learning techniques can enhance system reliability against evasion attacks.

The majority of previous studies focus on AI models' detection capabilities but often overlook efficiency, a key aspect introduced by Green AI. The concept of Green AI, which emphasizes the development of energy-efficient and environmentally friendly AI models, has gained traction in recent years. Schwartz et al. note that when thinking about the intelligent systems it is also important to think of the performance and energy consumption with the future generation AI solutions suggesting factors such as carbon footprint to take in account when an model evaluation is done [31]. This perspective is especially dear to IoT environments since resources are often a major limitation there.

In this context, the choice of programming languages and FS techniques plays a crucial role in the development of efficient IDS. In a research by Pereira et al. the 27 programming languages were compared regarding the runtime, memory consumption, and energy usage using ten problems from the Computer Language Benchmark Game [25]. The main aim of this repository is not the creation of new benchmarks, but rather, the evaluation of the performance of programming languages for the pre-specified tasks. According to research, C appeared to be the most efficient language in terms of runtime, memory usage, and power efficiency.

Another key factor that affects the efficiency of AI-based IDS is FS. Dimensional reduction of input data boosts the performance and energy efficiency of ML models. Ahmadi et al., for instance did establish that applying FS on IDS enhanced detection and reduced computational costs conducting a study using a combination of Correlation-based, IG, and Chi-square to identify the most relevant features, especially when using decision tree classifiers [1,6,32].

Looking at IDS, specially designed for IoT, numerous works has been dedicated to detecting various types of attacks. Many data sets have been proposed and used to evaluate IDS AI models for IoT setting and among those BotIoT is highly recognized [3]. Developed by Koroniotis et al., the BotIoT dataset imitates several IoT-based attacks and is widely cited in the literature of the IoT field [26]. In the same way, despite the fact that the Hikari-22 is not an IoT dedicated dataset, it is a large collection of traffic data that can be very helpful to create a general benchmark to develop and evaluate IDS models. Hikari-22 is also used in IDS research community because of the variety of traffic and real life attack scenarios wherein the effectiveness of IDS in various network environments can be tested [12].

The incorporation of Green AI principles for IDS can be seen as a way of improving not just the security in networks, but efficiency as well. This way, the resource consumption of an IDS is reduced and the programming languages are chosen more appropriate by the researchers, as well as the FS techniques. Moreover, collections such as BotIoT or Hikari-22 are valuable to determine the strengths and weakness of these systems, and thus, contribute to enhance all the features, including performance and sustainability among others.

In most cases, there is more focus on quality metrics than footprint metrics. These gaps are addressed in this paper in the sense that not only the effects of different programming languages on IDS performance are investigated under the Green AI environment but also by integrating footprint measurements into the evaluation process. Thus, our work offers a better insight into improving the performance and environmental aspects of IDS, which is immensely important for the continuous growth of Green AI in cyber security.

3 Methods

This section describes the utilized programming languages, models, FS techniques, datasets, the employed data preprocessing steps, and the evaluation metrics considered. This paper was carried out on a single machine, used to optimize and train all the models, ensuring a consistent environment during the tests. The machine has 32 GB of RAM and an 8-core CPU.

This comparative evaluation was carried out on four different programming languages to retrieve insights on the impact language choice has on the efficiency and performance of the ML models.

3.1 Feature Selection Methods

FS is crucial for developing efficient ML models, particularly IDS for IoT networks [28,40]. It not only enhances performance but also reduces computational costs, aligning with the goals of Green AI. Our objective was to determine which of the features aid in the early detection of intrusions without using up a lot of resources. We employed three FS methods, Chi-Square, IG, and RFE, because they have been used in recent studies in IoT settings, obtaining good results [30,35,44]. Preliminary experiments helped in identifying the fact that it is possible to reduce the computational load by selecting one-third of the total features present in each of the two datasets.

Chi-Square [45] method compares two events as to their independence - in this case, a feature and the target class. From one of the measures called chi-square, it sorts features in ascending order, aiming at those features that seem to be more independent of the class label. This technique is especially helpful when dealing with categorical data because it allows for the identification of contributing features with the largest correlations to the target variable.

IG [4] determine an average reduction in entropy or uncertainty of the target variable provided by the feature in question. It sorts features on the basis of their usefulness in determining the class label and makes it possible for us to deploy features that considerably enhance the model's precision.

RFE [42] is a technique of recursively eliminating the attributes that have the least weights assigned by a given model until those attributes that are deemed to be most valuable are obtained.

With these FS methods, we made certain that not only were the models efficient in terms of their performance but also resource usage, which forms a part of the attempts being made towards creating sustainable AI solution for systems security.

3.2 Programming Languages

Given the significant influence that programming languages can exert on the performance and efficiency of an AI model [27], we implemented our approach in four distinct languages: Python, Java, R, and Rust. All of these languages come with their own benefits in relation to the execution times and efficiency factors and thus are suitable for this research.

Python in particular, characterized by rather simple and clear syntax, has received rather significant degree of attention, particularly in the context of AI and ML. Numerous libraries like TensorFlow, and Scikit-Learn make it the most preferred language in data analysis and AI creation [29]. Python is an ideal language for data science and for creating the first versions of ML systems, computer vision programs, natural language processing tools. However, the language is interpreted and has the Global Interpreter Lock meaning it is slower when it comes to processing intensive tasks compared to compiled languages [17].

R, meanwhile, excels with it statistical computing and data analysis property and as such it is well suited for probability modeling [14,23], simulating and data visualization which are key aspects in building AI systems. Using packages such as caret, R provides useful package even on data manipulation and visualization. It also includes packages for DL such as TensorFlow for R.

Java cannot be overestimated among AI agents as it gives the ability to integrate new AI components with existing systems of an enterprise using JVM without the need to rewrite existing business applications [18,36]. Java has a number of strong libraries for instance DeepLearning4j for neural network and Weka for ML algorithms. However, it has to be understood that Java may be more verbose and as such, the process of code development may take more time than if done using languages such as Python or R.

Although relatively less popular among the AI enthusiasts, **Rust** offers performance and memory safety in high-performance computing use-cases [20]. But because Rust is a compiled language, it executes faster which is paramount for large models that will take ages to train and infer. It poses an ownership concept which makes it safe for memory, and it avoids crashes thus suitable for ML. However, Rust is comparatively new and has a less developed ecosystem, though it also has rather fine-grained control over what is happening in the program, and thus may be more challenging to learn.

3.3 Datasets

There are many datasets available to test Network Intrusion Detection Systems (NIDS) and all of them have their own properties. So for this paper we wanted to include two datasets that are comparatively recent and thematically closest, one that focuses specifically on the IoT environment and another more general dataset for NIDS research. To this end, and as we shall show in the following sections, we selected the BotIoT dataset, for IoT security studies and the Hikari-22 dataset that can be used in NIDS studies in general. This makes it possible to perform a diverse analysis of the specialized and generalized network intrusion.

BotIoT [26] dataset was developed as part of a project to collect and create most of the type of malicious activities that can happen in IoT network. The applications for this dataset include utilizing the Cyber Range Lab of the Australian Centre for Cyber Security, some of which are smart refrigerators, thermostats or surveillance cameras. Since the BotIoT dataset has various labeled data that can be utilized for example in ML to detect and prevent IoT based threats. The presence of different attacks and realistic IoT environments make the given dataset quite useful for IDS and other security systems investigations.

Hikari-22 [12] is the more recent than BotIoT dataset, proposed to solve the lack of publicly available up-to-date datasets for cyber security appliances. It was created from traffic captured on the internet, either as a packet or flow. Afterward, the captured traffic is compiled into a specific data type containing network-related features, including labeling. The raw data is then parsed through various pre-processing steps until it reaches its final stage. This dataset includes encrypted synthetic attacks that are lacking in many others [13].

For both datasets, the three previously introduced FS methods were applied independently.

3.4 Models and Fine-Tuning

Five types of ML models were chosen for this paper: RF, XGB, LGBM, MLP and LSTM. Hyperparameters were tuned for each of the models on each of datasets through a grid search which involves experimenting with the best established hyperparameter combinations. The configurations were selected based on 5-fold cross-validation and the evaluation metric was the macro-average F1-score so that the method is not sensitive to the imbalance in the sets. The following models were selected along with the fine-tuned parameters of each model:

RF [7] is an ensemble learning method that builds multiple decision trees during training. Each tree in the forest casts a vote, and the prevailing response is the final estimate. It reduces overfitting and increases the accuracy of classification or regression tasks. Table 1 summarizes the fine-tuned configuration.

Table 1. Summary of RF configuration.

Hyperparameter	BotIoT Value	Hikari-22 Value
Criterion	Entropy	Gini
No. of estimators	128	128
Min samples split	2	2
Max. depth of a tree	None	8
Min. samples in a leaf	1	1

XGB [8] is a way of implementing extreme gradient boosting techniques and is efficient and scalable. It creates models one at a time so the models it creates are corrections or improvements upon the models prior to them. Table 2 summarizes the fine-tuned configuration.

Table 2. Summary of XGB configuration.

Hyperparameter	BotIoT Value	Hikari-22 Value
Booster	gbtree	gbtree
Learning rates	0.4	0.3
No. of estimators	128	32
Objective	multi:softmax	multi:softmax
Subsample	0.8	0.8
Tree Method	hist	hist

LGBM [16] is a gradient boosting used for developing tree-based ML algorithm. It is very efficient in performing data operations and specifically designed for handling huge data with minimum memory consumption, especially recommended for high-dimensional. Table 3 summarizes the fine-tuned configuration.

Table 3. Summary of LGBM configuration.

Hyperparameter	BotIoT Value	Hikari-22 Value
Learning rate	0.1	0.1
No. of estimators	32	64
Max. depth of a tree	−1	−1
Max no. of leaves per tree	32	32

MLP [2] is feedforward artificial neural networks. It also comprises more than one layer of neurons, and each neuron from a given layer is connected to all the neurons in the layer following it. They can be applied in tasks such as classifications, regression analysis, and to transform the data in to features, more especially in cases where the data is non-linear. Table 4 summarizes the fine-tuned configuration.

Table 4. Summary of MLP configuration.

Hyperparameter	BotIoT Value	Hikari-22 Value
Activation	Logistic	Tanh
Hidden Layers	(32, 64)	(64, 32)
Learning Rate	0.001	0.001
Batch size	64	64
Epoch	200	200

LSTM [15] is a kind of DL model that has the ability to remember past events, LSTM is sub type of recurrent neural network (RNN). Some of the specific features include the presence of a memory cell where data stored in the memory is held for a long duration in a retained mode of operation particularly in applications such as time series forecasting, text and language processing and analysis of sequential data. Table 5 summarizes the fine-tuned configuration.

Table 5. Summary of LSTM configuration.

Hyperparameter	BotIoT Value	Hikari-22 Value
Hidden Layers	(32, 32, 32)	(16, 32, 16)
Dropout rate	0.4	0.5
Learning rate	0.1	0.1
Batch size	32	32
Epoch	128	64

4 Results and Discussion

This section will focus on the assessment of the implemented ML models. Here, we evaluate their performance in achieving the classification task using two main types of metrics, quality metrics - accuracy, precision, recall and F1 - and footprint metrics - training and prediction time, both in seconds. For each dataset, two tables are presented: one displaying results without FS and another showcasing the best performance achieved among the three FS models.

4.1 BotIoT

Table 6 provides the obtained results for the models trained with the BotIoT dataset without FS. It is important to note that some models are not possible to implement in certain languages.

Table 6. Obtained results for the BotIoT dataset without Feature Selection.

Model	Lang.	Acc.	Prec.	Rec.	F1	Train. Time	Pred. Time
RF	Java	0.9998	0.8906	0.8070	0.8366	110.234	5.296
	Python	0.9998	0.8659	0.8296	0.8455	44.8593	1.4218
	R	0.9998	0.7687	0.9856	0.8638	303.7559	1.2278
	Rust	0.9998	0.9417	0.8002	0.8411	2905.2297	69.9858
XGB	Java	0.9999	0.9998	0.9998	0.9998	1.687	0.047
	Python	0.9998	0.8469	0.8174	0.8292	85.8593	1.625
	R	0.9998	0.8174	0.8485	0.8326	11.3276	0.1372
LigthGBM	Python	0.9941	0.5864	0.6978	0.6195	13.4843	1.5
	R	0.9991	0.719	0.6718	0.6946	7.3249	0.0991
MLP	Java	0.9991	0.4988	0.5000	0.4994	4442.911	10.98
	Python	0.9992	0.6351	0.6532	0.6436	1073.5625	2.125
	R	0.9487	0.4075	0.4857	0.4431	638.6015	7.826
	Rust	0.0115	0.2686	0.3302	0.2767	992.8198	140.0066
LSTM	Java	0.9606	0.9754	0.4297	0.9061	444.858	1.485
	Python	0.9995	0.7492	0.7492	0.679	3468.0638	9.8897
	R	0.9996	0.7772	0.9383	0.8502	34902.385	34.8341

The XGB and RF have the highest overall performance on quality metrics, especially in Java implementations. Nevertheless, there are certain issues related to the speed at which Java models are trained. XGB in Java presents an incredibly short train. time, while all quality metrics have values above 0.9998, beyond that LSTM in Java seems also having problems having a significantly high F1, despite its low recall. This raises questions about the reliability of Java's efficiency in training complex models with the actual state of ML libraries.

Despite these issues, is to stand up the case of Python with RF having an accuracy of 0.9998, combined with a strong F1 of 0.8455, making it a reliable model for various applications. RF in R also has an high accuracy and F1, 0.8638 which is biggest than Python, but the difference in train. time is high, 44.8593 s to Python and 303.7559 s to R. XGB despite having lightly worse results of F1 compared to RF models, in R they excel achieving a better balance between precision and result doing with a significant difference in train. time, with RF taking 303.7559 s and XGB taking only 11.3276 s.

In terms of train. time, LGBM models take the least time in all languages, especially in R, where the model taking only 3.7039 s. However, LGBM typically doesn't provide very high accuracy and F1 compared to the other models. On the other hand, MLP models, are usually the most time-consuming, especially for models implemented in Java as the train. time is striking 4442.911 s although the model was very accurate up to 0.9991. Nevertheless, the MLP model has a considerably lower F1, noticeably lower in Java, showing the poorest performance along all indicators.

Considering the programming languages, Python proves itself reasonable and balanced language to implement ML models, providing high scores on quality metrics and, at the same time, good footprint metrics. R, thus, also get good stats, it obtained similar quality metrics compared to Python, obtaining worse footprint metrics in RF but for XGB, LGBM and MLP it obtained a better footprint metrics. Java is quite capable in certain aspects, but it is less efficient in other areas, and there is inconsistency, making it less ideal when a steady model training is needed. Rust also showed good results in quality metrics, but footprint metrics were pretty bad.

Comparing the results of ML models with FS and ML models without FS for BotIoT it can be inferred that the general quality metric do not differ significantly across the programming languages. However, one of the most significant benefits of using FS is that it leads to reduced training and inference time, and this is observed. Table 7 provides the obtained results for the models trained with the BotIoT dataset with FS.

The patterns observed in the previous table are maintained to this one. RF and XGB keeps as the best models on quality metrics with balances footprint metrics, LGBM keeps with the best results on footprint metrics but not good results in footprint metrics and MLP with bad results in both metrics. Despite this improvements, Java continues to exhibit challenges even with FS for the XGB and LSTM models. Beyond that it is important to highlight the improvements made by FSn on Rust MLP model, without FS Rust MLP presents an F1 of 0.2767, pretty lower than the results obtained with FS, 0.7010. This global analysis highlights the necessity of the choice of FS techniques and work languages that are appropriate to the characteristics and conditions of the further application of ML models.

Table 7. Obtained results for the BotIoT dataset with Feature Selection.

Model	Lang.	FS Tech.	Acc.	Prec.	Rec.	F1	Train. Time	Pred. Time
RF	Java	IG	0.9997	0.8809	0.7936	0.8285	49.734	4.797
	Python	Chi-Square	0.9998	0.8673	0.8105	0.8345	77.7812	1.5937
	R	Chi-Square	0.9998	0.7723	0.9830	0.8650	77.9851	0.7614
	Rust	Chi-Square	0.9997	0.8742	0.8140	0.8414	1697.3741	72.6016
XGB	Java	ALL	0.9999	0.9998	0.9998	0.9998	3.297	0.031
	Python	Chi-Square	0.9997	0.9885	0.7425	0.7980	64.0468	1.625
	R	Chi-Square	0.9997	0.739	0.9883	0.8457	9.7582	0.1828
LigthGBM	Python	RFE	0.9980	0.5550	0.6665	0.5819	4.7187	2.6093
	R	IG	0.9995	0.6866	0.8074	0.7421	6.5932	0.1082
MLP	Java	IG	0.9991	0.4985	0.5000	0.4993	3564.804	8.937
	Python	RFE	0.9996	0.7466	0.6625	0.6958	840.0468	1.75
	R	RFE	0.999	0.4998	0.4985	0.4992	634.985	7.1586
	Rust	RFE	0.9995	0.7452	0.6704	0.7010	807.1418	110.7449
LSTM	Java	Chi-Square	0.9583	0.9741	0.4255	0.8997	431.983	0.984
	Python	IG	0.9996	0.9544	0.7216	0.7527	3634.3075	10.2833
	R	Chi-Square	0.9997	0.7234	0.9896	0.8358	11286.8694	15.4808

4.2 Hikari-22

Given the issues identified with the Java XGB and LSTM models implemented in the BotIoT dataset, a subsequent analysis of these models on the Hikari-22 dataset reveals that these problems persist. Nevertheless, the XGB and RF models remain robust and prove to have the best results on the quality measures. Notably, LGBM has become an alternate model yielding nearly similar quality metrics. For instance, the F1 for LGBM, RF, and XGB are 0.9395, 0.9397 and 0.9398 respectively which are nearly equal. Table 8 shows the results of models trained on the Hikari-22 dataset without FS.

However, significant differences in train. times remain. train. time for implementing the RF model in R was 219.841 s while that for the same implemented in Python was 43-5312 s only. Interestingly, the XGB model proved to be the quickest all in all, which was different from the results on the BotIoT dataset where LGBM model was faster. XGB took 12.3592 s in Python and LGBM took 15.7968 s, while in R XGB took 5.3232 s and LGBM 7.7844 s to complete the training phase.

Yet, the outcomes remain unwanted for MLP models, overall, the obtained results are low for both quality and footprint metrics. Even more, serious degradation of LSTM model in Python was observed, where the F1 constituted only 0.2505, decreased sharply compared to F1 that was obtained by the R LSTM model of 0.9328.

Table 8. Obtained results for the Hikari-22 dataset without Feature Selection.

Model	Lang.	Acc.	Prec.	Rec.	F1	Train. Time	Pred. Time
RF	Java	0.9845	0.9958	0.8830	0.9219	29.188	2.0
	Python	0.9853	0.9960	0.8896	0.9273	43.5312	0.5156
	R	0.9853	0.8896	0.9958	0.9397	219.8410	0.7301
	Rust	0.9845	0.9956	0.8831	0.9219	2009.5006	18.0371
XGB	Java	0.9999	0.9998	0.9998	0.9998	3.234	0.031
	Python	0.9853	0.9956	0.8896	0.9271	12.3593	0.375
	R	0.9853	0.8899	0.9956	0.9398	5.3232	0.0405
LigthGBM	Python	0.9853	0.9951	0.8898	0.9270	15.7968	1.125
	R	0.9853	0.8898	0.9951	0.9395	7.7844	0.0794
MLP	Java	0.9773	0.9274	0.8657	0.8899	2844.601	6.672
	Python	0.9482	0.5379	0.5060	0.5020	597.875	3.9843
	R	0.9556	0.386	0.6262	0.4776	227.6732	2.8128
	Rust	0.8108	0.6222	0.5553	0.5846	1879.8119	96.0487
LSTM	Java	0.9404	0.9404	0.25	0.9692	55.143	0.188
	Python	0.9421	0.4855	0.2541	0.2505	550.9377	3.8851
	R	0.9838	0.8783	0.9945	0.9328	15138.4405	24.7039

Table 9. Obtained results for the Hikari-22 dataset with Feature Selection.

Model	Lang.	FS Tech.	Acc.	Prec.	Rec.	F1	Train. Time	Pred. Time
RF	Java	RFE	0.9845	0.9958	0.8830	0.9219	14.532	1.687
	Python	RFE	0.9853	0.9960	0.8896	0.9273	20.375	0.5625
	R	RFE	0.9853	0.8896	0.9962	0.9399	49.3899	0.3268
	Rust	RFE	0.9845	0.9903	0.8858	0.9229	607.1009	14.9905
XGB	Java	ALL	0.9999	0.9998	0.9998	0.9998	3.109	0.031
	Python	IG	0.9853	0.9954	0.8899	0.9271	5.6093	0.125
	R	IG	0.9853	0.8899	0.9958	0.9398	3.9919	0.0464
LigthGBM	Python	RFE	0.9853	0.9956	0.8899	0.9272	10.5937	2.4687
	R	RFE	0.9853	0.8899	0.9956	0.9398	6.6603	0.1108
MLP	Java	RFE	0.9759	0.9097	0.8652	0.8822	1634.504	3.739
	Python	RFE	0.9616	0.6727	0.6145	0.6343	611.8593	2.1718
	R	IG	0.9515	0.5284	0.8368	0.6478	218.5325	2.6937
	Rust	RFE	0.8046	0.5741	0.5063	0.4620	1014.5972	49.0509
LSTM	Java	Chi-Square	0.9404	0.9404	0.25	0.9692	61.015	0.427
	Python	Chi-Square	0.9415	0.2354	0.25	0.2425	546.0953	3.7458
	R	IG	0.9852	0.8887	0.9955	0.9391	3722.1571	8.5553

From the point of view of the implemented language, once again, Python is an evenly balanced language for the implementation of ML models in terms of the achieved quality of the model, as well as its computational efficiency. However, a large gap of performance between LSTMs is an indication of a possible weakness. R again performs well in terms of quality, although its footprint is higher than A's, especially for the RF models. However, R provides a better footprint performance for footprint-related metrics compared to Python when performing XGB, LGBM, and MLP modelling. Java, however, is good in some specific areas, but as we have seen it is slow in computation and hence inaccurate and uneven in training models, which makes it inferior to Python in constantly changing environments that demand consistency in the model training. Thus, in spite of good condition of quality indicators, Rust still has the problem of unsatisfactory values in the context of footprint indicators.

Comparing the results of ML models with FS and ML models without FS for Hikari-22 it can be inferred that the general quality metric do not differ significantly across the programming languages. However, one of the most significant benefits of using FS is that it leads to reduced training and prediction time, and this is observed in all models, excepts on MLP and LSTM models in Python. Table 9 provides the obtained results for the models trained with the Hikari-22 dataset with FS.

As was the case in the previous evaluation, the trends present here give similar results. LGBM, RF, and XGB remain as the models with the best quality metrics while at the same having moderate footprint metrics. Among them, XGB remains to have the highest accuracy in footprint metrics while MLP show bad results in both metrics. However, the challenge is still present when it comes to the XGB and LSTM models after the application of FS, thus showing that Java is still a difficult task.

In particular, the application of FS has brought tangible changes in the effectiveness of the Rust LSTM model. In case of training without FS the Rust LSTM model took 15138.4405 s of train. time a duration markedly higher than the 3722.16 s achieved following the application of FS. This detailed examination of the approaches clearly demonstrates the need for proper choice of FS methods and programming languages that best suit the needs and circumstances of the chosen ML model.

5 Conclusions

This paper, reviewed details of Green AI and its significance in the field of intrusion detection, particularly in the IoT domain. By analyzing the performance of various programming languages and FS techniques, we aimed to identify strategies that minimize the environmental impact of AI systems while maintaining their effectiveness. Our experiments provided a comprehensive examination of how different programming languages and FS techniques can affect the energy usage and optimization of the models in AI.

From the considered programming languages, Python and R consistently achieved high-quality results with efficient resource usage, while Rust turned out to be one of the most future-looking language for high-performance computing, which might indicate that the language is going to be the important to the development of the future generation of AI frameworks based on the performance and sustainability paradigms. Also, our results showed the significance of FS, minimizing training time while giving equivalent results, which helps contribute to more efficient AI processes.

Thus, these results can be viewed as making a significant contribution to current attempts to design AI systems that are less damaging to the environment and provide useful recommendations to improve their prospective study and applications. As such, the incorporation of the Green AI principles into the development and implementation of AI models will prove crucial in realizing both the security and sustainability objectives in IoT settings. Future work, should continue improving the specifics of programming languages as well as FS strategies in order to achieve improved performance of the AI systems in different applications. Also, extending this paper with more ML models and also in real-world scenarios will give further understanding to potential of Green AI in solving the problems of energy shortage and carbon footprint in AI technologies.

Acknowledgements. This work was supported by the CYDERCO project, which has received funding from the European Cybersecurity Competence Centre under grant agreement 101128052. This work has also received funding from UIDB/00760/2020.

References

1. Ahmadi, S., et al: Efficient feature selection for intrusion detection systems. In: 2019 IEEE 10th Annual Ubiquitous Computing, Electronics & Mobile Communication Conference (2019). https://doi.org/10.1109/UEMCON47517.2019.8992960
2. Almeida, L.B.: Multilayer perceptrons. In: Handbook of Neural Computation, pp. C1–2. CRC Press (2020)
3. Andrade-Hoz, et al: Infrastructure-wide and intent-based networking dataset for 5G-and-beyond AI-driven autonomous networks. Sensors **24**(3) (2024). https://doi.org/10.3390/s24030783
4. Azhagusundari, et al: Feature selection based on information gain. Int. J. Innov. Technol. Explor. Eng. (IJITEE) (2013)
5. Bacchi, U.: This is the carbon footprint of your internet activity. Technical report, Thomson Reuters Foundation (2020)
6. Barot, V., Chauhan, S., Patel, B.: Feature selection for modeling intrusion detection. Int. J. Comput. Netw. Inf. Secur. **6**, 56–62 (2014). https://doi.org/10.5815/IJCNIS.2014.07.08
7. Breiman, L.: Random forests. Mach. Learn. **45**, 5–32 (2001)
8. Chen, T., Guestrin, C.: Xgboost: a scalable tree boosting system. In: Proceedings of the 22nd ACM SIGKDD International Conference on Knowledge Discovery and Data Mining, pp. 785–794 (2016)
9. European Union Agency for Cybersecurity: Cyber Europe 2022 - After action report - Findings from a PAN-EUROPEAN cyber crisis exercise. Publications Office of the European Union (2022).https://doi.org/10.2824/397622

10. European Union Agency for Cybersecurity, Svetozarov Naydenov, R., et al.: ENISA threat landscape 2022 - July 2021 to July 2022. Publications Office of the European Union (2022). https://doi.org/10.2824/764318
11. Ferrag, M.A., et al.: Deep learning for cyber security intrusion detection: approaches, datasets, and comparative study. J. Inf. Secur. Appl. **50**, 102419 (2020). https://doi.org/10.1016/j.jisa.2019.102419
12. Ferriyan, A., et al.: Hikari-22 dataset. Zenodo (2022). https://doi.org/10.5281/zenodo.6463389
13. Ferriyan, A., et al.: Generating network intrusion detection dataset based on real and encrypted synthetic attack traffic. Appl. Sci. **11**(17), 7868 (2021). https://doi.org/10.3390/app11177868
14. Giorgi, F., et al: The R language: an engine for bioinformatics and data science. Life **12** (2022). https://doi.org/10.3390/life12050648
15. Graves, A., Graves, A.: Long short-term memory. Supervised sequence labelling with recurrent neural networks, pp. 37–45 (2012)
16. Ke, G., et al: Lightgbm: a highly efficient gradient boosting decision tree. In: Advances in Neural Information Processing Systems, vol. 30 (2017)
17. Kwame, A.E., et al.: Qualitative assessment of compiled, interpreted and hybrid programming languages. Commun. Appl. Electron. **7**(7), 8–13 (2017). https://doi.org/10.5120/cae2017652685
18. Lang, S., et al.: Wekadeeplearning4j: a deep learning package for weka based on deeplearning4j. Knowl. Based Syst. **178**, 48–50 (2019). https://doi.org/10.1016/J.KNOSYS.2019.04.013
19. Li, J., et al: Feature selection: a data perspective. ACM Comput. Surv. **50**(6) (2017). https://doi.org/10.1145/3136625
20. Lin, Y., et al.: Rust as a language for high performance GC implementation. In: Proceedings of the 2016 ACM SIGPLAN International Symposium on Memory Management (2016). https://doi.org/10.1145/2926697.2926707
21. Lyu, et al.: A survey on feature selection techniques based on filtering methods for cyber attack detection. Information **14**(3), 191 (2023). https://doi.org/10.3390/info14030191
22. Nurse, J.R., et al.: Security risk assessment in internet of things systems. IT Prof. **19**(5), 20–26 (2017). https://doi.org/10.1109/MITP.2017.3680959
23. Paquot, M., Larsson, T.: Descriptive statistics and visualization with R. In: Paquot, M., Gries, S.T. (eds.) A Practical Handbook of Corpus Linguistics, pp. 375–399. Springer, Cham (2020). https://doi.org/10.1007/978-3-030-46216-1_17
24. Patterson, D., et al.: The carbon footprint of machine learning training will plateau, then shrink. Computer **55**(7), 18–28 (2022). https://doi.org/10.1109/MC.2022.3148714
25. Pereira, R., et al: Energy efficiency across programming languages: how do energy, time, and memory relate? In: Proceedings of the 10th ACM SIGPLAN International Conference on Software Language Engineering, SLE 2017, pp. 256–267. Association for Computing Machinery, New York (2017). https://doi.org/10.1145/3136014.3136031
26. Peterson, J.M., et al: A review and analysis of the bot-IoT dataset. In: 2021 IEEE International Conference on Service-Oriented System Engineering (SOSE), pp. 20–27. IEEE (2021)
27. Pinto, L.: The impact of AI programming languages on AI talent (2024). https://lumenalta.com/insights/ai-programming-languages-talent

28. Rahman, M.A., Asyhari, A.T., Wen, O.W., Ajra, H., Ahmed, Y., Anwar, F.: Effective combining of feature selection techniques for machine learning-enabled IoT intrusion detection. Multimedia Tools Appl. **80**(20), 31381–31399 (2021). https://doi.org/10.1007/s11042-021-10567-y
29. Raschka, S., et al.: Machine learning in python: main developments and technology trends in data science, machine learning, and artificial intelligence. Information **11**(4), 193 (2020). https://doi.org/10.3390/info11040193
30. Rihan, S.D.A., et al: Approach for detecting attacks on IoT networks based on ensemble feature selection and deep learning models. Sensors **23** (2023). https://doi.org/10.3390/s23177342
31. Schwartz, R., et al: Green AI (2019). https://arxiv.org/abs/1907.10597
32. Sheen, S., Rajesh, R.: Network intrusion detection using feature selection and decision tree classifier. In: TENCON 2008 - 2008 IEEE Region 10 Conference, pp. 1–4 (2008). https://doi.org/10.1109/TENCON.2008.4766847
33. Silva, M., et al: Efficient network traffic feature sets for IoT intrusion detection (2024). https://arxiv.org/abs/2406.08042
34. Taylor, L.: How much does the internet contribute to global emissions? (2021)
35. Thakkar, A., Lohiya, R.: Attack classification using feature selection techniques: a comparative study. J. Ambient. Intell. Humaniz. Comput. **12**(1), 1249–1266 (2020). https://doi.org/10.1007/s12652-020-02167-9
36. Vanam, M.K., et al.: High performance machine learning and data science based implementation using weka. Mater. Today Proc. (2021). https://doi.org/10.1016/J.MATPR.2021.01.470
37. Verdecchia, R., et al: Data-centric green AI an exploratory empirical study. In: 2022 International Conference on ICT for Sustainability (ICT4S). IEEE (2022). https://doi.org/10.1109/ict4s55073.2022.00015
38. Vitorino, J., et al.: A Comparative Analysis of Machine Learning Techniques for IoT Intrusion Detection. Springer (2022). https://doi.org/10.1007/978-3-031-08147-7_13
39. Vitorino, J., et al.: An Adversarial Robustness Benchmark for Enterprise Network Intrusion Detection. Springer (2024). https://doi.org/10.1007/978-3-031-57537-2_1
40. Vitorino, J., et al.: Reliable feature selection for adversarially robust cyber-attack detection. Ann. Telecommun. (2024). https://doi.org/10.1007/s12243-024-01047-z
41. Wu, C.J., et al: Sustainable AI: environmental implications, challenges and opportunities. In: Marculescu, D., et al (eds.) Proceedings of Machine Learning and Systems, vol. 4, pp. 795–813 (2022)
42. Yan, K., Zhang, D.: Feature selection and analysis on correlated gas sensor data with recursive feature elimination. Sens. Actuators B Chem. **212**, 353–363 (2015). https://doi.org/10.1016/j.snb.2015.02.025
43. Yigitcanlar, T., et al: Green artificial intelligence: towards an efficient, sustainable and equitable technology for smart cities and futures. Sustainability **13**(16) (2021). https://doi.org/10.3390/su13168952
44. Yin, Y., et al: IGRF-RFE: a hybrid feature selection method for MLP-based network intrusion detection on UNSW-NB15 dataset. J. Big Data **10**, 1–26 (2022). https://doi.org/10.1186/s40537-023-00694-8
45. Zhai, et al: A chi-square statistics based feature selection method in text classification. In: 2018 IEEE 9th International Conference on Software Engineering and Service Science (2018). https://doi.org/10.1109/ICSESS.2018.8663882

A Privacy-Preserving Behavioral Authentication System

Md Morshedul Islam(✉), Md Abdur Rafiq, and Md Ashraful Islam

Concordia University of Edmonton, Edmonton, AB, Canada
{mdmorshedul.islam,mrafiq,mislam7}@concordia.ab.ca

Abstract. A behavioral authentication (BA) system leverages the behavioral characteristics of users to verify their identity claims through a verification algorithm. A verification algorithm can be created by employing a machine learning (ML) classifier trained on user profiles, which improves overall system efficiency. However, similar to other ML systems, ML-based BA classifiers are vulnerable to privacy attacks that can leak sensitive behavioral data. To protect behavioral data, we propose a non-cryptographic approach suitable for low-computation devices. Before sharing the profiles with the verifier, users apply a random projection (RP) transformation to their behavioral profiles. This transformation ensures the correctness and security properties of the BA systems, as RP can preserve the Euclidean distances between vectors in a metric space with high probability. Our approach also satisfies key privacy-preserving properties of authentication systems, including renewability, unlinkability, and irreversibility. Extensive experiments on two behavioral datasets, combined with comprehensive security and privacy evaluations, demonstrate the effectiveness of our method. Moreover, our approach is general and can be applied to other BA systems.

Keywords: Privacy-preserving authentication · Random projection · Behavioral data · Privacy attacker

1 Introduction

In recent years, the world has experienced a major technological revolution, with smartphones emerging as one of the most impactful innovations. Recent studies have demonstrated the feasibility of extracting behavioral data, such as touch dynamics, keystroke dynamics, and gait dynamics, using smartphone sensors and peripherals. A behavioral authentication (BA) system [6,9,12,16] can leverage these captured data for user authentication. BA systems have also been used in multifactor authentication to strengthen other factors.

The two main components of a BA system are the prover and the verifier. A prover is client-side software (also called a profile generator) that runs on user devices, collects behavioral data to construct profiles, and sends them to the verifier. Typically, a verifier is an online server that uses all the collected profiles

K. Adi et al. (Eds.): FPS 2024, LNCS 15533, pp. 95–107, 2025.
https://doi.org/10.1007/978-3-031-87496-3_7

to train a machine learning (ML) classifier. The trained classifier can then be deployed on a Machine Learning as a Service (MLaaS) platform to evaluate verification requests. Recently, neural network (NN)-based classifiers have been developed for classifying mouse movements [6], gaits [16], and keystrokes [9].

Privacy of Behavioral Data. Behavioral data carry sensitive personal information that must be protected from various types of privacy attacks, such as model extraction attacks [10] and model inversion attacks [14]. A privacy attacker in a BA system can be an honest-but-curious verifier or any other external actors seeking to learn behavioral patterns from the system and link them to the user's identity. According to the ISO/IEC 24745 standard [23], a privacy-preserving authentication system should meet the following three requirements: (i) *renewability (cancelability)* - users should be able to refresh their compromised profiles; (ii) *unlinkability* - it should be infeasible for an attacker to link two or more profiles; and (iii) *irreversibility* - it should be practically impossible to infer users' behavioral patterns from a compromised profile. Biometric and behavioral biometric systems use templates of the profiles to ensure some of these properties. Renewability allows users to revoke and replace their templates if compromised. Unlinkability ensures that the distance or divergence between two templates, whether from the same or different sources, is indistinguishable, preventing cross-matching attacks [18]. Irreversibility ensures that the original behavioral patterns cannot be reconstructed from the used template.

Among all cryptographic and non-cryptographic approaches, cancelable biometrics, as first defined in [24], has the potential to ensure all three privacy properties. This method transforms a user's original biometric profile into a pseudo-template, which can be easily replaced if compromised. Cancelable biometrics can protect the privacy of the original profile if the transformation used is irreversible. The transformed profiles of cancelable biometrics can also be used to train an ML-based classifier if the transformation preserves the pairwise Euclidean distances among the profiles. However, finding a suitable transformation function that ensures all of these criteria is challenging.

Our Work. We utilize random projection (RP) to transform behavioral profiles and then use them to train a BA classifier. Here, RP transforms profile vectors from a high-dimensional space to a lower-dimensional one using an individual random matrix that acts as a secret known only to the user. RP preserves the relative Euclidean distances among the vectors in a metric space with high probability. Consequently, a BA classifier trained with RP-transformed data can ensure system performance while maintaining privacy. The contributions of this paper include: (i) the proposal of a privacy-preserving BA system that guarantees all three privacy properties while ensuring system performance; (ii) performing security and privacy analysis under diverse adversarial conditions; and (iii) validating the system through experiments, with results consistent with the theoretical analysis.

The structure of the paper is as follows. Section 2 presents the related work, while Sect. 3 covers the privacy-preserving BA system. An ML-based privacy attack is introduced in Sect. 4, and the experimental results are outlined in Sect. 5. Lastly, Sect. 6 provides the conclusion of the paper.

2 Related Work

BA System. A profile $\mathbf{X}$ in a BA system consists of m vectors $\{\mathbf{x_1}, \mathbf{x_2}, \cdots, \mathbf{x_m}\}$ of dimension d, where each dimension represents a feature and each vector corresponds to a behavioral measurement. During registration, a BA verifier collects N profiles to train an NN-based classifier $\mathtt{C}(\cdot)$. A verification request is a tuple $(u_i, \mathbf{Y})$ consisting of (i) an identity u_i and (ii) n behavioral samples $\mathbf{Y} = \{\mathbf{y_1}, \mathbf{y_2}, \cdots, \mathbf{y_n}\}$, where $n < m$. The verification algorithm $\mathtt{Ver}(\cdot, \cdot)$ uses $\mathtt{C}(\cdot)$ to generate n prediction vectors $\hat{y_1}, \hat{y_2}, \cdots, \hat{y_n}$, which are then used for an authentication decision, accept or reject. A BA system must ensure correctness and security, measured by false acceptance rate (FAR) and false rejection rate (FRR), where FAR is the probability of granting a request from an unauthorized user and FRR is the probability of denying a request from an authorized user.

The KL divergence $D_{KL}(\mathbf{X}||\mathbf{Y})$ quantifies how much the distribution $\mathbf{Y}$ diverges from $\mathbf{X}$. Since KL divergence is asymmetric, Jensen-Shannon (JS) divergence [21], addresses this by providing a symmetric measure $D_{JS}(\mathbf{X}||\mathbf{Y}) = \frac{1}{2}(D_{KL}(\mathbf{X}||\mathbf{Z}) + D_{KL}(\mathbf{Y}||\mathbf{Z}))$, where $\mathbf{Z} = \frac{1}{2}(\mathbf{X} + \mathbf{Y})$ is the mixture distribution representing their average. JS divergence can evaluate profile similarity by interpreting profiles as probability distributions. We apply the k-NN divergence estimator [26] to estimate $D_{KL}(\cdot||\cdot)$ due to its reliability with small sample sizes. The estimated $D_{KL}(\cdot||\cdot)$ is then used in the JS divergence to effectively measure the similarity between two profiles.

Privacy-Preserving Authentication System. Privacy-preserving biometric and behavioral biometric authentication systems are classified into key binding (fuzzy vault [13] and fuzzy commitment [4]), key generation [27] and cancelable biometric [24] systems. Key-binding and key-generation systems are not suitable for noisy BA systems, particularly those using ML classifiers for authentication. Cancelable biometrics [25,29] are commonly used in BA systems, with random projection (RP) being the most popular method, where feature vectors are projected onto a random subspace. References [22,25,28] detail RP-based methods in cancelable biometrics. Most RP-based approaches rely on traditional distance-based verification, and only a few employ ML algorithms. In addition, some privacy-preserving systems use cryptographic techniques, including homomorphic encryption [2], zero-knowledge proofs [20], and blockchain [19].

Random projection (RP). RP projects a vector $\mathbf{x_i}$ from a high-dimensional space to $\mathbf{x'_i}$ in a lower-dimensional space. The RP of a profile $\mathbf{X}$ is given by $\mathbf{X'} = \frac{1}{\sqrt{k}\sigma_r}\mathbf{RX}$, or more simply $\mathbf{X'} = \mathbf{RX}$. RP is an inherently lossy process, which means that some information about the original data is lost during projection. The foundation of RP is the Johnson-Lindenstrauss (JL) lemma [17],

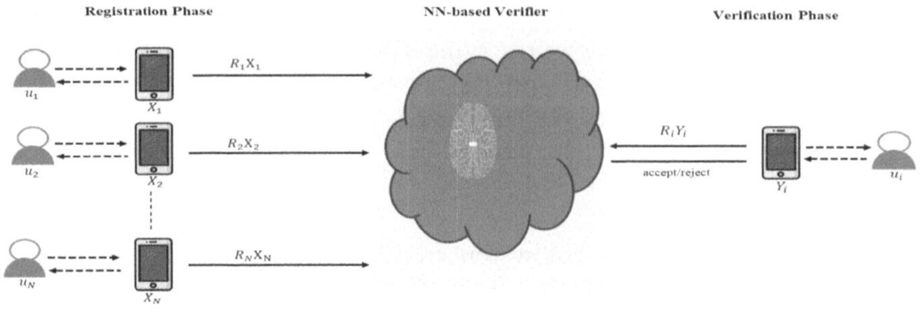

Fig. 1. In the proposed BA system, the verifier trains a neural network classifier with projected profiles and uses projected verification data for authentication decisions.

with an extension [7] suggesting a minimum dimension reduction to preserve the distances between the vectors. Mathematical analysis of RP operations [3] shows that compact points in vector space can be projected into random space while approximately preserving distances. RP-based methods were analyzed for privacy in biometric data [22] and behavioral biometrics [25]. To speed up the computation, [1] introduced a discretized version, generating $\mathbf{R}$ components (+1, 0, −1) with probabilities $Pr(x = +1) = \frac{1}{2\phi}$, $Pr(x = 0) = 1 - \frac{1}{\phi}$, $Pr(x = -1) = \frac{1}{2\phi}$. This discrete distribution was later adapted in [25] for behavioral profiles.

3 A Privacy-Preserving BA System

Figure 1 shows the block diagram of the proposed privacy-preserving BA system. RP makes the system suitable for low computation devices. Details of registration and verification phases are provided below.

Registration Phase. After obtaining a profile $\mathbf{X}$ from a user u_i, the user device generates a random matrix $\mathbf{R}_i$ and applies it to project $\mathbf{X}$ as $\mathbf{X}' = \mathbf{R}_i\mathbf{X}$. RP uses a Lipschitz mapping $f : \mathbb{R}^d \rightarrow \mathbb{R}^k$ to reduce the profile's dimensionality from d to k. To simplify computation, a discrete distribution is employed for RP with ϕ set to 3. The device then transmits the projected profile $\mathbf{X}'$ to the verifier. The verifier gathers N projected profiles $\mathbf{X}'_1, \mathbf{X}'_2, \cdots, \mathbf{X}'_N$, and trains an NN-based BA classifier $\mathtt{C}(\cdot)$ using them. In this setup, the verifier can act as a third-party service provider deploying $\mathtt{C}(\cdot)$ through an MLaaS platform. The generation of $\mathbf{R}$ for RP is based on a seed. In our proposed system, each user has a secret random seed, which they memorize and use later to generate the random matrix.

Verification Phase. During the verification phase, the user's device transforms the newly connected verification profile to $\mathbf{Y}' = \mathbf{R}_i\mathbf{Y}$ using a random matrix $\mathbf{R}_i$ generated from memorized seed and then sends a verification request $(u_i, \mathbf{Y}')$

to the verifier. The verification algorithm $\texttt{Ver}(\cdot,\cdot)$ uses the BA classifier $\texttt{C}(\cdot)$ to classify the verification data. The output of $\texttt{C}(\cdot)$ consists of n prediction vectors $\hat{y}$ for the n vectors in $\mathbf{Y}'$. The verification algorithm aggregates these outputs into a single binary decision (accept or reject) and notifies the user.

3.1 Analysis

Renewability Analysis. To ensure the renewability property, each user should be able to revoke an old projected profile and replace it with a new one in the system. In our proposed privacy-preserving BA system, a user u can achieve this by changing the secret $\mathbf{R}_i$ to $\mathbf{R}_j$, which generates a new projected profile $\mathbf{X}'_j = \mathbf{R}_j\mathbf{X}$ from $\mathbf{X}$ and a new verification profile $\mathbf{Y}'_j = \mathbf{R}_j\mathbf{Y}$ from $\mathbf{Y}$. The user can then update $\texttt{C}(\cdot)$ by replacing $\mathbf{X}'_i$ (where $\mathbf{X}'_i = \mathbf{R}_i\mathbf{X}$) with the new projected profile $\mathbf{X}'_j$. For u, the new verification request becomes $(u, \mathbf{Y}'_j)$. In this updated system, the performance of the BA system should be largely preserved, which is confirmed in Sect. 5.1 by the experimental results.

Unlinkability Analysis. It is important for a privacy-preserving BA system to ensure the infeasibility of correlating transformed profiles. For example, if an attacker acquires two projected profiles $\mathbf{X}'_i$ and $\mathbf{X}'_j$ belonging to user u, it should be computationally infeasible to determine whether these protected profiles originate from the same source. The unlinkability property prevents cross-matching attacks [18] and reduces the risk of tracing an individual enrolled in multiple systems using the same behavioral profile. The unlinkability property is satisfied if the symmetric divergence between two protected profiles from the same source, but projected using two different $\mathbf{R}$ matrices is indistinguishable from the symmetric divergence between protected profiles from different sources. In Sect. 5.1, we validated the unlinkability property of our proposed privacy-preserving BA system by comparing the distributions of these symmetric divergences measured by the JS divergence estimator.

Irreversibility Analysis. Two key factors contribute to the irreversibility of our proposed scheme: the difficulty of finding the secret $\mathbf{R}$ and extracting features from compromised projected profiles. In this section, we analyze brute-force attacks to find the correct $\mathbf{R}$ and use the "minimum-norm" solution to extract behavioral features. In Sect. 4, we present an ML-based attack model to evaluate an attacker's ability to recover features from projected profiles.

To find the secret $\mathbf{R}$, consider a scenario where the details of RP are known, except $\mathbf{R}$. The matrix can be estimated by trying all possible combinations. The random matrix $\mathbf{R}$ has dimensions $k \times d$, with each element being $+1$, 0, or -1. Thus, the worst-case complexity of guessing $\mathbf{R}$ is $O(3^{k\times d})$, which grows exponentially with k and d. Moreover, these attacks do not guarantee success as the attacker cannot confirm whether a guessed key is correct.

To extract behavioral features, consider a scenario where the projected profile $\mathbf{X}'$ is known. If the original profile $\mathbf{X}$ is unknown, the system of linear equations

$\mathbf{X}' = \mathbf{R}\mathbf{X}$ has $d - k$ degrees of freedom. Among all possible solutions, the solution $\hat{\mathbf{X}} = \mathbf{R}^T(\mathbf{R}\mathbf{R}^T)^{-1}\mathbf{X}'$, known as the minimum-norm solution, minimizes the Euclidean norm $|\hat{\mathbf{X}}| = \sqrt{\sum_{t=1}^{m} \hat{x}_t^2}$ [8], allowing recovery of a profile $\mathbf{X}$. However, in [25], the authors demonstrate that for behavioral data, RP is an effective privacy-preserving transformation against the minimum-norm solution for both known and unknown $\mathbf{R}$. They also derived theoretical privacy bound for this system and verified their claims experimentally.

4 ML-Based Privacy Attack

This section evaluates the privacy of our proposed BA system against ML-based attacks, which can uncover complex relationships between projected and plain profiles, posing a significant threat to privacy-preserving mechanisms. In our scenario, we assume the attacker has: (i) knowledge of the verification process $\mathtt{Ver}(\cdot,\cdot)$, including the architecture and input-output dimensions of the trained $\mathtt{C}(\cdot)$; (ii) access to projected profiles of the BA system through an honest-but-curious verifier, model inversion attacks, or other attack methods; (iii) access to publicly available profile generator software of the BA system for collecting auxiliary profiles; and (iv) knowledge of the distribution and dimension of $\mathbf{R}$. In the worst case, the attacker may also obtain the secret $\mathbf{R}$ if the seed is compromised.

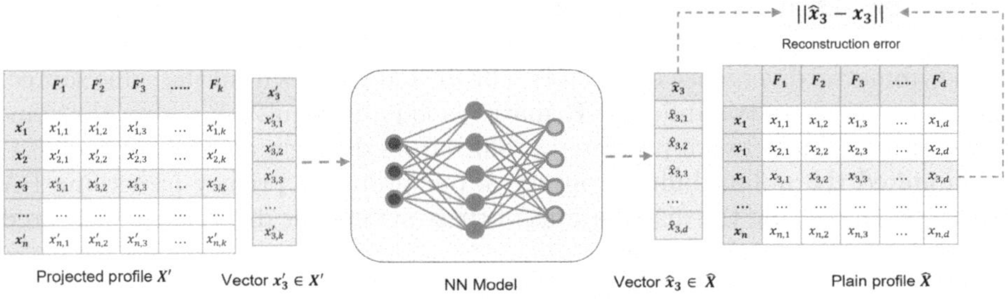

Fig. 2. The attack model $\mathtt{M_P}(\cdot)$ is trained to reconstruct a plain profile $\hat{\mathbf{X}}$ from a projected profile $\mathbf{X}'$. The reconstruction error is calculated as the average difference between the vectors of $\hat{\mathbf{X}}$ and the ground truth profile $\mathbf{X}$.

Train an Attack Model. The goal of this privacy attack is to reconstruct the plain profiles from the projected profiles and extract the behavioral pattern. For this purpose, the attacker trains an ML-based attack model $\mathtt{M_P}(\cdot)$. The details of each step in the $\mathtt{M_P}(\cdot)$ training process are described below.

- The attacker uses the profile generator to collect the necessary auxiliary profiles. Although there is no limit on the number of auxiliary profiles, having more profiles results in a more generalized attack model.

- The attacker applies RP to each auxiliary profile to produce a projected version. The **R** for RP is generated either using a compromised seed or by leveraging knowledge of the distribution. To increase the number of projected auxiliary profiles and improve the generalization of $\mathtt{M_P}(\cdot)$, the attacker can apply multiple instances of **R** to each auxiliary profile.
- To train $\mathtt{M_P}(\cdot)$, the attacker uses the projected auxiliary profiles as training data and the original auxiliary profiles as the ground truth. The attacker's goal is to generate plain profiles that closely match the corresponding profiles. Figure 2 illustrates the training process of $\mathtt{M_P}(\cdot)$.

The trained $\mathtt{M_P}(\cdot)$ is then used to generate plain profiles from the compromised projected profiles, aiming to recover behavioral patterns of target users.

Privacy Evaluation. We evaluate the privacy of our system by analyzing the statistical similarity between recovered profiles and their original counterparts.

Definition 1. *(ϵ-Distribution-privacy:) Suppose* $\mathtt{M_P}(\cdot)$ *is applied to a projected profile* $\mathbf{X}'$ *to recover its plain profile. A privacy-preserving BA system is said to offer* ϵ*-distribution-privacy against a privacy attacker if the best ML-based approach produces a profile* $\hat{\mathbf{X}}$ *where no more than* ϵ *percent of features pass a statistical similarity test with corresponding features of the original profile* $\mathbf{X}$.

We consider two scenarios for this privacy attack: (i) the adversary knows the distribution of **R**, and (ii) the adversary knows the secret **R**. The second scenario represents the extreme case. If **R** is unknown, the attacker generates a random matrix from the known distribution of **R**, which is publicly available information. If the attacker knows **R**, they directly use the known matrix. In both scenarios, the attacker projects the auxiliary profiles using the respective matrix before training $\mathtt{M_P}(\cdot)$. Our privacy-preserving BA system should limit the attacker from recovering more than ϵ percent of features on average per profile. Since RP is inherently a lossy process, causing some information about the original profile to be lost during the initial projection, attackers cannot perfectly reconstruct the original behavioral patterns from the projected profiles in either scenario. We validate this through experiments in Sect. 5.2.

5 Experimental Results

We implemented and evaluated our approach on voice [11] and drawing pattern [15] data sets. The voice data includes 86 users with 120 observations each, while the drawing data consists of 193 users with 80 to 240 observations each. There are 104 features in the voice data and 65 features in the drawing data.

Experiment Setup. We downloaded, cleaned[1], and normalized the profile data, and separated 20.0% of the data from each profile for testing purposes. Using the Synthetic Minority Over-sampling Technique (SMOTE) [5],

[1] Replacing "NaN" and "Infinity" with zero and removing duplicate rows.

we increased the sample sizes for the remaining data by generating new data points through interpolation. We then split the profiles into two groups: Group 1 (68 voice and 155 drawing pattern profiles, about 80%) was used to train and validate the ML-based BA classifier, while Group 2 (18 voice and 38 drawing pattern profiles) served as auxiliary profiles. For random projection, we generated $\mathbf{R}$ following the discrete distribution discussed before, where $\phi = 3$. Using the JL lemma [7], we calculated the minimum acceptable k for an $\mathbf{R}^{k \times d}$, ensuring a 0.99 distance-preserving probability, which is 73 for voice data and 46 for drawing data. Details of the JL lemma are provided in [7].

5.1 Privacy-Preserving BA Classifier

In this section, we design the NN architecture for BA classifiers, train them on plain and projected profiles, and assess their accuracy, security, renewability, and unlinkability.

Table 1. The performance of $\mathtt{C}(\cdot)$ is assessed at: before applying RP, after applying RP, and after renewing training profiles. The minimal variations in FRR and FAR validate the correctness, security, and renewability of both privacy-preserving BA systems.

Data Set	Before RP		After RP		Updated $\mathtt{C}(\cdot)$	
	FRR	FAR	FRR	FAR	FRR	FAR
Voice data	1.90	0.94	0.44	0.45	1.33	0.12
Drawing data	1.07	0.69	1.03	0.33	2.08	3.60

Performance of BA Classifiers for Plain Profiles. We developed two hierarchical NN architectures for both BA classifiers, incorporating dense, batch normalization, ReLU activation, and dropout layers, with a softmax layer for output. From Group 1, 80% of the voice and drawing data was used for training, and 20% for evaluating the classifiers. We then tested system performance using the reserved test data. Table 1 presents the FRR and FAR of both BA systems before applying RP to plain profiles.

Performance of BA Classifiers for Projected Profiles. For RP, we set k to 94, and 56 for voice and drawing data, respectively, and kept the NN architecture the same, with different numbers of layers and nodes in each layer. After training, we achieved 95.65% and 97.34% accuracy for voice and drawing data, respectively. For correctness testing, each profile was projected using the same $\mathbf{R}$ employed during training, yielding 99.56% and 98.97% accuracy (0.44% and 1.03% FRR). The security tests used incorrect $\mathbf{R}$, resulting in accuracy dropping to 0.45% and 0.33%, respectively, which represent the FAR of the systems. Table 1 shows the performance of our privacy-preserving systems closely match with original BA systems.

Renew Training Profile. To evaluate the renewability property of our privacy-preserving BA system, we projected each plain training profile using a new $\mathbf{R}$ and then updated $\mathtt{C}(\cdot)$. For voice data, the updated BA classifiers achieved 96.32% training accuracy and 94.60% accuracy for drawing data. In security tests, we used test data projected by the wrong $\mathbf{R}$, yielding FAR values of 0.12% and 3.60%, as expected. When the test datasets were projected using the correct $\mathbf{R}$, system correctness increased to 98.67% (1.33% FRR) for voice and 97.92% (2.08% FRR) for drawing data, which validates the renewability property of our BA system. Table 1 shows the performance of our proposed BA system after renewing the training profiles.

Similarity of Divergence Distributions. To ensure unlinkability, the JS divergence distribution should differ from the distribution of valid claims (same source, same $\mathbf{R}$) when profiles from the same source are projected with different $\mathbf{R}$ matrices (case 1), but should remain close to the distribution of invalid claims (different sources, different $\mathbf{R}$) (case 2). Figure 3 (a-b) shows the divergence distributions for these two cases. We then applied the Kolmogorov-Smirnov (KS) test to evaluate the null hypothesis that the two divergence distributions compared are close. For case 1, we consistently obtained p-values much lower than 0.05, and for case 2, p-values were consistently higher than 0.05. This indicates that the divergences in case 1 follow different distributions, while in case 2, they follow the close distribution, or there is insufficient evidence to conclude otherwise. These results suggest that an attacker cannot link the projected profiles in our BA system based on their symmetric divergence.

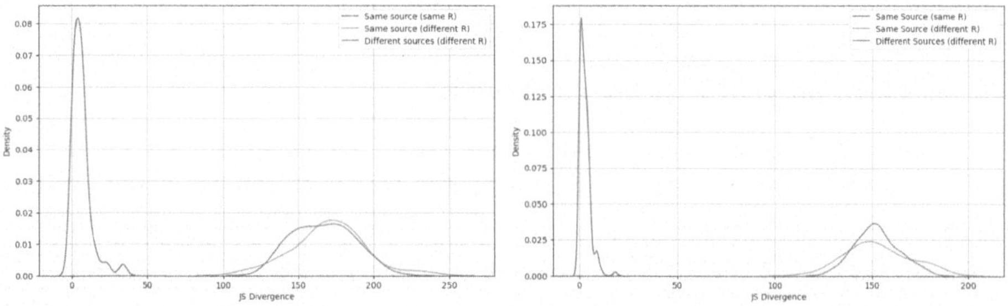

(a) Voice data (b) Drawing data

Fig. 3. In both BA systems, the JS divergence differs from valid claims when same-source profiles are projected with different $\mathbf{R}$ matrices but aligns with invalid claims.

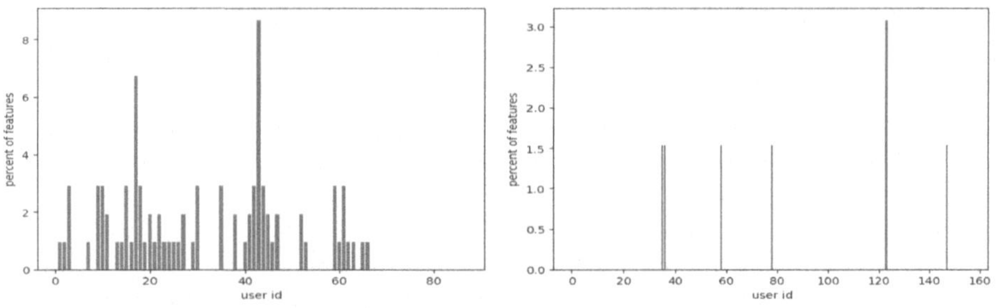

(a) Voice data (b) Drawing data

Fig. 4. Performance of $\mathtt{M_P}(\cdot)$ with a known distribution of $\mathbf{R}$ shows low average feature recovery for compromised profiles: 1.96% for voice data and 1.75% for drawing data.

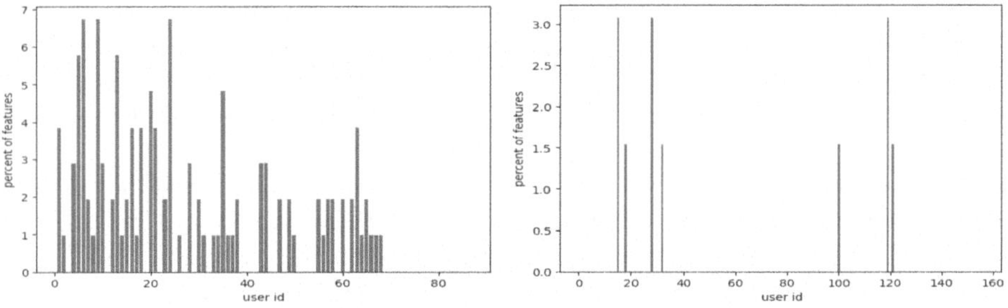

(a) Voice data (b) Drawing data

Fig. 5. Performance of $\mathtt{M_P}(\cdot)$ with a known $\mathbf{R}$ shows low average feature recovery for compromised profiles: 2.43% for voice data and 2.14% for drawing data.

5.2 Performance of ML-Based Attack

To recover BA features, we trained an ML-based attack model $\mathtt{M_P}(\cdot)$ and then applied it to reconstruct plain profiles from the compromised projected profiles.

Train an Attack Model. We designed two hierarchical NN architectures for $\mathtt{M_P}(\cdot)$, one for each dataset. The purpose of building a hierarchical model is that each layer in an NN can capture more complex non-linear relationships between projected and corresponding plain profiles. Both architectures included dense, batch normalization, and ReLU layers. The final layer uses a sigmoid function to keep the output to [0, 1]. We projected auxiliary profiles using newly generated $\mathbf{R}$ matrices for unknown $\mathbf{R}$ (case 1) and existing $\mathbf{R}$ matrices for known $\mathbf{R}$ (case 2) and then used them to train $\mathtt{M_P}(\cdot)$. In both cases, we used "mean-square-error" as the loss function and "RMSProp" as the optimizer with a learning rate of 0.001. Case 1 resulted in training losses of 0.013 and 0.011 and validation losses of 0.013 and 0.0012 after 50 epochs. Case 2 with known $\mathbf{R}$ achieved similar losses for both datasets.

Recover Feature. The trained $\mathtt{M_P}(\cdot)$ is now used to generate plain profiles from each intercepted projected profile. Using the KS test, we estimate the similarity between the features of the recovered and ground-truth profiles. Figure 4 (a-b) shows the percentage of features that passed the KS test for each profile when the attacker knows the distribution of $\mathbf{R}$. The attacker recovered at least one feature from 43 out of 86 voice profiles, and 6 out of 155 drawing profiles, but the average feature recovery rate per profile remains very low: 1.96% for voice data and 1.75% for drawing data. Figure 5 (a-b) shows the results when the attacker knows $\mathbf{R}$, increasing the recovered voice profiles to 48 and drawing profiles to 7, with average feature recovery rates of 2.43% and 2.14% per profile, respectively. However, these recovered features are insufficient to reveal users' behavioral patterns or to be useful for future attacks.

5.3 Results Comparison

We compare the performance of our proposed BA system with existing RP-based systems mentioned in related work. The comparison focuses on performance, privacy properties, and resilience against various attacks. While some related works excel in specific areas, our system demonstrates competitive performance by balancing authentication accuracy with privacy. Furthermore, it provides robust protection against diverse privacy threats, including advanced ML-driven attacks. A summary of the comparisons is presented in Table 2.

Table 2. Comparison of RP-based cancelable authentication systems.

System	FAR, FRR	Privacy Property	Attack Resilience
Wang et al. [28]	18.19%	Ensure 2 out of 3	Cross match, Known R
Taheri et al. [25]	Below 6.0%	Ensure 2 out of 3	Known and unknown R
Peng et al. [22]	Below 1.0%	Ensure all 3	Cross match, Known R, Brute-force
Our Work	Below 4.0%	Ensure all 3	ML driven, Cross match, Known and unknown R

6 Conclusion

We proposed a privacy-preserving BA system designed for low-computation devices, ensuring profile irreversibility through the one-way property of RP. Renewability and unlinkability are achieved by using a unique $\mathbf{R}$ for each user in RP. Our experimental results on two behavioral datasets, along with comprehensive security and privacy evaluations, validate the effectiveness of our method. Beyond BA systems, our approach has broader applicability to domains such as biometric authentication and high-dimensional data publishing. Future work will extend its applicability to multi-modal biometric authentication and federated learning systems.

Acknowledgment. This research was supported by Concordia University of Edmonton (CUE), Edmonton, AB, Canada, through the Seed Grant program.

References

1. Achlioptas, D.: Database-friendly random projections: Johnson-lindenstrauss with binary coins. J. Comput. Syst. Sci. **66**, 671–687 (2003)
2. Baig, A.F., Eskeland, S., Yang, B.: Privacy-preserving continuous authentication using behavioral biometrics. Int. J. Inf. Secur. **22**(6), 1833–1847 (2023)
3. Bingham, E., Mannila, H.: Random projection in dimensionality reduction: applications to image and text data. In: Proceedings of the seventh ACM SIGKDD, pp. 245–250. ACM (2001)
4. Chauhan, S., Sharma, A.: Improved fuzzy commitment scheme. Int. J. Inf. Technol. **14**(3), 1321–1331 (2022)
5. Chawla, N.V., Bowyer, K.W., Hall, L.O., Kegelmeyer, W.P.: SMOTE: synthetic minority over-sampling technique. J. Artif. Intell. Res. **16**, 321–357 (2002)
6. Chong, P., Elovici, Y., Binder, A.: User authentication based on mouse dynamics using deep neural networks: a comprehensive study. IEEE Trans. Inf. Forensics Secur. **15**, 1086–1101 (2019)
7. Dasgupta, S., Gupta, A.: An elementary proof of a theorem of Johnson and Lindenstrauss. Random Struct. Algorithms **22**(1), 60–65 (2003)
8. Demmel, J.W., Higham, N.J.: Improved error bounds for underdetermined system solvers. SIAM J. Matrix Anal. Appl. **14**(1), 1–14 (1993)
9. Deng, Y., Zhong, Y.: Keystroke dynamics advances for mobile devices using deep neural network. Recent Adv. User Authentication Using Keystroke Dyn. Biometrics **2**, 59–70 (2015)
10. Gong, X., Wang, Q., Chen, Y., Yang, W., Jiang, X.: Model extraction attacks and defenses on cloud-based machine learning models. IEEE Commun. Mag. **58**(12), 83–89 (2020)
11. Gupta, S., Buriro, A., Crispo, B.: A chimerical dataset combining physiological and behavioral biometric traits for reliable user authentication on smart devices and ecosystems. Data Brief **28**, 104924 (2020)
12. Islam, M.M., Safavi-Naini, R.: POSTER: a behavioural authentication system for mobile users. In: Proceedings of the 2016 ACM Conference on Computer and Communications Security (CCS '16), pp. 1742–1744. ACM (2016)
13. Islam, M.M., Safavi-Naini, R.: Fuzzy vault for behavioral authentication system. In: ICT Systems Security and Privacy Protection: 35th IFIP TC 11 International Conference, SEC 2020, Maribor, Slovenia, September 21–23, 2020, Proceedings 35, pp. 295–310. Springer (2020)
14. Islam, M.M., Safavi-Naini, R.: Model inversion for impersonation in behavioral authentication systems. In: SECRYPT, pp. 271–282 (2021)
15. Islam, M.M., Safavi-Naini, R., Kneppers, M.: Scalable behavioral authentication. IEEE Access **9**, 43458–43473 (2021)
16. Jung, D., et al.: Deep neural network-based gait classification using wearable inertial sensor data. In: 2019 41st Annual International Conference of the IEEE Engineering in Medicine and Biology Society (EMBC), pp. 3624–3628. IEEE (2019)
17. Kaski, S.: Dimensionality reduction by random mapping: fast similarity computation for clustering. In: 1998 IEEE International Joint Conference on Neural Networks Proceedings. IEEE World Congress on Computational Intelligence (Cat. No. 98CH36227). vol. 1, pp. 413–418. IEEE (1998)

18. Kelkboom, E.J., Breebaart, J., Kevenaar, T.A., Buhan, I., Veldhuis, R.N.: Preventing the decodability attack based cross-matching in a fuzzy commitment scheme. IEEE Trans. Inf. Forensics Secur. **6**(1), 107–121 (2010)
19. Kim, S., Mun, H.J., Hong, S.: Multi-factor authentication with randomly selected authentication methods with did on a random terminal. Appl. Sci. **12**(5), 2301 (2022)
20. Mir, O., Roland, M., Mayrhofer, R.: DAMFA: decentralized anonymous multi-factor authentication. In: Proceedings of the 2nd ACM International Symposium on Blockchain and Secure Critical Infrastructure, pp. 10–19 (2020)
21. Nielsen, F.: On a variational definition for the jensen-shannon symmetrization of distances based on the information radius. Entropy **23**(4), 464 (2021)
22. Peng, J., Gupta, B.B., Abd El-Latif, A.A.: A biometric cryptosystem scheme based on random projection and neural network. Soft. Comput. **25**, 7657–7670 (2021)
23. Secretary, I.: Information technology-security techniques-biometric information protection. Int. Organ. Stand., Stand. ISO/IEC **24745**, 2011 (2011)
24. Soutar, C., Roberge, D., Stoianov, A., Gilroy, R., Kumar, B.V.: Biometric encryption using image processing. In: Optical Security and Counterfeit Deterrence Techniques II. vol. 3314, pp. 178–188. SPIE (1998)
25. Taheri, S., Islam, M.M., Safavi-Naini, R.: Privacy-enhanced profile-based authentication using sparse random projection. In: Proceedings of the IFIP SEC'17, pp. 474–490. Springer (2017)
26. Wang, Q., Kulkarni, S.R., Verdú, S.: Divergence estimation for multidimensional densities via k-nearest-neighbor distances. IEEE Trans. Inf. Theory **55**(5), 2392–2405 (2009)
27. Wang, Y., Li, B., Zhang, Y., Wu, J., Ma, Q.: A secure biometric key generation mechanism via deep learning and its application. Appl. Sci. **11**(18), 8497 (2021)
28. Wang, Y., Plataniotis, K.N.: An analysis of random projection for changeable and privacy-preserving biometric verification. IEEE Trans. Syst., Man, Cybern., Part B (Cybernetics) **40**(5), 1280–1293 (2010)
29. Yang, W., Wang, S., Kang, J.J., Johnstone, M.N., Bedari, A.: A linear convolution-based cancelable fingerprint biometric authentication system. Comput. Secur. **114**, 102583 (2022)

Automated Exploration of Optimal Neural Network Structures for Deepfake Detection

Yuto Toshikawa[1(✉)], Ryo Iijima[1,2], and Tatsuya Mori[1,3,4]

[1] Waseda University, Shinjuku, Japan
toshi@nsl.cs.waseda.ac.jp
[2] Advanced Industrial Science and Technology (AIST), Tokyo, Japan
[3] National Institute of Information and Communications Technology (NICT), Tokyo, Japan
[4] RIKEN Center for Advanced Intelligence Project (AIP), Tokyo, Japan

Abstract. The proliferation of Deepfake technology has raised concerns about its potential misuse for malicious purposes, such as defaming celebrities or causing political unrest. While existing methods have reported high accuracy in detecting Deepfakes, challenges remain in adapting to the rapidly evolving Deepfake technology and developing efficient and effective detectors. In this paper, we propose a novel approach to address these challenges by utilizing advanced Neural Architecture Search (NAS) methods, specifically focusing on DARTS, PC-DARTS, and DU-DARTS. Our experimental results demonstrate that the PC-DARTS method achieves the highest test AUC of 0.88 among the techniques investigated, with a learning time of only 2.86 GPU days. This highlights the efficiency and effectiveness of our approach in automatically building Deepfake detection models. Moreover, the models using NAS exhibit competitive performance compared to state-of-the-art architectures such as XceptionNet, EfficientNet, and MobileNet. Our results suggest that the automatic search process using advanced NAS methods can quickly and easily construct adaptive and high-performance Deepfake detection models, indicating a new and promising direction for combating the ever-evolving Deepfake technology.

Keywords: Deepfake · detection · NAS · image recognition · deep learning

1 Introduction

The advancement of Deepfake technology has led to increasingly realistic synthetic videos, posing risks in malicious applications such as misinformation and identity manipulation. An example is the March 2022 Deepfake of Ukrainian President Volodymyr Zelenskyy, which, though debunked, highlighted the technology's potential for harm [2]. This has spurred an urgent need for effective detection methods.

K. Adi et al. (Eds.): FPS 2024, LNCS 15533, pp. 108–120, 2025.
https://doi.org/10.1007/978-3-031-87496-3_8

Table 1. Deepfake Datasets and Their Details

Dataset	Generation	Real Videos	Fake Videos	Release
UADFV [10]	1st	49	49	2018.11
DeepfakeTIMIT [9]	1st	–	620	2018.12
FaceForensics++ [14]	1st	1,000	2,000	2019.01
DeepFakeDetection [1]	2nd	363	3,068	2019.09
DFDC Preview [5]	2nd	1,131	4,119	2019.10
Celeb-DF [11]	2nd	590	5,639	2019.11
Deeper Forensics [8]	3rd	48,475	11,000	2020.05
DFDC [4]	3rd	23,654	104,500	2020.06

Current Deepfake detection largely relies on deep learning models, which perform well on datasets like FaceForensics++. For instance, Thing et al. [16] achieved a test AUC of 0.9945 using EfficientNet, while Dang et al. [3] reported 0.9969 with XceptionNet. However, while these models perform well on their training datasets, they struggle with newer, more sophisticated Deepfakes. Li et al. [11] demonstrated this by showing that XceptionNet, achieving a test AUC of 0.997 on FaceForensics++, dropped to 0.482 when tested on the newer Celeb-DF dataset. This sharp decline underscores the need for adaptable detection models capable of handling evolving Deepfake techniques.

Developing such adaptive models is resource-intensive, and we hypothesize that Neural Architecture Search (NAS) could offer a solution. Although not initially purposed for this task, NAS has shown success in discovering architectures optimized for various vision applications, reducing dependency on manual design. Methods like DARTS [12], PC-DARTS [18], and DU-DARTS [15] achieve strong performance across vision tasks. Our study explores the application of NAS for Deepfake detection, testing DARTS, PC-DARTS, and DU-DARTS on the challenging Celeb-DF dataset to assess NAS's ability to construct robust detection models.

We compare these NAS-discovered models to existing manually designed architectures, evaluating NAS's feasibility for adaptive Deepfake detection.

Implementation code is available at: https://github.com/deepfake-detection-nas/deepfake-detection-nas.

2 Background

2.1 Deepfake Datasets

As research on Deepfake detection has advanced, datasets have evolved across different generations, each marked by improvements in data quality and sample size. First-generation datasets (2018) include lower quality Deepfakes, while the second (2019) and third generations (2019–2020) provide high-quality Deepfakes and larger datasets. Table 1 summarizes major datasets, focusing on generation, size, and release dates.

The Celeb-DF and DFDC Preview datasets are benchmark datasets commonly used. Celeb-DF [11] was designed to produce visually higher quality Deepfakes with fewer artifacts, offering 5,639 fake videos based on 590 real YouTube videos.

Table 2. Recent SoTA in Deepfake Detection Research

Author (Year)	Model Structure	Test Data	Accuracy	AUC
Thing (2023) [16]	XceptionNet	Celeb-DF	97.68	0.9977
	EfficientNetB7	Celeb-DF	96.43	0.9988
	ViT	Celeb-DF	87.21	0.9754
	XceptionNet	DFDC	80.08	0.9596
	EfficientNetB7	DFDC	92.02	0.9761
	ViT	DFDC	86.62	0.9341
Nguyen (2019) [13]	CapsuleNet	Celeb-DF	93.10	-
Zhao (2020) [19]	ResNet-50	Celeb-DF	-	0.6680

2.2 State of the Art in Deepfake Detection Techniques

The detection of Deepfakes has become a global challenge, with numerous methods for detecting Deepfakes being published. Research in this field has been focused on proposing various detection techniques using deep learning. Table 2 presents the recent State of the Art (SoTA) in Deepfake detection research.

Current SoTA technologies have reported very high test accuracy and AUC. Especially, the study by Thing et al. in 2023 [16] evaluated many advanced network architectures, confirming the possibility of highly accurate detection. However, despite such high-precision results, several significant challenges remain. The first challenge is whether the datasets and models constructed can flexibly adapt to the evolution of Deepfake technology. Deepfake technology is evolving rapidly, and models that could detect with high accuracy in the past may become ineffective against new generation methods. The second challenge is the high computational costs and the challenges associated with manual model design. Many SoTA models require advanced computational resources, and their architecture is manually designed by skilled experts. Considering these challenges, even if it seems that sufficient accuracy has been achieved with existing methods, the rapid evolution of Deepfakes and cost issues demand new approaches.

2.3 Neural Architecture Search (NAS)

Neural Architecture Search (NAS) automates the optimization of neural networks, significantly reducing the manual effort and expertise required. NAS typically involves three steps: defining a search space, selecting a search strategy, and determining a performance estimation strategy.

Two types of NAS strategies include "multi-trial" and "one-shot" methods. Multi-trial methods like NAS-RL require extensive computational resources, while one-shot methods (e.g., DARTS [12], PC-DARTS [18]) use supernetworks to reduce computational costs, although weight-sharing may impact independence among architectures (Table 3).

Table 3. Comparison of NAS Methods.

Method	Main Features	Computational Cost	Application Scope
DARTS	Differentiable search space, uses gradient descent	High	Wide range of datasets
PC-DARTS	Partial channel connections, Edge normalization reduces computational cost	Low	Wide range of datasets, especially when computational resources are limited
DU-DARTS	Reduces uncertainty, selects optimal operations	Medium to High	Various datasets for balancing accuracy and efficiency

DARTS enables efficient search by continuously optimizing structure choices using gradient descent, though it may face stability issues with complex architectures. PC-DARTS reduces computational demands by sampling channels per layer, making it effective in resource-limited settings. DU-DARTS explicitly reduces uncertainty through a categorical distribution, facilitating high-performance searches with lower computational costs.

3 Evaluation of NAS for Deepfake Detection

3.1 Workflow Overview

The experimental workflow is as follows:

1. **Image Preprocessing:** Convert all videos from the Deepfake dataset into images and extract faces. This preprocessing stage includes image denoising and normalization. (3.2)
2. **Definition of Model Search Space:** Define the space of model architectures to be searched for each of the algorithms: DARTS, PC-DARTS, and DU-DARTS. (3.3)
3. **Training and Evaluation:** Conduct the search with each algorithm based on the defined model search space. Perform training with the searched model structure three times and evaluate the performance of the model structure using the average of these results. (3.4)

3.2 Image Preprocessing

Image preprocessing involves face extraction and random augmentation for time efficiency. The MTCNN [7] is used to extract faces, discarding those with detection accuracy below 90%, which accounts for only 0.005% of images. Extracted faces have a 10% padding and are resized to 128×128 (Fig. 1).

3.3 Model Search Space Definition

The model search space includes eight operations, allowing various transformations on input data. These include convolutional and pooling layers, with parameters like kernel size and convolution type, enhancing structural flexibility.

Specifically, the operations include a "none" operation, which performs no transformation, and pooling operations such as a 3×3 max pooling and a 3×3 average pooling, providing ways to downsample the feature maps. The search space also includes skip connections, which pass the feature map directly to the

Fig. 1. Overview diagram of the preprocessing for the image data

Table 4. Definition of the Model Search Space

Operation	Description
none	Do nothing
max_pool_3×3	3×3 max pooling
avg_pool_3×3	3×3 average pooling
skip_connect	Skip connection (passes the feature map directly to the next layer if the size matches)
sep_conv_3×3	3×3 separable convolution (Depthwise Separable Convolution)
sep_conv_5×5	5×5 separable convolution
dil_conv_3×3	3×3 dilated convolution (Dilated Convolution)
dil_conv_5×5	5×5 dilated convolution

next layer if the size matches, enabling a flexible flow of information across layers. For convolutional transformations, the model search space offers separable convolutions (Depthwise Separable Convolution) with kernel sizes of 3×3 and 5×5, as well as dilated convolutions (Dilated Convolution) with the same kernel size options. The separable and dilated convolutions allow the model to capture features at varying levels of granularity and spatial context, adding to the flexibility and diversity within the search space (Table 4).

The network architecture consists of 10 cells, each with four steps, resulting in 8^{14} combinations per cell, making up a search space of approximately 2.5822×10^{134} for a 10-cell network. This space diversity significantly affects search efficiency and outcome.

3.4 Evaluation Method

This study aims to automate the search for the optimal neural network architecture for Deepfake detection. We employ three algorithms-DARTS, PC-DARTS, and DU-DARTS-to search for model structures, comparing their performance against high-performance models, including XceptionNet, EfficientNetB7, and MobileNetV3-large, all trained on the same dataset for fair benchmarking.

Table 5. Random modification processes of the image data.

Rotation	-15 to $+15°$
Width Shift (Vertical)	-15% to $+15\%$
Width Shift (Horizontal)	-15% to $+15\%$
Scaling	1 to 1.1 times
Horizontal Flip	True

Performance evaluation primarily considers test accuracy and AUC to quantify detection effectiveness. GPU-days are also recorded to assess both performance and training efficiency. Additionally, we analyze structural characteristics unique to each algorithm's output, identifying features that enhance Deepfake detection.

Each search is repeated three times per algorithm, with the average results enhancing reliability and minimizing variability. This study ultimately aims to provide deeper insights into optimal architectures for Deepfake detection, contributing toward more advanced and effective detection methods.

4 Performance Evaluation

4.1 Experimental Setup

Dataset Selection and Utilization

In order to automatically search for the optimal neural network structure in Deepfake detection, this study adopts the Celeb-DF dataset, which is known for its high-quality Deepfake generation technology and extensive data volume. Due to its widespread use in Deepfake detection research, Celeb-DF is considered a reliable dataset for evaluating model performance under realistic conditions.

However, due to the high computational cost and time associated with using the entire dataset, only a portion of Celeb-DF is used in this study. Specifically, we use 80% of the dataset for training, 10% for validation, and the remaining 10% for testing. From these segments, 1% is randomly selected for use in experiments to streamline search times and increase computational efficiency.

Data Preprocessing, Augmentation, and Sampling
We outline the process undertaken to enhance data diversity and strengthen the robustness of our models. Initially, we apply several preprocessing steps to the Celeb-DF dataset to prepare it for effective Deepfake detection. To augment data diversity, we implement five types of random augmentation processes during training: image rotation, width shift, zooming, and horizontal flipping. These augmentations aim to expose the model to a variety of conditions, thereby improving its ability to recognize Deepfakes. Specific details of these augmentation techniques, such as applying image rotation within a range of -15 to $15°$, are detailed in Table 5.

Table 6. Overview of the Celeb-DF dataset after preprocessing.

	Proportion (%)	Number of Image Data
Total Data Before Preprocessing	100	2,342,039
Training Data	80	19,826
Validation Data	10	2,218
Test Data	10	1,369

Table 7. Performance Comparison of Discovered Models and Existing Models.

Model Structure	Test Accuracy	Test AUC	GPU-days	Number of Parameters
DARTS	91.64%	0.7798	9.47	4,885,858
PC-DARTS	85.21%	0.8750	2.86	766,978
DU-DARTS	91.76%	0.7834	6.06	2,442,929
XceptionNet	87.81%	0.8956	–	20,809,001
EfficientNet	83.05%	0.8763	–	63,789,521
MobileNet	78.12%	0.8597	–	4,203,313

Following the augmentation phase, we proceed to split the data. The preprocessed and augmented face images from the Celeb-DF dataset are divided into three distinct sets: 80% are allocated for training, 10% for validation, and the remaining 10% for testing purposes. To ensure the study is manageable and respects computational limits, we randomly select 1% of the data from each of these subsets for the experimental evaluations. Table 6 provides an overview of the dataset post-preprocessing and splitting, indicating the partitioning criteria and dataset distribution used in our experiments. Moreover, Fig. ?? displays samples from the preprocessed and subsequently split Celeb-DF dataset, offering a glimpse into the data utilized for training and evaluation.

Model Training and Configuration
Model training and architecture search were executed on a RAIDEN GPU server [6] with Tesla V100 GPUs. Parameters [17] include an initial learning rate of 0.1 and a weight decay of 0.0003. Each model was trained for 50 epochs, ensuring optimal learning without overfitting.

4.2 Detection Accuracies

Table 7 presents a comparison of the performance between the optimal Deepfake detection model structures discovered using DARTS, PC-DARTS, and DU-DARTS, against the performance of state-of-the-art (SoTA) Deepfake detection models. The evaluation metrics include test accuracy, test AUC, and the training time required (measured in GPU-days). These metrics are utilized to assess and contrast the effectiveness of the discovered models with those of existing benchmark models. For the newly discovered models, each experiment was conducted three times, with their average values used for the comprehensive evaluation.

The results in Table 7 demonstrate that the models discovered using DARTS and DU-DARTS have remarkably high test accuracies, which is essential for effective Deepfake detection. In contrast, while PC-DARTS has lower test accuracy, its high test AUC indicates significant robustness to data variability, demonstrating its usefulness. This highlights the importance of evaluating model performance using multiple metrics rather than relying on a single metric. In addition, training time, measured in GPU days, is critical in determining a model's practicality in real-world settings. DARTS, while showing commendable accuracy, requires longer training times. Conversely, PC-DARTS stands out for its efficiency, offering an excellent test AUC with significantly reduced training time. DU-DARTS represents a balanced approach between the two, demonstrating a mix of effectiveness and efficiency. These results highlight the different trade-offs between model search speed and performance, and guide the selection of appropriate models for Deepfake detection in different operational scenarios.

Overall, the discovered model structures successfully balance the trade-off between parameter efficiency and accuracy, maintaining an optimal balance. Specifically, PC-DARTS demonstrates superior performance in test AUC, highlighting its advantage considering test AUC as a highly effective metric for robustness against data variability. These results suggest that using NAS for automatic model search is a promising approach for Deepfake detection tasks.

4.3 Identified Model Structures

Finally, we explore the optimal model structures for Deepfake detection that were identified through the use of DARTS, PC-DARTS, and DU-DARTS, respectively. The structures of the Normal Cell and Reduction Cell discovered by each algorithm are shown in Figs. 2, 3, and 4. The model structures presented are those that demonstrated the highest test AUC in three trials conducted, thus are considered as the optimal design for Deepfake detection and represent the best performance of each algorithm.

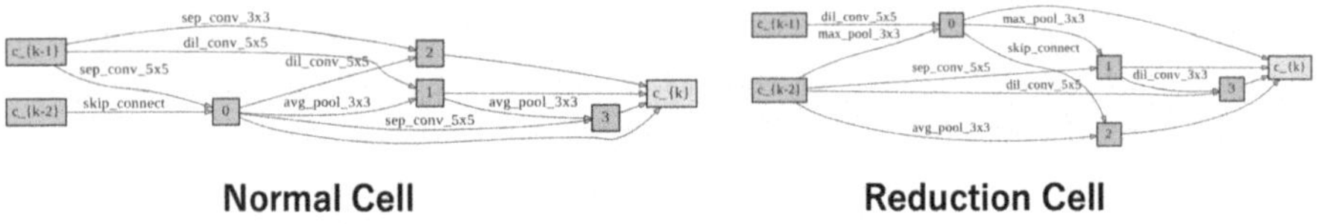

Fig. 2. Cell structure explored by DARTS.

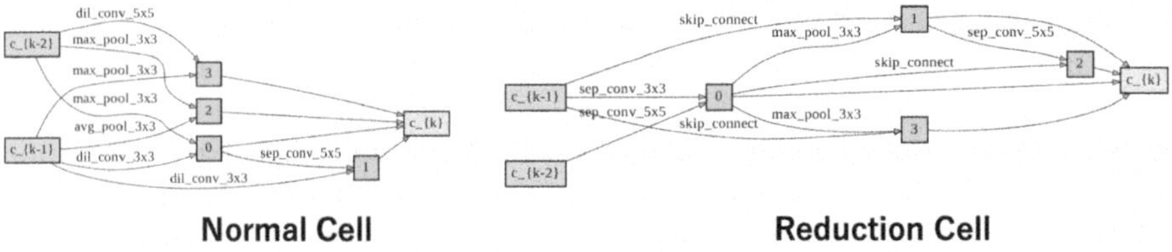

Fig. 3. Cell structure explored by PC-DARTS.

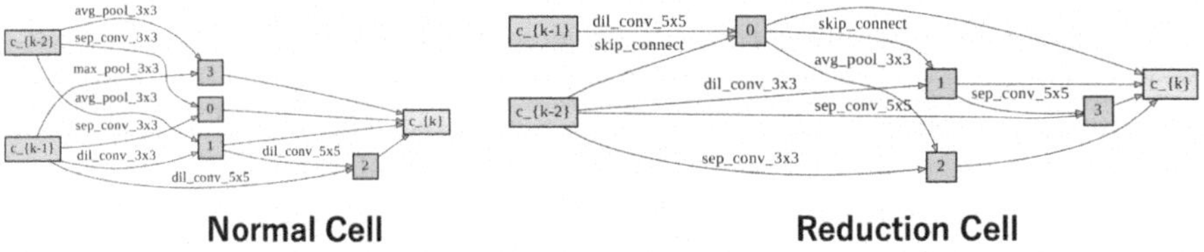

Fig. 4. Cell structure explored by DU-DARTS.

The analysis of the Normal Cell structure by DARTS, as shown in Fig. 2, reveals that a combination of different operations effectively contributes to enhancing the model's expressive power. Particularly, the integration of various types of convolution operations, repeated multiple times, is believed to enhance the capability to capture fine features of Deepfakes. However, the frequent use of convolution operations with large filter sizes in this structure might pose a problem, especially in scenarios dealing with large datasets, due to increased demands on computational resources. On the other hand, in the Reduction Cell, pooling layers and convolution layers with large filters are strategically chosen to achieve effective feature extraction and dimensionality reduction, playing a crucial role in capturing spatial hierarchies. However, there may be a lack of adoption of skip connections to balance overall network computational efficiency.

PC-DARTS is designed to specialize in searching under computational resource constraints, and as a result, the Normal Cell shown in Fig. 3 adopts many operations with smaller filter sizes that are computationally efficient compared to DARTS. This characteristic is particularly desirable for applications in resource-constrained environments or where real-time processing is required. In the Reduction Cell, the choice of operations also reflects a balance between expressive power and computational cost, overall prioritizing a design focused on computational cost and efficiency. These observations suggest that PC-DARTS proposes an efficient and effective model structure suitable for deployment in practical environments.

The analysis of the Normal Cell structure by DU-DARTS, as shown in Fig. 4, reveals a unique operation configuration that demonstrates high adaptability to specific data characteristics and distributions. This allows for effective capture of subtle texture and shape variations in Deepfake detection. In the Reduction Cell, convolution layers are predominantly used as the main operation, efficiently extracting features unique to Deepfakes and contributing to the overall accuracy of the model. These observations suggest that DU-DARTS aims to provide a more suitable model structure for the unique challenges of Deepfake detection, striving for high performance.

5 Discussion

5.1 Limitations

Firstly, regarding the dataset, while the Celeb-DF used in this study is a commonly used dataset, to conduct a broader and more detailed search for the best model structure for Deepfake detection, it would be desirable to use multiple different datasets. However, in that case, the computational cost and time could increase significantly, so only a part of Celeb-DF was used in this study. Furthermore, if all data were used, the computational cost and time would increase significantly, so only a part of the dataset was used in this study. Since the training of existing model structures was conducted with the same amount of data, it is considered that there is no problem in comparing with this study, but ideally, it would be desirable to be able to search using all data.

Furthermore, in this study, Deepfake videos from the Celeb-DF dataset were converted into images, and then the face parts were extracted from those images using MTCNN. If the accuracy of MTCNN was below 90%, the image was not recognized as a face and was not subjected to Deepfake detection. As a result, a limitation arises that the detection performance of the Deepfake detection model depends greatly on the face extraction accuracy of MTCNN. Especially, if MTCNN fails to extract faces properly, the detection accuracy as a Deepfake detection model may decrease. Evaluating the impact of the face region identification algorithm on the entire system is an important issue for future research. However, it is considered that the impact on this study is limited because, among those not recognized by MTCNN as faces, many were covered faces or non-human faces such as characters.

Moreover, defining the search space, selecting appropriate evaluation methods, hardware constraints, and others are conditions that should be considered. In addition, this study does not perform interpretation or analysis of the searched architectures. These can be considered as important issues that should be deeply explored in the search for the optimal network architecture for Deepfake detection.

5.2 Future Research

This study has revealed several significant obstacles to effective deepfake detection, underscoring crucial avenues for future research. To address these challenges and advance the field, two key areas of focus have emerged as the subject of research in the near future. The first significant challenge is the incorporation of a variety of data sets in the field of deepfake detection research. It is imperative to utilize datasets beyond Celeb-DF or incorporate data generated under varied conditions to validate the model's generalizability and robustness. This approach has the potential to result in notable enhancements in the accuracy and reliability of detection. However, it also presents challenges, including increased computational costs and extended time requirements. To address these issues, future research should investigate the use of advanced parallel computing techniques, develop more efficient learning methods, and create standardized benchmarks incorporating multiple datasets.

A second crucial area for future research is a comprehensive reassessment of the search space definition and the selection of evaluation methods. The methodology employed in this study may not represent the optimal approach for all scenarios, despite its effectiveness. Future research should concentrate on enhancing the diversity of architectural searches by integrating diverse activation functions, loss functions tailored for deepfake detection, and innovative layer types. Moreover, researchers should investigate the potential of dynamic or adaptive search spaces, which could evolve in response to the characteristics of emerging Deepfake techniques. The development of more sophisticated evaluation metrics and the implementation of multi-objective optimization techniques will also be of great importance in achieving a balance between accuracy, efficiency, and robustness in model selection.

It is expected that significant advancements in the field of Deepfake detection will result from the resolution of the aforementioned challenges through focused research efforts. These efforts could result in enhanced accuracy and reliability of detection systems across a diverse range of Deepfake types, the development of more adaptable models capable of rapidly responding to novel Deepfake generation techniques, and a more nuanced understanding of the fundamental features most effective for Deepfake detection.

6 Conclusion

This study explored automated neural architecture search (NAS) methods, specifically DARTS, PC-DARTS, and DU-DARTS, for optimizing Deepfake detection models. Using the Celeb-DF dataset, these NAS methods were evaluated through repeated training, revealing that PC-DARTS achieved competitive results with a test accuracy of 85.21% and an AUC of 0.8750. This performance rivals established models like XceptionNet, EfficientNet, and MobileNet, highlighting the potential of NAS in developing robust Deepfake detection models.

Our results indicate that NAS can identify architectures that perform comparably to manually designed models, providing a strong basis for future improvements in Deepfake detection. Future work will focus on enhancing computational efficiency while maintaining accuracy, an essential aspect for real-world applications. Additionally, as Deepfake techniques continue to advance, ensuring model robustness across varied datasets will be crucial for developing scalable and adaptable detection solutions.

Acknowledgments. This work was supported by computational resources provided by the RAIDEN supercomputer at the RIKEN Center for Advanced Intelligence Project (AIP).

References

1. Google AI blog: contributing data to deepfake detection research (2019). https://blog.research.google/2019/09/contributing-data-to-deepfake-detection.html. Accessed 20 Jan 2024
2. Allyn, B.: Deepfake video of zelenskyy could be 'tip of the iceberg' in info war, experts warn (2022). https://www.npr.org/2022/03/16/1087062648/deepfake-video-zelenskyy-experts-war-manipulation-ukraine-russia. Accessed 07 Mar 2024
3. Dang, H., Liu, F., Stehouwer, J., Liu, X., Jain, A.K.: On the detection of digital face manipulation. In: Proceedings of the IEEE/CVF Conference on Computer Vision and Pattern Recognition (CVPR), pp. 5781–5790 (2020)
4. Dolhansky, B., et al.: The deepfake detection challenge (DFDC) dataset (2020)
5. Dolhansky, B., Howes, R., Pflaum, B., Baram, N., Ferrer, C.C.: The deepfake detection challenge (DFDC) preview dataset. In: CVPR 2019 (2019)
6. FUJITSU: The AI research computer system "raiden" introduced at riken was significantly expanded to become the largest in Japan (2018). https://pr.fujitsu.com/jp/news/2018/04/20.html. Accessed 20 Jan 2024
7. ipazc: ipazc/mtcnn: Mtcnn face detection implementation for tensorflow, as a pip package. https://github.com/ipazc/mtcnn. Accessed 20 Jan 2024

8. Jiang, L., Li, R., Wu, W., Qian, C., Loy, C.C.: Deeperforensics-1.0: a large-scale dataset for real-world face forgery detection (2020)
9. Korshunov, P., Marcel, S.: Deepfakes: a new threat to face recognition? Assessment and detection. IDIAP-RR-18-2018 (2018)
10. Li, Y., Chang, M.C., Lyu, S.: In ictu oculi: exposing AI generated fake face videos by detecting eye blinking. In: WIFS 2018 (2018)
11. Li, Y., Yang, X., Sun, P., Qi, H., Lyu, S.: Celeb-DF: a large-scale challenging dataset for deepfake forensics. In: CVPR 2020 (2020)
12. Liu, H., Simonyan, K., Yang, Y.: Darts: differentiable architecture search. In: ICLR 2019 (2019)
13. Nguyen, H.H., Yamagishi, J., Echizen, I.: Use of a capsule network to detect fake images and videos. In: ICASSP 2019 (2019)
14. Rössler, A., Cozzolino, D., Verdoliva, L., Riess, C., Thies, J., Nießner, M.: Faceforensics++: learning to detect manipulated facial images. In: ICCV 2019 (2019)
15. Lu, S., et al.: DU-DARTS: decreasing the uncertainty of differentiable architecture search. In: BMVC 2021 (2021). Accessed 20 Jan 2024
16. Thing, V.L.L.: Deepfake detection with deep learning: convolutional neural networks versus transformers. In: IEEE Cyber Security and Resilience Conference 2023 (2023)
17. Toshikawa, Y.: Automated exploration of optimal neural network structures for deepfake detection. https://github.com/deepfake-detection-nas/deepfake-detection-nas/blob/main/pc-darts/train_search_celeb.py. Accessed 10 Nov 2024
18. Xu, Y., et al.: PC-darts: partial channel connections for memory-efficient architecture search. In: ICLR 2020 (2020)
19. Zhao, T., Xu, X., Xu, M., Ding, H., Xiong, Y., Xia, W.: Learning self-consistency for deepfake detection. In: ICCV 2021 (2021)

An Empirical Study of Black-Box Based Membership Inference Attacks on a Real-World Dataset

Yujeong Kwon, Simon S. Woo, and Hyungjoon Koo(✉)

Sungkyunkwan University, Suwon, South Korea
{shr2008,swoo,kevin.koo}@g.skku.edu

Abstract. The recent advancements in artificial intelligence drive the widespread adoption of Machine-Learning-as-a-Service platforms, which offers valuable services. However, these pervasive utilities in the cloud environment unavoidably encounter security and privacy issues. In particular, a membership inference attack (MIA) poses a threat by recognizing the presence of a data sample in a training set for the victim model. Although prior MIA approaches underline privacy risks repeatedly by demonstrating experimental results with standard benchmark datasets such as MNIST and CIFAR. However, the effectiveness of such techniques on a real-world dataset remains questionable. We are the first to perform an in-depth empirical study on black-box based MIAs that hold realistic assumptions, including six metric-based and three classifier-based MIAs with the high-dimensional image dataset that consists of identification (ID) cards and driving licenses. Additionally, we introduce the Siamese-based MIA that shows similar or better performance than the state-of-the-art approaches and suggest training a shadow model with autoencoder-based reconstructed images. Our major findings show that the performance of MIA techniques against too many features may be degraded; the MIA configuration or a sample's properties can impact the accuracy of membership inference on members and non-members.

Keywords: Membership Inference Attack · Machine Learning

1 Introduction

Today, the advancements in artificial intelligence technologies lead to the wide adoption of Machine Learning as a Service (MLaaS) across various sectors and services. (*e.g.*, ChatGPT [25], Claude [2], DALL-E [26]). While MLaaS stores a model in the cloud [1,22] and processes cloud and processes the vast amounts of data remotely every day, the pervasive utilities inevitably expose a severe threat to security and privacy such as information leaks. One such concern is a membership inference attack [33] (hereinafter dubbed MIA) where an adversary attempts to determine the presence of a data sample in a training dataset while building a model. A successful inference can accidentally reveal sensitive information such

K. Adi et al. (Eds.): FPS 2024, LNCS 15533, pp. 121–137, 2025.
https://doi.org/10.1007/978-3-031-87496-3_9

as a patient's medical record. Meanwhile, from a non-adversarial perspective, an MIA technique can be utilized to evaluate the effectiveness of machine unlearning [4] that aims to forget a particular instance or a class (*e.g.*, data deletion request to comply with regulations such as General Data Protection Regulation (GDPR) [21] and California Consumer Privacy Act (CCPA) [35].

Recent advances in MIA introduce varying techniques depending on the attacker's knowledge; black-box based [5,7,8,11,18,19,23,30,31,34,36,38,40] and white-box based [17,24] MIAs. The former setting requires a strong assumption that the adversary is aware of a victim model's architecture, parameters, and dataset, while the latter assumes that part of that information has been known. However, prior MIA approaches [5,8,11,18,19,24,30,31,34,36,38,40] evaluate their effectiveness with a standard (well-known) and (relatively simple) benchmark datasets such as MNIST [9], CIFAR-10 [15], and CIFAR-100 [15]. Besides, each MIA technique has different assumptions, rendering the potential applicability on a (high dimensional and complex) real-world dataset questionable.

In this work, we provide an in-depth empirical study of black-box based MIAs including six metric-based black-box MIAs and three classifier-based black-box MIAs; the effectiveness of different MIA approaches under the same setting with both traditional benchmark (*e.g.*, CIFAR-10 [15]) and real-world datasets (KID34K [27]: identification cards and driving licenses). We introduce a Siamese-based MIA that adopts a prediction vector generated by a shadow model alone, where the model learns the distances from sample pairs (*i.e.,* decreasing the distance between same-label-pair samples and increasing the distance between different-label-pair samples). Notably, our Siamese-based MIA achieved high performance (*i.e.,* 70% AUC) with CIFAR-10 among other state-of-the-art techniques, however, it did not work with KID34K. Additionally, we conduct thorough analyses in varying settings: training a shadow model with reconstructed images with an Autoencoder [3] so that the model can learn essential features, and splitting KID34K in a way that better discloses membership.

In summary, our major findings indicate that ① the performance of existing MIA approaches may not be persistent in a real-world dataset that contains too many features, ② the accuracy of membership inference on members and non-members can vary depending on the configuration, and ③ a sample's properties can significantly impact on the success of an MIA.

The following summarizes our contributions:

- To the best of our knowledge, we first apply an MIA to a (high dimensional) real-world dataset, demonstrating the effectiveness of MIA.
- We conduct varying experiments on different black-box MIA techniques under the same setting, including six metric-based and three classifier-based MIAs.
- We propose a Siamese-based MIA that learns the distance difference between member and non-member samples, being capable of similar membership inference performance even with limited information.
- We empirically show that reconstructed images by an autoencoder can potentially assist in training a shadow model for better MIA performance.
- We perform an in-depth analysis with different configurations: splitting a training dataset, confusion matrices, and visualizations.

2 Related Work

We survey varying MIAs, classifying them primarily into white-box based [16,17, 24] and black-box based MIAs. The latter can be fallen into two types depending on the model construction: a metric-based attack [5,7,11,23,31,34,36,38] (generating a shadow model) and a classifier-based [8,18,19,30,40] attack (generating both shadow and classification models). Besides, we explore defense strategies [6,13,14,24,29] against MIAs.

White-Box Based MIAs: A white-box MIA assumes that the attacker has complete knowledge of the internal parameters of a victim model and significant information about the training dataset. As one may expect, such supplementary information enhances overall attack performance [24] by utilizing the intermediate computations of the victim model as inputs to build an MIA attack model. However, assuming that the adversary is aware of a significant portion of the private training dataset is unrealistic. Later, Liu et al. relaxed such an assumption on a training dataset [17]. Note that our work focuses on black box-based MIAs with a realistic setting.

Black-Box Based MIAs: A black-box MIA assumes that the attacker has query access to a victim model with the knowledge of its structure and the distribution of its training dataset. A classifier-based MIA [8,18,19,30,40] infers membership during attack model training from the outputs of a shadow model. TrajectoryMIA [18] leverages differences in the loss trajectory of a victim model during the training and testing stages. Note that knowledge distillation has been employed by training a shadow model because a black-box setting does not allow the attacker to directly obtain the victim model's loss trajectory. Meanwhile, a metric-based MIA [5,7,11,23,31,34,36,38] uses specific metrics derived from the model's outputs to determine membership. The intuition behind this technique is that the victim model has been overfitted. In ensemble models like EnsembleMIA [31], the performance improves as the number of models used increases, but privacy decreases. The fused method of ensemble models enables membership inference by averaging prediction confidence values, amplifying differences between training, and testing sample confidences to facilitate membership inference. MIB [11] infers membership by adding triggers to victim samples and verifying if the model has been backdoored.

Defenses Against MIAs: In general, an overfitted model can be victimized by MIAs. In response, RELAXLOSS [6] and HEMP [24] employ regularization to mitigate the overfitting problem. For example, RELAXLOSS [6] leverages a training loss of a victim model with a threshold to prevent model overfitting: adopting a gradient descent during training when the loss exceeds the threshold or either a gradient ascent or posterior probability flattening otherwise. Similary, HAMP [24] attempts to mitigate overfitting with label smoothing. Meanwhile,

DMIG [13] utilizes synthetic data (*e.g.*, reconstructed images) for training a model to provide incomplete prediction vectors. MemGuard [14] appends a noise to prediction vectors to degrade the attack model's performance. Another direction leverages differential privacy to defend against MIAs, such as DPSGD [29].

3 Background

3.1 Membership Inference Attacks

Problem Definition: An MIA aims to accurately infer whether a specific sample has been part of the training dataset for a machine learning model. Formally, we define an MIA as in Eq. 1: the attack model $g(\theta_\alpha, f)$ determines the membership in a trained machine learning model of $f(\theta_v, x)$ when a target sample x is given. Note that 1 represents that x is a member or 0 otherwise.

$$g(\theta_\alpha, f(\theta_v, x)) \rightarrow \{0, 1\} \tag{1}$$

Impact: On one hand, MIAs can pose a severe threat in terms of privacy when sensitive information (*e.g.*, medical records) has been trained. On the other hand, MIAs can be utilized in the field of machine unlearning to verify its effectiveness (*e.g.*, the unlearning request has been applied).

Types and Assumptions: Based on the knowledge of an attacker, MIAs can be predominately categorized into white-box and black-box attacks. The former setting [16,24] requires a strong assumption that an adversary owns the knowledge of a victim model's architecture, its model algorithm and parameters, and even a dataset. Some approaches [17,24] assume that an attacker has complete access to the victim model, being able to observe intermediate training information such as model parameters or gradients for further inference. Meanwhile, the latter setting relaxes the assumption that the adversary has limited knowledge (*e.g.*, model architecture [8,18,19,30,31], dataset distribution [5,23,34,38], or target samples [11]) about the victim model (*i.e.*, distinguishing a membership with queries and corresponding outputs).

3.2 Black-Box MIAs

This work merely focuses on black-box MIAs that hold more realistic configurations than white-box ones, which can be classified mainly into metric-based and classifier-based MIAs (Hu et al. [12]).

Metric-Based MIAs: Metric-based MIAs [5,7,11,23,31,34,36,38] involve querying a model to obtain a prediction vector. Simply put, prediction vectors from querying a model can be computed using a specific metric, followed by comparing those predictions with a pre-defined threshold. Note that metric-based MIAs may use shadow models (for accuracy) that approximate a target victim model, or may not use them (for efficiency). Hu et al. [12] introduce the following four types (each technique exploits different aspects of the model's output): ① a correctness-based attack infers membership if the prediction vector accurately predicts the label; ② a loss-based attack infers membership if the loss of the prediction vector is smaller than the training loss, using a loss metric; ③ a confidence-based attack infers membership when the maximum prediction confidence exceeds a specified threshold; and ④ an entropy-based attack infers membership if a prediction vector's entropy is smaller than a specified threshold.

Classifier-Based MIAs: A classifier-based MIA [8,18,19,30,40] involves shadow model(s)(M^S) to mimic a victim model (M^V), leveraging it to create an attack dataset (D^A) labeled with either a member or a non-member. Then, an attack model (M^A) is trained to infer the membership of a given sample.

4 Empirical Study on Black-Box Based MIAs

4.1 On the Effectiveness of Black-Box Based MIAs

This work reproduces experiments with six metric-based MIAs and three classifier-based MIAs. Section 6.2 describes the effectiveness of previous MIAs.

Metric-Based MIAs: First, the threshold-based attack [34] (loss-based) infers membership of a sample by querying the target model (*i.e.*, victim) to obtain prediction vectors and comparing their loss with a predefined threshold. Second, the threshold entropy-based attack [34] (entropy-based) infers membership of a sample by querying the target model to obtain prediction vectors and comparing their entropy loss with a predefined threshold. Third, the likelihood ratio attack (LiRA) [5] (loss-based) infers membership using loss values and logits obtained from querying a shadow model (whose structure is the same as a target model). The subsequent three attacks are dubbed as the descriptions from the implementation of Ye et al. [39]. Fourth, the population metric attack (loss-based) [39] is a model-dependent MIA that applies different attack thresholds for each target model, leveraging the dependency of loss thresholds on each model to enhance performance. Fifth, the shadow metric attack [33,39] (correctness-based) is a label-dependent MIA where the adversary infers membership using predicted labels obtained from querying the model. The adversary uses the most limited knowledge to perform the attack. Lastly, the reference metric attack [39] (loss-based) is a sample-dependent MIA where the adversary applies different attack thresholds for the target data samples. This attack trains multiple reference models using data samples excluding the target and evaluates losses for specific records. Similar to MIAs designed for summary statistics and graphical models, it uses reference models to compute the probability of the null hypothesis.

Classifier-Based MIAs: First, logistic regression-based attack [34] trains a neural network with prediction confidences from a shadow model as features to infer membership. Second, SAMIA [40] utilizes a self-attention mechanism to infer a membership. In a nutshell, applying neural network pruning to both shadow and victim models enhances the model's memorization of training data, potentially improving the performance of membership inference. Third, the confidence-based neural network attack [33] adopts confidence vectors generated by a shadow model to train an attack model for membership inference.

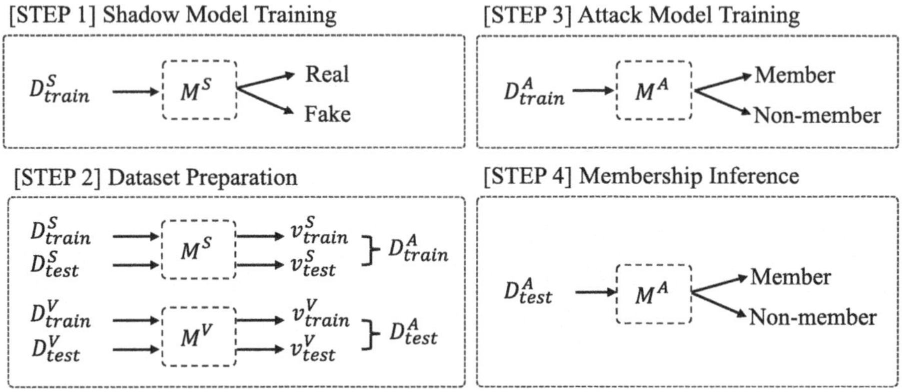

Fig. 1. Overall Siamese-based MIA workflow. An adversary generates a shadow model that mimics a target (victim) model for binary classification (Step 1). Next, the attacker prepares a dataset (Step 2) that is fed to the Siamese architecture, followed by training an attack model (Step 3). Once complete, membership can be deduced (Step 4) with the attack model. D and M represent a dataset and a model with their superscripts that denote a set (*i.e.*, victim, shadow, attack) and their subscripts that denote a usage (*i.e.*, training or testing).

4.2 Our Approach: Siamese-Based MIA

We propose the Siamese network-based MIA (Fig. 2) approach that learns distances between member and non-member samples.

Assumptions: Similar to the general black-box scenario, we assume that an adversary only has a query access to the victim model (M^V) with the knowledge of its architecture. Besides, the adversary owns a shadow dataset (D^S_{train}) that follows the same distribution as the victim model's training dataset (D^V_{train}).

Overall Workflow: Unlike the previous classifier-based MIA approach [40] that uses multiple factors (*e.g.*, confidence vector, prediction vector, one-hot label, confidence sensitivity), we use the confidence vectors generated by the shadow model (M^S) alone for training. This reduces the training time of the attacker model (M^A), saving computing resources. Figure 1 concisely illustrates the overall workflow of our Siamese-based MIA that consists of the following four stages.

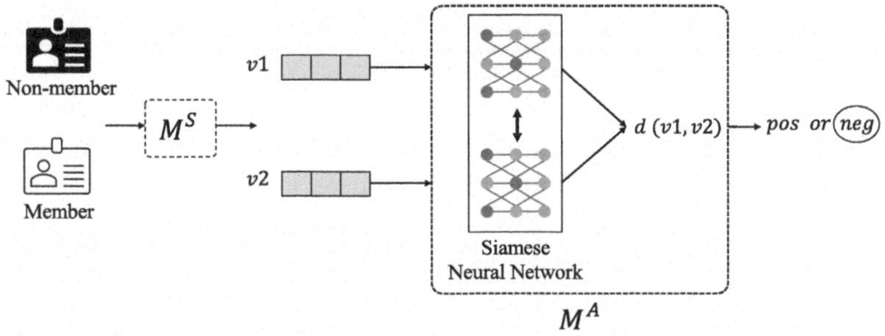

Fig. 2. Overview of our Siamese-based MIA. Taking the two predicted vectors from the member and non-member samples as input, we train an attack model so that a distance can get close for positive sets or distant for negative sets.

(Step 1) Shadow Model Training: With the assumption that the distribution of a shadow dataset follows that of a victim, we divide the entire dataset into shadow and victim datasets, each consisting of 50%. Then, we split the shadow dataset into training and test sets, representing members and non-members so that the attacker can train M^S.

(Step 2) Dataset Preparation: Obtaining the predicted vectors from M^S trained on D^S_{train}, we label those vectors for the training dataset as members and those for the test dataset as non-members. We prepare a positive set (*e.g.*, member to member or non-member to non-member pairs) and a negative set (*e.g.*, member to non-member pairs) for training M^A with the Siamese network.

(Step 3) Attack Model Training: With D^A from M^S, the adversary trains M^A. The Siamese network-based attack model learns distances between samples, aiming to decrease the distance between same-label-pair samples while increasing it between different-label-pair samples. The distance (d) between the two inputs can be computed as $d = \|p_\theta(v_1), p_\theta(v_2))\|_2$ between the two vectors where v_1 and v_2 are the output vectors of the Siamese neural network. Equation 2 represents the contrastive loss function of Siamese that minimizes the distance where y represents the label (0 or 1) for the input pairs.

$$L(v_1, v_2, y) = y\|v_1 - v_2\|^2 + (1 - y) \cdot \max(0, m^2 - \|v_1 - v_2\|^2) \tag{2}$$

Table 1. We split KID34K [27] into training and testing sets, each divided in half according to a victim and shadow set; 25% for D^S_{train}, D^V_{train}, D^S_{test}, and D^V_{test}. Besides, we define two datasets: D_{rd} that randomly splits each dataset and D_{sp} that splits by the individual user (*i.e.*, realistic assumption to check the membership of a single person). G, P, and S represent a set of samples whose labels are `Genuine`, `Print`, and `Screen`. It is noted that we define a desirable set by combining sample groups: *e.g.*, $G|P$ represents a union of `Genuine` and `Print` samples.

			Train Set (Member: 50%)						Test Set (Non-Member: 50%)					
			Victim (D^V_{train})			Shadow (D^S_{train})			Victim (D^V_{test})			Shadow (D^S_{test})		
Dataset	**Class**	**Label**	$G\|P$	$G\|S$	All	$G\|P$	$G\|S$	All	$G\|P$	$G\|S$	All	$G\|P$	$G\|S$	All
D_{rd}	`Real`	`Genuine`	3,073	3,073	3,073	3,073	3,073	3,073	3,073	3,073	3,073	3,073	3,073	3,073
	`Fake`	`Print`	1,813	0	1,813	1,801	0	1,801	1,813	1,813	1,813	1,801	1,801	1,801
		`Screen`	0	3,478	3,478	0	3,488	3,488	3,478	3,478	3,478	3,478	3,478	3,478
	Total		4,886	6,551	8,364	4,874	6,561	8,362	8,364	8,364	8,364	8,352	8,352	8,352
D_{sp}	`Real`	`Genuine`	3,335	3,335	3,335	3,335	3,335	3,335	3,335	3,335	3,335	3,335	3,335	3,335
	`Fake`	`Print`	1,707	0	1,707	1,706	0	1,706	1,707	1,707	1,707	1,706	1,706	1,706
		`Screen`	0	2,997	2,997	0	2,996	2,996	2,997	2,997	2,997	2,996	2,996	2,996
	Total		5,042	6,332	8,039	5,041	6,331	8,037	8,039	8,039	8,039	8,037	8,037	8,037

Note that m is a hyperparameter that defines the lower bound distance between samples of different classes.

(Step 4) Membership Inference: Now, the adversary can infer membership with M^A via M^V. Suppose that the adversary has non-member and unknown samples for membership inference. Then, those samples are fed into the victim model, producing predicted vectors. Finally, the attack model takes the vectors, producing the output of 1 for a member sample, or 0 otherwise.

4.3 Image Reconstruction with an Autoencoder

To the best of our knowledge, we first conduct varying MIAs against one of the real-world datasets, KID34K [27] (Sect. 6.1), rather than a common dataset like CIFAR-10 [15] or MNIST [9]. This is challenging because KID34K contains high-resolution images (*i.e.*, 512×800) with two-class classification (*i.e.*, `Real` or `Fake`). Our experimental results (Sect. 6.2) demonstrate that the performance of most existing approaches (including our Siamese-based MIA) has been considerably degraded.

We hypothesize that a shadow model learns excessive features (due to high dimensions). To extract significant features for decision-making, we adopt an autoencoder [3] that allows for compressing an input image to a lower dimension (*i.e.*, latent vector). Then, we reconstruct images that retain essential features for training a shadow model.

5 Implementation

Victim and Shadow Models: We adopt ResNet20 [10] and ResNet50 [10] as the victim and shadow models provided by the PyTorch [28]'s `timm` library (PyTorch Image Models) [37]. We set the Adam optimizer with $\beta_1 = 0.9$, $\beta_2 = 0.99$, and $\epsilon = 10^{-3}$, and the training epochs to 100 for both models. Each model's training took around 4 h with approximately 8,000 samples. Another hyperparameter is the number of shadow models for each MIA: two for the logistic regression attack [34] and LiRA [5], five for SAMIA [40] and the confidence-based neural network attack [33], and only one for our Siamese-based MIA. It is noteworthy to mention that increasing the number of shadow models does not guarantee higher MIA performance at all times.

Siamese-Based MIA: We developed the Siamese-based MIA framework based on the original Siamese structure with PyTorch [28]. Training the model with around 8,000 samples took about 3 h. We set up the Adam optimizer with $\epsilon = 10^{-3}$ and the model training epochs to 100.

Image Reconstruction with an Autoencoder: We implemented the Autoencoder [3] architecture with PyTorch [28] for creating reconstructed images. The autoencoder training took approximately 12 h with around 8,000 samples from our shadow dataset. We set up the Adam optimizer with $\epsilon = 10^{-6}$ and the training epochs to 200.

6 Evaluation

6.1 Experimental Setup

Our experiments were conducted on a server equipped with an Intel(R) Xeon(R) Gold 5218 CPU @ 2.30GHz, 500GB RAM, and three Matrox Electronics Systems MGA G200e [Pilot] with 480GB of memory.

Datasets: For evaluating the effectiveness of varying black-box based MIAs, we use both a common (CIFAR-10 [15]) and a real-world (KID34K [27]) dataset. CIFAR-10 [15] is an image dataset that consists of different objects with a $3 \times 32 \times 32$ resolution, which contains 10 classes, with 6,000 samples per class, a total of 60,000 samples. KID34K [27] is an image dataset comprising identification cards and driving licenses with a $3 \times 512 \times 800$ resolution. It contains two classes: `Real` and `Fake`. The `Real` class contains samples with `genuine` labels, while the `Fake` class includes samples labeled as `print` (*i.e.,* paper-printed image) or `screen` (*i.e.,* screen-captured image). There are 10,488, 13,728, and 10,444 samples for `genuine`, `screen`, and `print`, respectively. Table 1 shows how we split KID34K into training and test datasets with each dividing in half to a victim and a shadow set.

Evaluation Metrics: We adopt F1 and AUC (Area Under Curve) as evaluation metrics. F1 is the harmonic mean of precision and recall. AUC is computed as the area under the ROC (Receiver Operating Characteristic) curve, which illustrates the change in TPR (True Positive Rate) with respect to FPR (False Positive Rate) variations.

Research Questions: We define the following three research questions (RQs) to answer the effectiveness and applicability of various MIAs.

- RQ1. How effective are black-box based MIAs (including our Siamese-based MIA) on a previous benchmark dataset (*i.e.*, CIFAR-10 [15])(Section 6.2)?
- RQ2. How well do the MIAs perform against a real-world dataset (KID34K [27]) (Sect. 6.3)?
- RQ3. How well the reconstructed images improve MIA performance on a real-world dataset (Sect. 6.4)?

Table 2. Empirical results of varying MIAs against the victim model trained on CIFAR-10. The re-evaluation of metric-based MIAs demonstrates discrepancies (< 0.6) with the original performance. While binary classifier-based approaches show better performance, our Siamese-based MIA ranks the highest AUC (0.7).

Attack Technique	Base Approach	AUC
MIA Evaluation (Threshold attack) [34]	Metric-based (Loss)	0.52
MIA Evaluation (Threshold entropy attack) [34]	Metric-based (Entropy)	0.51
LiRA [5]	Metric-based (Loss)	0.58
Privacy Meter (Population metric attack) [39]	Metric-based (Loss)	0.50
Privacy Meter (Shadow metric attack) [33,39]	Metric-based (Correctness)	0.50
Privacy Meter (Reference metric attack) [39]	Metric-based (Loss)	0.50
MIA Evaluation (Logistic regression attack) [34]	Classifier-based	0.51
SAMIA [40]	Classifier-based	0.67
Confidence-based neural network attack [33]	Classifier-based	0.64
Siamese-based MIA (Ours)	Classifier-based	0.70

6.2 Comparison of Different Black-Box MIA Approaches (RQ1)

Using CIFAR-10, we conduct experiments with nine black-box MIA techniques as a baseline, comparing them with our Siamese-based MIA. Table 2 summarizes comparison results with the CIFAR-10 dataset. Our findings show that ① metric-based MIAs tend to have discrepancies with the original performance (< 0.6), ② binary-classifier-based MIAs better perform than metric-based ones, and ③ our Siamese-based MIA achieves the highest AUC (0.7) with efficiency.

Table 3. We conduct a variety of MIA experiments on a real-world dataset. The baselines are SAMIA and the confidence-based neural network, which demonstrates high performance. We prepare a shadow dataset with different configurations to demonstrate that overall MIA performance can be affected by i) a data sample (by splitting it into D_{rd} and D_{sp}), ii) reconstructed images, and iii) MIA approach. In our experiment, combining SAMIA with reconstructed images of D_{sp} using an autoencoder shows the best performance. A, P, and R represent accuracy, precision, and recall while A_m and A_n denote the accuracy of a member and a non-member. (*) means our Siamese-based MIA. A bold number represents better performance between original and reconstructed corpus from D_{sp}.

Corpus	Selection	D_{train}	Method	A_m	A_n	A	P	R	F1	AUC
Original	D_{rd}	$G\|P$	SAMIA	0.17	0.83	0.50	0.50	0.50	0.45	0.50
	D_{rd}	$G\|S$	SAMIA	0.30	0.70	0.50	0.50	0.50	0.48	0.50
	D_{rd}	*All*	SAMIA	0.21	0.79	0.50	0.50	0.50	0.45	0.50
	D_{sp}	$G\|P$	SAMIA	0.99	0.25	0.62	0.77	0.62	0.56	0.62
	D_{sp}	$G\|S$	SAMIA	0.61	0.45	0.53	0.55	0.53	0.53	0.53
	D_{sp}	*All*	SAMIA	0.73	0.35	**0.54**	0.56	0.54	0.52	**0.54**
	D_{rd}	$G\|P$	Confidence-based	0.18	0.83	0.50	0.51	0.50	0.45	0.50
	D_{rd}	$G\|S$	Confidence-based	0.75	0.25	0.50	0.50	0.50	0.47	0.50
	D_{rd}	*All*	Confidence-based	0.20	0.81	0.50	0.50	0.50	0.45	0.50
	D_{sp}	$G\|P$	Confidence-based	0.35	0.99	**0.67**	0.79	0.67	**0.63**	**0.67**
	D_{sp}	$G\|S$	Confidence-based	0.53	0.56	0.54	0.56	0.54	0.54	0.54
	D_{sp}	*All*	Confidence-based	0.70	0.38	**0.54**	0.56	0.54	0.53	**0.54**
	D_{rd}	$G\|P$	Siamese-based*	0.14	0.85	0.50	0.50	0.50	0.42	0.50
	D_{rd}	$G\|S$	Siamese-based*	0.15	0.85	0.50	0.50	0.50	0.43	0.50
	D_{rd}	*All*	Siamese-based*	1.00	0.00	0.50	0.25	0.50	0.33	0.50
	D_{sp}	$G\|P$	Siamese-based*	0.19	0.83	0.51	0.53	0.51	0.45	0.51
	D_{sp}	$G\|S$	Siamese-based*	0.13	0.82	0.48	0.47	0.48	0.41	0.47
	D_{sp}	*All*	Siamese-based*	0.17	0.82	**0.50**	0.51	0.50	0.44	**0.50**
Reconstructed	D_{sp}	$G\|P$	SAMIA	0.40	0.93	**0.66**	0.74	0.66	**0.64**	**0.66**
	D_{sp}	$G\|S$	SAMIA	0.67	0.41	**0.54**	0.56	0.54	0.53	**0.54**
	D_{sp}	*All*	SAMIA	0.56	0.50	0.53	0.54	0.53	**0.53**	0.53
	D_{sp}	$G\|P$	Confidence-based	0.36	0.95	0.66	0.75	0.66	0.62	0.66
	D_{sp}	$G\|S$	Confidence-based	0.60	0.49	0.54	0.56	0.54	0.54	0.54
	D_{sp}	*All*	Confidence-based	0.63	0.44	0.53	0.55	0.53	0.53	0.53
	D_{sp}	$G\|P$	Siamese-based*	0.54	0.50	**0.52**	0.54	0.52	**0.51**	**0.52**
	D_{sp}	$G\|S$	Siamese-based*	0.16	0.80	0.48	0.48	0.48	**0.42**	**0.48**
	D_{sp}	*All*	Siamese-based*	0.22	0.75	0.49	0.50	0.49	**0.45**	0.49

6.3 Effectiveness of Black-Box MIAs on a Real-World Dataset (RQ2)

We assess varying black-box MIAs against KID34K [27], one of the real-world datasets as a victim model. Notably, we choose the two MIA techniques (*i.e.*, SAMIA [40] and confidence-based neural network [33]) that exhibit relatively higher performance. Table 3 presents a handful of interesting findings. First, the results indicate that an MIA approach against a common dataset may not be persistent in a real-world dataset. For example, the AUCs of our Siamese-based approach demonstrate slightly behind SAMIA and the confidence-based technique. Second, membership inference accuracy on a member (A_m) and a non-member (A_n) sample can largely vary depending on a configuration and a dataset. Even with the same approach (*e.g.*, SAMIA), the accuracy on deducing a non-member (A_n) is higher than a member (A_m) in a random selection setting, however, the other way around in a user split setting. Third, it is possible that the success of an MIA may vary depending on the sample's property (*e.g.*, randomly selected sample VS. member-oriented sample) as well as an MIA technique.

6.4 Effectiveness of Autoencoder-Reconstructed Images (RQ3)

Table 3 indicates that attack models using reconstructed images improves (or is on par with) attack success rates (both F1 score and AUC) where overall SAMIA with the autoencoder-generated samples ranks the highest (AUC of 0.66). For instance, our proposed Siamese-based MIA showed a 5.8% increase in F1 in the $G|P$ setting with D_{sp}. For SAMIA [40], an 8.1% increase in F1 was achieved in the same configuration, observing overall increases in most other settings. However, in the case of confidence-based neural network attack [33], AUC increase was limited (around 0.3 %) in the $G|P$ configuration with D_{sp}. Additionally, our experiment on the effectiveness of a different size of latent vectors (*e.g.*, 128 vs. 512) shows limited impact on the performance of a shadow model. Note that we use $d = 128$. Table 4 summarizes the experimental results of three shadow models: SAMIA, confidence-based, and Siamese-based MIAs.

Table 4. Experimental results of shadow models' performance using the whole D_{train} (*i.e.*, *All*) according to a dimension (d) in a latent space. We adopt $d = 128$ because of the little gap in performance.

Method	d	A	P	R	F1	AUC
SAMIA	128	0.53	0.54	0.53	0.53	0.53
	512	0.53	0.54	0.53	0.53	0.53
Confidence-based	128	0.53	0.55	0.53	0.53	0.53
	512	0.53	0.55	0.53	0.53	0.53
Siamese-based*	128	0.49	0.50	0.49	0.45	0.49
	512	0.50	0.51	0.50	0.48	0.50

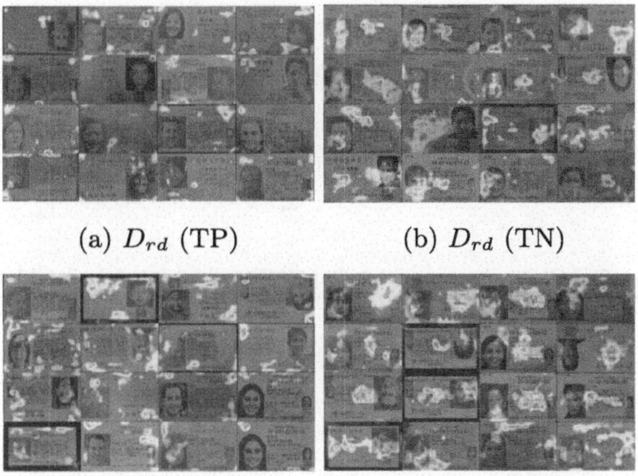

(a) D_{rd} (TP) (b) D_{rd} (TN)

(c) D_{sp} (TP) (d) D_{sp} (TN)

Fig. 3. Grad-CAM [32] results of a shadow model that is trained on the randomly picking dataset (D_{rd}) and the individually splitting dataset (D_{sp}). The model sees more features in D_{sp} for true positive samples (*e.g.*, `Real` → `Real`) than those in D_{rd}. Meanwhile, the model recognizes relatively plentiful features in both D_{rd} and D_{sp} for true negative samples (*e.g.*, `Fake` → `Fake`). TP and TN denote a true positive and negative.

6.5 In-depth Analysis of Black-Box MIAs on a Real-World Dataset

This section delves into in-depth analysis of the results of our MIA experiments in Table 3. According to the description of the KID34K [27] dataset, it contains the images of identification cards from 37 users and driver licenses from 45 users, with a total of 46 users. Because the random selection of a dataset (D_{rd}) lowers the performance of a shadow model, we split it based on an individual sample (D_{sp}). We visualize the results of SAMIA with D_{sp} using t-SNE in Fig. 4. In the $G|P$ cases (*e.g.*, datasets picking `genuine` and `print` labels) of both original and reconstructed images, the model recognizes clear boundaries for membership decisions. Additionally, Fig. 3 illustrates Grad-CAM [32], showing that the shadow model with D_{sp} identifies more features than that with D_{rd} for true positive samples (Fig. 3 (a) and Fig. 3 (c)).

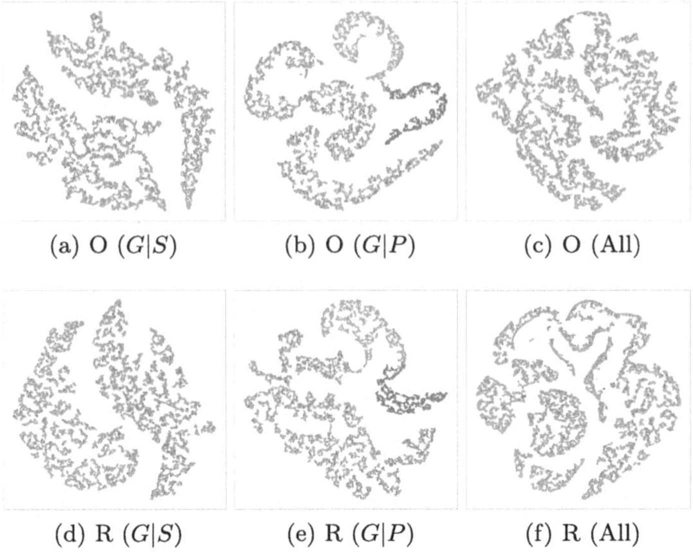

Fig. 4. t-SNE [20] results of SAMIA with D_{sp}. This visualization illustrates the reason why the shadow model trained with D_{train} that consists of $G|P$ (*e.g.*, relatively clear boundaries for decision-making) achieves the highest F1 and AUC (Table 3). O and R denote the original and reconstructed images, respectively.

7 Discussion and Limitations

Threats to Validity: We empirically demonstrate that MIA results may vary depending on the configuration, the distribution of a dataset, the number of classes, and the characteristics of a sample as well as an approach. We believe that a single counterexample can be allusive to convey that MIAs against arbitrary datasets can be ineffective. However, the results with other real-world datasets may be possibly inconsistent with ours: *i.e.,* the dataset in our experiment is not fully representative with different features (financial or health data). As a final note, this work focuses solely on black-box MIAs under relaxed assumptions; hence the results with white-box MIAs may be different.

Usage of Reconstructed Images for MIAs: Although using autoencoder-generated images for training a shadow model enhances the success rate of MIAs, we observe the degradation of the shadow model's performance (around 16%). While an adversary can adopt this strategy for reducing dimensions, optimizing the size of a latent vector that encompasses essential features is an open problem.

Machine Learning Bill of Materials (ML-BOM) and MIAs: As the demand for reliability in machine learning services increases, a comprehensive inventory that documents the whole process of model creation, deployment, and maintenance is needed. This request inspires the Machine Learning Bill of Materials (ML-BOM), ensuring transparency, accountability, traceability, and compliance. We expect that the assumption of white-box based MIAs become feasible upon the broad adoption of ML-BOM in the near future.

Trade-offs between Membership Inference Attacks and Defenses: In general, defending against MIAs often involves trade-offs between model performance (*i.e.,* usability, accuracy) and security (*i.e.,* privacy, robustness). For instance, a model with high-performance could be susceptible and targetable to MIAs; however, security mitigations such as differential privacy, model distillation, or adopting multiparty computation could be prone to reduce performance with additional overheads.

8 Conclusion

Lately, the prevalent utilities of machine learning-based applications have raised concerns about security and privacy issues. An MIA that determines the presence of a sample in a training set can pose a severe threat, when sensitive information such as one's medical record, driver license, passport, or identification card information is inadvertently revealed. In this work, we conduct an empirical study focusing on black-box based MIAs against a real-world dataset, KID34K dataset, which contains driver license and identification card information. Through extensive experimental evaluation, our findings reveal that the performance of existing MIAs could be degraded and impacted by their settings or a sample's properties.

Acknowledgments. We thank the anonymous reviewers for their constructive feedback. This work was partially supported by three grants from Institute of Information & Communications Technology Planning & Evaluation (IITP), funded by the Korean government (MSIT; Ministry of Science and ICT): No. 2022-0-00688; No. RS-2024-00337414; and No. 2022-0-01199. Additional support was provided by the Basic Science Research Program through the National Research Foundation of Korea (NRF), funded by the Ministry of Education of the Government of South Korea (Grant No. NRF-2022R1F1A1074373). Any opinions, findings, and conclusions or recommendations expressed in this material are those of the authors and do not necessarily reflect the views of the sponsor.

References

1. Amazon: Cloud computing services - amazon web services. https://aws.amazon.com/ko/ (2024)
2. Anthropic: Generate code with claude. https://claude.ai (2024)
3. Baldi, P.: Autoencoders, unsupervised learning, and deep architectures. In: ICML Workshop on Unsupervised and Transfer Learning (2012)
4. Bourtoule, L., et al.: Machine unlearning. In: IEEE Symposium on Security and Privacy (2021)

5. Carlini, N., Chien, S., Nasr, M., Song, S., Terzis, A., Tramer, F.: Membership inference attacks from first principles. In: IEEE Symposium on Security and Privacy (2022)
6. Chen, D., Yu, N., Fritz, M.: RelaxLoss: Defending membership inference attacks without losing utility. arXiv preprint arXiv:2207.05801 (2022)
7. Chen, Y., Shen, C., Shen, Y., Wang, C., Zhang, Y.: Amplifying membership exposure via data poisoning. Advances in Neural Information Processing Systems (2022)
8. Choquette-Choo, C.A., Tramer, F., Carlini, N., Papernot, N.: Label-only membership inference attacks. In: International Conference on Machine Learning (2021)
9. Deng, L.: The MNIST database of handwritten digit images for machine learning research. IEEE Sig. Process. Mag. (2012)
10. He, K., Zhang, X., Ren, S., Sun, J.: Deep residual learning for image recognition. In: IEEE Conference on Computer Vision and Pattern Recognition (2016)
11. Hu, H., Salcic, Z., Dobbie, G., Chen, J., Sun, L., Zhang, X.: Membership inference via backdooring. arXiv preprint arXiv:2206.04823 (2022)
12. Hu, H., Salcic, Z., Sun, L., Dobbie, G., Yu, P.S., Zhang, X.: Membership inference attacks on machine learning: a survey. ACM Comput. Surv. (2022)
13. Hu, L., et al.: Defending against membership inference attacks with high utility by GAN. IEEE Trans. Dependable Secure Comput. (2022)
14. Jia, J., Salem, A., Backes, M., Zhang, Y., Gong, N.Z.: MemGuard: defending against black-box membership inference attacks via adversarial examples. In: Proceedings of the 2019 ACM SIGSAC Conference on Computer and Communications Security (2019)
15. Krizhevsky, A.: The CIFAR-10/100 dataset. https://www.cs.toronto.edu/~kriz/cifar.html (2024)
16. Leino, K., Fredrikson, M.: Stolen memories: Leveraging model memorization for calibrated {White-Box} membership inference. In: USENIX Security Symposium (2020)
17. Liu, H., et al.: Trustworthy AI: a computational perspective. ACM Trans. Intell. Syst. Technol. (2022)
18. Liu, Y., Zhao, Z., Backes, M., Zhang, Y.: Membership inference attacks by exploiting loss trajectory. In: ACM SIGSAC Conference on Computer and Communications Security (2022)
19. Liu, Y., et al.: {ML-Doctor}: Holistic risk assessment of inference attacks against machine learning models. In: USENIX Security Symposium (2022)
20. Van der Maaten, L., Hinton, G.: Visualizing data using t-SNE. J. Mach. Learn. Res. (2008)
21. Mantelero, A.: The EU proposal for a general data protection regulation and the roots of the 'right to be forgotten'. Comput. Law Secur. Rev. (2013)
22. Microsoft: Microsoft azure: Cloud computing services. https://azure.microsoft.com/en-us (2024)
23. Murakonda, S.K., Shokri, R.: ML privacy meter: Aiding regulatory compliance by quantifying the privacy risks of machine learning. arXiv 2007.09339 (2020)
24. Nasr, M., Shokri, R., Houmansadr, A.: Comprehensive privacy analysis of deep learning: passive and active white-box inference attacks against centralized and federated learning. In: IEEE Symposium on Security and Privacy, pp. 739–753 (2019)
25. OpenAI: ChatGPT. https://openai.com/index/chatgpt/ (2022)
26. OpenAI: Dall e. https://openai.com/index/dall-e/ (2024)

27. Park, E.J., Back, S.Y., Kim, J., Woo, S.S.: KID34K: a dataset for online identity card fraud detection. In: ACM International Conference on Information and Knowledge Management (2023)
28. Paszke, A., et al.: PyTorch: an imperative style, high-performance deep learning library. In: Advances in Neural Information Processing Systems (2019)
29. Rahimian, S., Orekondy, T., Fritz, M.: Differential privacy defenses and sampling attacks for membership inference. In: ACM Workshop on Artificial Intelligence and Security (2021)
30. Rezaei, S., Liu, X.: On the difficulty of membership inference attacks. In: IEEE/CVF Conference on Computer Vision and Pattern Recognition (2021)
31. Rezaei, S., Shafiq, Z., Liu, X.: Accuracy-privacy trade-off in deep ensemble: a membership inference perspective. In: IEEE Symposium on Security and Privacy (2023)
32. Selvaraju, R.R., Cogswell, M., Das, A., Vedantam, R., Parikh, D., Batra, D.: Grad-CAM: visual explanations from deep networks via gradient-based localization. In: IEEE International Conference on Computer Vision (2017)
33. Shokri, R., Stronati, M., Song, C., Shmatikov, V.: Membership inference attacks against machine learning models. In: IEEE Symposium on Security and Privacy (2017)
34. Song, L., Mittal, P.: Systematic evaluation of privacy risks of machine learning models. In: USENIX Security Symposium (2021)
35. de la Torre, L.: A guide to the California consumer privacy act of 2018. Available at SSRN 3275571 (2018)
36. Wen, Y., et al.: Canary in a coalmine: Better membership inference with ensembled adversarial queries. arXiv preprint arXiv:2210.10750 (2022)
37. Wightman, R.: PyTorch image models. https://github.com/rwightman/pytorch-image-models (2019)
38. Ye, J., Maddi, A., Murakonda, S.K., Bindschaedler, V., Shokri, R.: Enhanced membership inference attacks against machine learning models. In: ACM SIGSAC Conference on Computer and Communications Security, pp. 3093–3106 (2022)
39. Ye, J., Maddi, A., Murakonda, S.K., Shokri, R.: Privacy auditing of machine learning using membership inference attacks. arXiv preprint arXiv:2108.04417 (2021)
40. Yuan, X., Zhang, L.: Membership inference attacks and defenses in neural network pruning. In: USENIX Security Symposium (2022)

New Trends of Machine Leaning and AI Applied to Cybersecurity

ModelForge: Using GenAI to Improve the Development of Security Protocols

Martin Duclos[1](✉), Ivan A. Fernandez[1], Kaneesha Moore[1], Sudip Mittal[1], and Edward Zieglar[2]

[1] Mississippi State University, Mississippi, Mississippi State, MS 39762, USA
{md128,iaf28,kkm267}@msstate.edu, mittal@cse.msstate.edu, evziegl@nsa.gov
[2] National Security Agency, Fort George G. Meade, Maryland, MD 20755, USA

Abstract. Formal methods can be used for verifying security protocols, but their adoption can be hindered by the complexity of translating natural language protocol specifications into formal representations. In this paper, we introduce ModelForge, a novel tool that automates the translation of protocol specifications for the Cryptographic Protocol Shapes Analyzer (CPSA). By leveraging advances in Natural Language Processing (NLP) and Generative AI (GenAI), ModelForge processes protocol specifications and generates a CPSA protocol definition. This approach reduces the manual effort required, making formal analysis more accessible. We evaluate ModelForge by fine-tuning a large language model (LLM) to generate protocol definitions for CPSA, comparing its performance with other popular LLMs. The results from our evaluation show that ModelForge consistently produces quality outputs, excelling in syntactic accuracy, though some refinement is needed to handle certain protocol details. The contributions of this work include the architecture and proof of concept for a translating tool designed to simplify the adoption of formal methods in the development of security protocols.

Keywords: Formal Methods · Security Protocols · CPSA · NLP · Generative AI · LLM · Protocol Analysis

1 Introduction

The current standards process used by the Internet Engineering Task Force (IETF) for reviewing security protocols is hindered by a lack of verification of the stated protocol properties. This shortcoming primarily arises from the absence of formal proofs, which are essential for thorough verification. In an effort to enhance the standards process, the IETF is encouraging protocol developers to incorporate formal methods analysis and validation into their work [6]. Formal methods are mathematical techniques used to prove the correctness and security properties of protocols. However, formal methods analysis is a complex area that demands specialized expertise, rendering it inaccessible to some security protocol developers [5]. This paper aims to support the IETF's efforts by

K. Adi et al. (Eds.): FPS 2024, LNCS 15533, pp. 141–155, 2025.
https://doi.org/10.1007/978-3-031-87496-3_10

simplifying formal methods analysis and validation, thereby making these tasks more accessible to security protocol developers.

One approach to formal methods analysis, as described by Meadows [13] and originally suggested by Kemmerer [8], involves modeling a protocol in a formal language. A verification system is then employed to validate these models against the stated protocol properties (e.g., secrecy and authentication). Protocol developers perform analysis and verification using tools such as Cryptographic Protocol Shapes Analyzer (CPSA), Maude-NPA, Tamarin, and ProVerif. However, this task is both tedious and labor-intensive, often requiring a *domain expert* to parse and convert protocol specifications-typically expressed in natural language [7,17,18]-into models or protocol definitions compatible with a formal methods tool [6]. Consequently, accurately translating protocol specifications into a usable form for formal methods tools poses a significant challenge [5].

As illustrated in Fig. 1, the current IETF standards process could be improved by making formal methods analysis tools more accessible to protocol developers. Increased accessibility would likely encourage security protocol developers to integrate these tools into their workflow, enabling them to perform protocol analysis during the specification development phase, even before submitting a protocol proposal to the IETF. We envision an enhanced workflow where a translator tool is capable of accepting protocol specifications and turning them into protocol definitions or models for a formal methods tool. Such a system could potentially automate a portion of the creation of security protocol definitions, reducing the manual effort required and improving efficiency. Subsequently, this translator tool would align with one of the goals of the Usable Formal Methods Research Group (UFMRG), established by the IETF in January 2023 [6], which seeks to understand how formal methods can be incorporated into the development of specifications for security protocols.

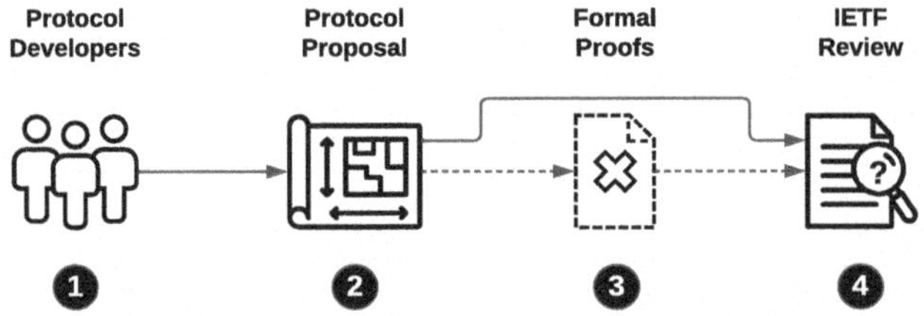

Fig. 1. Overview of the IETF standards process for security protocols, highlighting the lack of formal verification at key stages. ModelForge aims to automate aspects of formal methods analysis to address these gaps. (1) Developers design a new protocol, (2) compile protocol specifications into a proposal, (3) often submitting it without formal proofs, (4) leaving the IETF to establish formal proofs during review.

Building on our objective of making formal methods analysis more accessible, we propose ModelForge, a translating tool that leverages recent advances in Natural Language Processing (NLP) and Generative AI (GenAI). Our tool feeds protocol specifications into a fine-tuned Large Language Model (LLM), which then automatically generates candidate protocol definitions or models. ModelForge is specifically designed with CPSA as the target protocol analyzer, requiring the LLM to output the protocol definitions using CPSA syntax. The CPSA formal methods tool necessitates a protocol definition (model) and a partial description of an execution (protocol skeleton) as inputs, both formatted as structured text using symbolic expressions (s-expressions) [10]. The structured output candidates generated by ModelForge will need to be reviewed and revised by a domain expert. This step is to ensure that protocol definitions accurately represent the protocol specifications before undergoing analysis. This novel approach has the potential to enhance the overall efficiency of the secure protocol formal analysis process by reducing the manual effort and complexity associated with translating specifications into the format required by CPSA, thereby making formal analysis more accessible.

Our key contributions are: 1) the development of an architecture for translating natural language protocol specifications into CPSA protocol definitions, 2) the validation of this architecture through a proof-of-concept implementation, and 3) the evaluation of various LLMs in translating protocol specifications into CPSA protocol definitions. In summary, our paper presents a methodology that lowers the barriers to adopting formal methods tools in the field of security protocol development and analysis.

To address the complexity and inaccessibility of formal methods in security protocol development, as we discussed in the introduction, we now focus on key concepts and related work in formal methods, NLP, and Generative AI, which provide the basis for our proposed solution, ModelForge.

2 Background and Related Work

Despite advancements in Natural Language Processing (NLP), translating protocol specifications into formal definitions remains a challenge across various tools, including CPSA. Automating this translation process offers a potential solution. This section reviews related work in formal methods, NLP, and large language models (LLMs) as a foundation for addressing this challenge.

2.1 Internet Engineering Task Force

The Internet Engineering Task Force (IETF) develops standards and security protocols through the Request for Comments (RFC) process, which relies heavily on natural language to promote discussion and consensus. In January 2023, the IETF established the Usable Formal Methods Research Group (UFMRG) to promote the use of formal methods in protocol standards development [6].

2.2 Formal Methods in Protocol Analysis

Protocol developers and researchers can utilize different formal methods tools to verify the security goals of a protocol. In the context of such tools, formal methods are expressive mathematical models used to prove theorems constructed from a protocol's stated properties. These methods fall under domains such as model checking and logical inference. As defined by Lal et al., the emphasis within model checking lies in exploring all possible states and transitions in a systematic nature, using abstractions to optimize the verification analysis. Whereas, logical inference, the domain in which our work resides, uses mathematical reasoning of the system to determine the validity of the protocol analysis [9].

2.3 Cryptographic Protocol Shapes Analyzer

The MITRE Corporation developed the Cryptographic Protocol Shapes Analyzer (CPSA) [10], an open-source tool for analyzing cryptographic protocols using logical inference within a strand-space model. CPSA acts as a model finder, exploring protocol behaviors through roles, messages, variables, and their assumptions, defined using a LISP (LISt Processing)-like syntax."

CPSA uses partial executions, known as skeletons, which instantiate strands and roles with variable assumptions to identify possible protocol behaviors. Figure 2 shows an example from the CPSA manual. In a Dolev-Yao network [4], where an adversary can intercept, alter, and fabricate messages, CPSA finds all distinct protocol executions and outputs them as shapes [11].

Shapes represent distinct protocol executions, and each contains analysis sentences that capture "all that can be learned from a CPSA run" [14], enabling derivation of security goals and proofs. We selected CPSA for our work due to our familiarity with the tool and access to experts.

2.4 Large Language Models

LLMs are versatile models trained on large datasets to perform a wide range of tasks across various domains. Their development goes back to the rise of foundational models in natural language processing (NLP) [1]. Foundational models are designed to be highly adaptable, using diverse training data to enable fine-tuning for multiple tasks. However, their broad training scope can lead to limitations in accuracy when applied to specialized fields.

2.5 ChemLLM

Foundational LLMs like OpenAI's ChatGPT and Meta's Llama are widely used, but specialized domains, such as chemistry, benefit from domain-specific models. Zhang et al. [20] emphasize that foundational models often lack chemical knowledge and propose ChemLLM, a chemistry-specific LLM fine-tuned from a foundational model. They also demonstrate the use of synthetic data to train the model when organic data is limited.

```
(defprotocol blanchet basic
  (defrole init
    (vars (a b akey) (s skey) (d data))
    (trace (send (enc (enc s (invk a)) b))
           (recv (enc d s)))
    (uniq-orig s))
  (defrole resp
    (vars (a b akey) (s skey) (d data))
    (trace (recv (enc (enc s (invk a)) b))
           (send (enc d s)))
    (uniq-orig d)))

(defskeleton blanchet
  (vars (a b akey) (s skey) (d data))
  (defstrand init 2 (a a) (b b) (s s) (d d))
  (deflistener d)
  (non-orig (invk b)))

(defskeleton blanchet
  (vars (a b akey) (s skey) (d data))
  (defstrand resp 2 (a a) (b b) (s s) (d d))
  (deflistener d)
  (non-orig (invk a) (invk b)))
```

Fig. 2. Blanchet's Protocol, defined in CPSA syntax, consists of two steps. First, the initiator (init) sends a symmetric key s to the responder (resp), signed with init's private key (a) and encrypted with resp's public key (b). Then, resp sends data d back to init, encrypted with s.

2.6 StrucBench

Extending LLMs beyond simple text generation can be challenging. Tang et al. [19] note that LLMs, such as GPT-4, struggle with generating intricate formatted text including complex structured data (e.g., tables). These limitations are likely due to the way LLMs are trained to mimic patterns of human language and the token requirements for structured output. Tang et al. propose the Format Chain-of-Thought (FormatCOT) methodology for generate fine-tuning pairs via self-instruction. To address the research gaps with LLMs used for structured output including systemic analyses, they also introduce the STRUC-BENCH benchmark that focuses on structured text generation (e.g., HTML, LaTeX).

3 ModelForge Architecture

In this section, we present the modular architecture of ModelForge, a translator designed to convert natural language secure protocol specifications into CPSA protocol definitions. Figure 3 illustrates how the architecture centers around a fine-tuned LLM for generating protocol definitions in response to user defined queries. Like CPSA, ModelForge is designed for researchers and developers working with cryptographic protocols and formal methods. The main components and data flow are illustrated in Fig. 3.

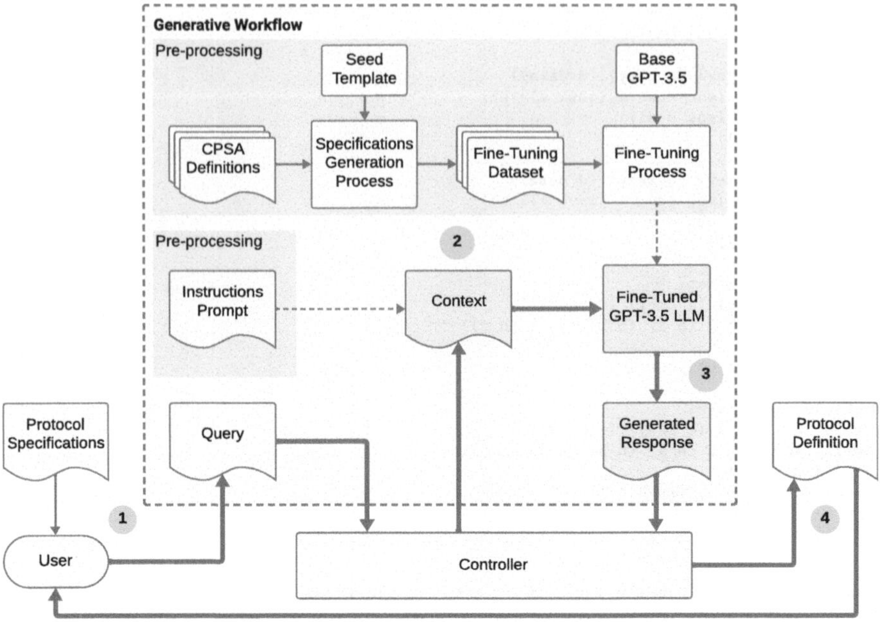

Fig. 3. ModelForge architecture: (1) A user submits protocol specifications as a query. (2) The controller combines the query with an instruction prompt and sends it to the fine-tuned LLM. (3) The LLM generates a CPSA protocol definition. (4) The output is then delivered to the user for validation.

3.1 Query

A user-provided query serves as both the input and the starting point for ModelForge. The query consists of a natural language protocol specifications. Figure 4 presents an example of a simple user query.

3.2 Generative Workflow

The keystone of the generative workflow in our architecture is a fine-tuned LLM, a subset of generative AI focused specifically on text generation. In our use case, this model generates a CPSA protocol definition from natural language specifications, aiding in the formal methods analysis of security protocols.

3.3 Pre-processing

Before the generative workflow can be utilized, several components must be initialized as part of a pre-processing sequence. These components, highlighted in a darker shade in Fig. 3, consist of pre-processing tasks, loosely categorized into dataset-related, fine-tuning, and configuration tasks.

```
Protocol Description: Alice and Bob require a secure protocol for mutual
authentication over an insecure network. Using the specifications below, create
a CPSA protocol definition. The protocol must employ public-key encryption[...]

Initiation Sequence: Alice sends a message to Bob including Alice's identity (a)
and her nonce (n1), encrypted with Bob's public key. Upon receiving Alice's
message, Bob sends to Alice the nonce (n1) received from Alice, his identity
(b), and his nonce (n2), encrypted with Alice's public key. Alice decrypts Bob's
message then sends Bob's nonce (n2) back to him.
```

Fig. 4. Example of a user-submitted query for a secure protocol using public-key encryption. This query serves as input for ModelForge.

3.4 Fine-Tuning Dataset

One of the initial challenges we faced was the scarcity of CPSA protocol definitions available to us for our fine-tuning goal. To address this issue, we utilized GPT-4, to generate ten seed templates of CPSA protocol definitions. These templates served as the question portion of a question-and-answer (Q&A) pair. GPT-4 was further employed to generate corresponding protocol specifications, creating synthetic Q&A pairs of CPSA protocol definitions and their associated specifications. After forming these pairs, GPT-4 was leveraged once again to introduce variance into the existing set of Q&A pairs, thereby increasing the number of pairs available for the fine-tuning process.

3.5 Fine-Tuning Process

With a curated dataset of synthetic Q&A pairs in place, the next step involved fine-tuning a pre-trained LLM to ensure it could accurately generate protocol definitions, a task requiring domain-specific adjustments. Fine-tuning is a method used to update the weights of a pre-trained model by further training it on specific data. This process is referred to as supervised fine-tuning when it uses labeled data tailored to a particular task [3]. In other words, fine-tuning enables us to modify the LLM in two ways: 1) inject it with additional knowledge, and 2) altering its behavior to perform specific tasks more effectively. In Sect. 4.4, we detail the fine-tuning process associated with OpenAI's GPT-3.5 model, the LLM selected for ModelForge.

3.6 Configuration

The configuration components are the settings and parameters that guide the behavior of the LLM during the generation process. In our architecture, this consists of a single but important configuration component: a pre-defined instructions prompt. This prompt includes specialized instructions and a placeholder for the user query.

3.7 Context

The context is obtained by concatenating two components: 1) the user query and 2) the instructions prompt. These two components form the context, and is later fed by the controller as an input into the LLM for processing.

3.8 Fine-Tuned LLM

Core to our architecture, is an LLM responsible for translating the input into an output that contains a CPSA protocol definition. To accomplish this task, the LLM relies on three types of knowledge: 1) knowledge acquired during an initial pre-training phase, 2) knowledge gained through the fine-tuning process, and 3) context-specific knowledge provided by the user query. In Sect. 4.4, we detail the specifics of using GPT-3.5-turbo from OpenAI, the LLM we selected for the implementation of our translator.

3.9 Generated Response

The output out of the LLM consists of structured text, made of symbolic expressions that form a CPSA protocol definition. See Fig. 5 for an output example.

```
(herald "Mutual Authentication Protocol
 with Public Key Encryption")

(defprotocol mutual-auth basic
   (defrole init
     (vars (a name) (b name) (n1 text) (n2 text)
     (pubk data))
     (trace
       (send (enc (cat a n1) (pubk b)))
       (recv (enc (cat n1 n2) (pubk a)))
       (send n2)))
```

Fig. 5. Example of a generated CPSA protocol definition by ModelForge, illustrating the output format using s-expressions for protocol roles and trace sequences.

3.10 Controller

The controller's role is to orchestrate the sequence of execution between the architectural components. Additionally, the controller is responsible for initializing the system and setting up the necessary parameters and states.

3.11 Data Flow

As illustrated in Fig. 3, the flow of data through the main components of the architecture is described below.
(1) User Query: The process begins when a user submits a query containing secure protocol specifications, similar to the example in Fig. 4.
(2) Query and Prompt Concatenation: The next step consists of concatenating the user query with instructions prompt. This will form the input for the LLM.
(3) LLM Response Generation: The combined input is then fed into a fine-tuned LLM, which is instructed to generate a CPSA protocol definition based on the secure protocol specifications contained within the input.
(4) Output Delivery: Finally, the controller receives the response generated by the LLM and directs it back to the user.

4 Experimental Results

In this section, we present the findings from our experiments, including both a quantitative and qualitative evaluation methods of our fine-tuned translator model. We also provide information on the technical setup of our experiment, along with details on the survey instrument used to collect data for the evaluation. Finally, we present and discuss the results, offering insights into the effectiveness of our approach.

4.1 Evaluation

To assess the effectiveness of ModelForge in generating CPSA protocol definitions, we conducted an evaluation using both quantitative and qualitative methods. The evaluation involved 4 participants with relevant experience ranging from less than one year to 10 or more years. These participants reviewed the outputs generated by various LLMs, rating their correctness, clarity, and completeness, while also providing feedback on the outputs' strengths and weaknesses. This allowed us to gather valuable data on the LLMs' effectiveness in meeting the requirements of CPSA protocol definitions. The data collection was carried through a survey implemented using Google Forms. The survey presented participants with three distinct queries and a total of nine corresponding CPSA protocol definitions. Table 1 provides the specific criteria and definitions used in the survey.

Table 1. Evaluation criteria for assessing CPSA protocol definitions, including correctness, clarity, and completeness for formal analysis.

Criterion	Description
Correctness	Output uses proper CPSA syntax.
Clarity	Output is easy to read and well-structured.
Completeness	Output covers the main aspects of the query.

4.2 Quantitative Method

Our quantitative portion of the evaluation, focused on assessing how well ModelForge, along with other popular LLMs (see Table 2), could generate an output that aligns with the syntactical requirements of CPSA, readability of protocol definitions, and the intent of the user query.

To assess the protocol definitions, we collected ratings from subject-matter experts who evaluated how closely each model's output approximated a complete, accurate and easily readable CPSA protocol definition.

For each output, experts were asked to rate its correctness, clarity, and completeness on a scale from 1 to 5, with 1 indicating an unusable output and 5 indicating a very good output. Table 1 provides the criteria used in the survey.

The experts' ratings provided data on each LLM's performance, highlighting their ability or inability in generating CPSA protocol definitions. A summary of the ratings provided by the experts is presented in Table 3.

4.3 Qualitative Method

For the qualitative portion, we again asked the same experts to provide feedback on the strengths and weaknesses of the generated CPSA protocol definitions. Experts were asked to describe the strengths and weaknesses of each generated protocol definition, providing detailed feedback on aspects that are critical for the practical application of CPSA protocols but difficult to quantify. We present a summary of the qualitative results in Table 4.

4.4 Experimental Setup

To gather experimental results for ModelForge, we implemented a proof of concept based on the architecture depicted in Fig. 3. This setup enabled us to evaluate the performance of ModelForge by having human experts rate the outputs it generated. Below, we describe the technical details of our implementation.

Framework: At the core of our implementation is LlamaIndex, a modern data framework for LLM-based applications, built using Python [2,12,15,16]. We chose LlamaIndex due to our familiarity with the framework and its ease of use in working with LLMs.

LLM and Fine-Tuning: Building on the LlamaIndex framework, we used a fine-tuned version of OpenAI's GPT-3.5-turbo model to generate CPSA protocol definitions from natural language specifications. The base model, *gpt-3.5-turbo*, was fine-tuned to handle the structured nature of CPSA syntax.

Our fine-tuning process utilized a carefully curated dataset of 340 synthetic Q&A pairs, partitioned into a 70% training set and a 30% testing set. The model underwent 3 epochs of training, processing a total of 568,200 tokens. This resulted in a training loss of 0.2976 and a validation loss of 0.3902, indicating effective generalization of the task of generating CPSA protocol definitions from input specifications.

For the generation phases of both the fine-tuning dataset and protocol definitions, we intentionally set the temperature parameter to 0. This parameter controls the randomness of the LLM's outputs. This choice of temperature encourages more deterministic results, prioritizing consistency and adherence to the protocol specifications over creative variations. By minimizing randomness, we aimed to ensure that ModelForge's outputs aligned with the structured nature of CPSA syntax (see Sect. 2) and the specific requirements of each protocol definition.

4.5 Results

Using our experimental setup, we evaluated the performance of ModelForge as well as other LLMs (see Table 2) for comparison. In Tables 3 and 4 we present the results for both quantitative and qualitative methods of our evaluation.

Table 2. List of additional LLMs evaluated alongside ModelForge.

LLM	Author	Parameters	Description
Claude 3.5	Anthropic	Unknown	Conversational model for dialogue and interactive tasks.
LLama 3	Meta	70B	Multilingual model for a wide variety of tasks.
GPT-4o	OpenAI	>175B	Versatile model capable of a wide variety of tasks.
Codestral	Mistral AI	22B	Specialized in generating and understanding code.

The results of our quantitative study found in Table 3, summarizes the experts' survey ratings across the three queries and nine models evaluated. The data reflects the experts' assessments of each model's correctness, clarity, completeness, as defined in Table 1. These ratings provide valuable insights into the relative effectiveness of ModelForge, compared to other leading LLMs.

ModelForge, as indicated by the results, demonstrates consistent performance across correctness, clarity, and completeness, particularly excelling with Query 2, where it achieved some of the highest ratings across all models. However, there is room for improvement with Query 3, where GPT-4o outperformed ModelForge. Despite this, ModelForge remains competitive, consistently ranking among the top-performers overall.

From a qualitative perspective, the feedback on the strengths and weaknesses provided by survey participants was also insightful. As summarized in Table 4, ModelForge was regarded as having the best instance of CPSA syntax among the evaluated models, but it still exhibited specific weaknesses, particularly in

Table 3. Normalized average ratings provided by experts for each query and model. Metrics include correctness, clarity, and completeness for CPSA protocol definitions.

Query	Model	Correctness	Clarity	Completeness
Query 1	Codestral	0.00	0.50	0.33
	Claude 3.5	0.50	0.50	0.33
	GPT-4o	0.25	0.50	0.42
	LLama 3.1	0.00	0.00	0.00
	ModelForge	0.67	0.75	0.67
Query 2	Codestral	0.00	0.17	0.08
	Claude 3.5	0.75	0.92	0.83
	GPT-4o	0.00	0.00	0.00
	LLama 3.1	0.00	0.17	0.25
	ModelForge	0.83	0.92	0.92
Query 3	Codestral	0.00	0.33	0.25
	Claude 3.5	0.50	0.50	0.50
	GPT-4o	0.80	0.80	0.80
	LLama 3.1	0.00	0.00	0.33
	ModelForge	0.75	0.50	0.50

protocol handling, such as issues with the use of public keys. While the structure and syntax of its outputs were praised, the feedback highlighted opportunities for further refinement to achieve greater CPSA compatibility.

Table 4. Summary of qualitative feedback on ModelForge's performance, highlighting strengths in CPSA syntax generation and areas requiring improvement.

Aspect	Feedback
Strengths	Best CPSA syntax so far. Strong structure and formatting, recognized as clear.
Weaknesses	Public key issue: Sending out the public key, which was not part of the protocol definition. Limited CPSA compliance, needs refinement for full compatibility.

5 Limitations and Future Work

While our evaluation in Sect. 4.1 demonstrates that ModelForge can generate syntactically correct CPSA definitions, particularly excelling in certain queries, there are notable limitations. In this section, we explore some of these limitations and propose avenues for future improvement.

ModelForge's initial outputs generally adhered to the CPSA syntax format, however, they often required corrections. As such, human experts should remain an integral part of any workflow. More precisely, a domain expert should carefully review the AI-generated CPSA protocol definitions to ensure they are correct, complete, and secure. A Human-in-the-Loop validation is an efficient way to increase automation while minimizing risks caused by limitations.

One notable limitation of ModelForge is that it performs better when variable names are provided as part of the user query. This presents a challenge when translating documents such as RFCs, where variable names are not always explicitly stated. To address this challenge, future work could explore methods such as reinforcement learning from human feedback to establish a basis for automatically inferring or generating variable names.

Another significant challenge arises when working with RFCs, which often contain a considerable amount of unnecessary content to form a protocol definition. One potential solution to this issue could involve training a separate AI model designed to parse and extract only the necessary content for translation into a protocol definition.

Addressing these limitations, such as inferring variable names and content extraction from RFCs, will be key milestones in enhancing ModelForge's capabilities. Future research could explore larger-scale evaluations and the development of additional models to handle more complex protocol features. In conclusion, our work demonstrates the potential of AI-driven tools in simplifying formal methods analysis, moving us closer to the IETF's goal of integrating formal methods into security protocol development.

6 Conclusion

In this paper, we presented ModelForge, a novel translating tool designed to facilitate the integration of formal methods analysis into the development of security protocols. Our evaluation, detailed in Sect. 4.1, demonstrates ModelForge's strong performance. It consistently performs well and, in several instances, even outperforms more recent foundational LLMs. It is important to note that only ModelForge had been fine-tuned for the specific task, further highlighting the effectiveness of domain-specific language models.

Looking ahead, future research could involve larger-scale evaluations across a broader range of protocol specifications, as well as the development of an ensemble of models to handle more complex features within CPSA, such as Diffie-Hellman algebra, goals, and listeners.

Overall, the contributions of our work represent a step towards making formal methods more accessible, supporting the Internet Engineering Task Force's (IETF) efforts to improve the verification of security protocol standards.

Acknowledgments. This work was supported by the PATENT Lab (Predictive Analytics and Technology Integration Laboratory) in the Department of Computer Science and Engineering at Mississippi State University. The authors would also like to thank the participants who completed the survey. We extend our sincere gratitude to Enis Golaszewski for his invaluable guidance in utilizing CPSA, which significantly contributed to this research.

Disclosure of Interests. The authors have no competing interests to declare that are relevant to the content of this article.

References

1. Bommasani, R., et al.: On the opportunities and risks of foundation models (2021)
2. Braunschweiler, N., Doddipatla, R., Keizer, S., Stoyanchev, S.: Evaluating large language models for document-grounded response generation in information-seeking dialogues (2023). https://arxiv.org/abs/2309.11838
3. Brown, T., et al.: Language models are few-shot learners. Adv. Neural. Inf. Process. Syst. **33**, 1877–1901 (2020)
4. Dolev, D., Yao, A.C.C.: On the security of public key protocols. In: 22nd Annual Symposium on Foundations of Computer Science (SFCS 1981), pp. 350–357 (1981)
5. Gritzalis, S., Spinellis, D., Georgiadis, P.: Security protocols over open networks and distributed systems: formal methods for their analysis, design, and verification. Comput. Commun. **22**(8), 697–709 (1999)
6. Internet Engineering Task Force (IETF): Usable Formal Methods Proposed Research Group (UFMRG) (2023). https://datatracker.ietf.org/doc/charter-irtf-ufmrg/01/. Accessed 1 Aug 2024
7. Kaufman, C., Hoffman, P.E., Nir, Y., Eronen, P., Kivinen, T.: Internet Key Exchange Protocol Version 2 (IKEv2). RFC 7296 (2014). https://doi.org/10.17487/RFC7296, https://www.rfc-editor.org/info/rfc7296
8. Kemmerer, R.: Using formal methods to analyze encryption protocols. IEEE J. Select. Areas Commun. **7**(4), 448–457 (1989)
9. Lal, S., Jain, M., Chaplot, V.: Approaches to formal verification of security protocols (2011). https://api.semanticscholar.org/CorpusID:18414398
10. Liskov, M.D., Ramsdell, J.D., Guttman, J.D., Rowe, P.D.: The Cryptographic Protocol Shapes Analyzer: A Manual for CPSA 4.1. The MITRE Corporation (2023). version 4.3
11. Liskov, M.D., Rowe, P.D., Thayer, F.J.: Completeness of CPSA. Tech. rep, Citeseer (2011)
12. Liu, J.: Llamaindex (2022). https://doi.org/10.5281/zenodo.1234, https://github.com/jerryjliu/llama_index, release date: 2022-11-01
13. Meadows, C.: Applying formal methods to the analysis of a key management protocol. J. Comput. Secur. **1**(1), 5–35 (1992)
14. Ramsdell, J.D.: CPSA and formal security goals (2015)
15. Rau, A., et al.: A context-based chatbot surpasses radiologists and generic ChatGPT in following the ACR appropriateness guidelines. Radiology **308**(1), e230970 (2023)
16. Rau, S., et al.: A retrieval-augmented chatbot based on GPT-4 provides appropriate differential diagnosis in gastrointestinal radiology: a proof of concept study. Eur. Radiol. Exp. **8**(1), 60 (2024)

17. Rescorla, E.: The Transport Layer Security (TLS) Protocol Version 1.3. RFC 8446 (2018). https://doi.org/10.17487/RFC8446, https://www.rfc-editor.org/info/rfc8446
18. Simpson, W.A.: PPP Authentication Protocols. RFC 1334 (1992). https://doi.org/10.17487/RFC1334, https://www.rfc-editor.org/info/rfc1334
19. Tang, X., Zong, Y., Zhao, Y., Cohan, A., Gerstein, M.: Struc-Bench: Are large language models really good at generating complex structured data? (2023)
20. Zhang, D., et al.: ChemLLM: A chemical large language model (2024)

Detecting Energy Attacks in the Battery-Less Internet of Things

Luca Mottola[1,2,3](✉) and Thiemo Voigt[1,2]

[1] RI.SE Sweden, Kista, Sweden
[2] Uppsala University, Uppsala, Sweden
[3] Politecnico di Milano, Milan, Italy
luca.mottola@polimi.it

Abstract. We present a technique to detect energy attacks in the battery-less Internet of Things (IoT). Battery-less IoT devices rely on ambient energy harvesting and are employed in a multitude of applications, including safety-critical ones such as biomedical implants. Due to scarce energy intakes and limited energy buffers, their executions become *intermittent*, alternating periods of active operation with periods of recharging energy buffers. Evidence exists that demonstrates how exerting limited control on ambient energy one can create situations of *livelock*, *denial of service*, and *priority inversion*, without physical device access. We call these situations *energy attacks*. Using concepts of approximate intermittent computing and machine learning, we design a technique that can detect energy attacks with 92%+ accuracy, that is, up to 37% better than the baselines, and with up to one fifth of their energy overhead. By design, our technique does not cause any additional energy failure compared to the regular intermittent processing.

1 Introduction

Ambient energy harvesting allows Internet of Things (IoT) devices to eliminate their dependency on traditional batteries [12]. This enables previously unattainable deployments, including safety-critical settings such as biomedical implants [1,18,23,33]. Harvested energy is generally highly variable in time, yet energy buffers, such as capacitors, are generally limited. System shutdowns due to energy depletion are unavoidable and computing becomes *intermittent* [5].

Computing Intermittently. Figure 1 shows an example execution. The ambient charges the IoT device's onboard capacitor until voltage V_{on} is reached that causes the device to power on. The device senses, computes, and communicates as long as the capacitor charge remains above a threshold V_{off}. The device then switches off, waiting for the capacitor to reach V_{on} again. This pattern may occur on tiny time scales; for example, computing simple error correction codes on a battery-less IoT device may require as many as 16 energy cycles [11].

K. Adi et al. (Eds.): FPS 2024, LNCS 15533, pp. 156–173, 2025.
https://doi.org/10.1007/978-3-031-87496-3_11

Due to resource constraints, applications run with no operating system support [5]. When the device powers off at V_{off}, the system state would normally be lost. Intermittently-computing IoT systems use checkpointing [4,8,11,54,61] or task-based programming [44,62] to create persistent state on non-volatile memory (NVM). These systems operate as the device approaches V_{off}, allowing them to retain the application state across energy failures. Operations on NVM, however, are extremely energy hungry [46].

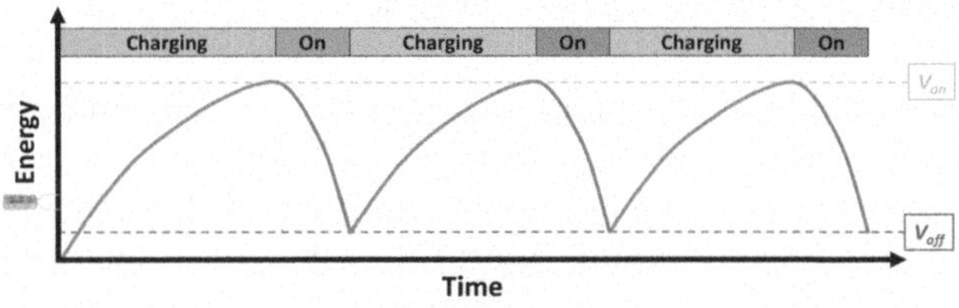

Fig. 1. Example intermittent execution.

Energy Attacks. Evidence exists that shows how exerting limited control on ambient energy may steer intermittent executions in unintended ways [49]. We call these situations *energy attacks*. The simplest scenario consists, for example, in physically blocking a solar panel that powers the device, leading to a denial of service. Such an attack, however, would be straightforward to detect, as the system would suddenly and completely stop working.

Curically, much more subtle situations exist, where attackers may potentially do much more harm than with a complete denial of service situation that is immediately recognized and redressed. Energy attacks are indeed reported that that create situations of *livelock*, *priority inversion*, and *denial of service* [49]. Unlike the simple scenario above, these attacks create situations that are deceptively similar to legitimate executions.

Following a definition of the system and attack model in Sect. 3, in Sect. 4 we tackle the problem of *detecting* energy attacks. Intuitively, this means understanding when ambient energy provisioning does not follow the "natural" patterns. The problem appears as a case of *anomaly detection* [17]. Three peculiar requirements exist: detecting energy attacks *i)* accurately and *ii)* with low latency, while doing so *iii)* right on the IoT devices, as opposed to an external system, to spare the energy overhead of radio operations necessary to offload data to a third party. Our technique uses concepts of approximate intermittent computing [9,59] and machine learning to ensure that, by design, the attack detection process does not cause additional energy failures compared to the regular intermittent processing, imposing minimal overhead.

Section 5 reports on the accuracy and overhead of our detection technique, based on 500K+ data points obtained using real-world energy traces, compared with two baselines. The results indicate that our technique is 92%+ accurate, which is up to 37% better than the baselines, and imposes an overhead that is up to one fifth of the baselines. Further, the detection performance is largely independent of the energy patterns and robust to previously unseen attacks.

Following detection of an energy attack, the system should apply countermeasures. In Sect. 6, we explore the multiple dimensions of the problem, articulate the related trade-offs, and inspire the design of defense techniques.

2 Background and Related Work

Our work is an example of the many ongoing efforts at running inference processes of machine learning models on resource-constrained devices [6]. We specifically tailor an existing machine learning technique for detecting energy attacks on a batter-less IoT device running intermittently. In the following, we provide background information and survey related works in closely related areas.

Power Attacks in Data Centers. Energy attacks resemble similarities with power attacks in data centers. Malicious workloads may generate power spikes on multiple servers at the same time, which causes branch circuit breakers to trip, leading to power outages [29,40]. Detection techniques include machine learning applied to performance logs [19] and modeling user behaviors that may indicate the infrastructure is under-performing [40].

Common with our problem is that energy is part of the attack vector. However, the technology is extremely different, for example, in terms of workloads and hardware platforms. Moreover, in contrast to the attack model we describe in Sect. 3, attackers do not directly manipulate the energy provisioning channel and need access to the target data center or must be informed of its layout. In contrast, the attacks described by Mottola et al. that we consider [49], do not require physical access to the target device.

Security in Battery-Powered IoT. IoT devices are difficult to secure due to resource constraints, which complicates the use of mainstream security mechanisms and protocols [57]. Battery-powered IoT devices enable peculiar attacks, for example, in an attempt to drain batteries [36,48,51]. Low-power radios make IoT devices vulnerable to denial of service attacks, for example, due to intentional jamming [35]. Multi-hop networks require specialized network stacks that open to new kinds of attacks, in particular at the routing layer, motivating new security mechanisms ranging from hardware-based solutions [52] to methods for attack detection and mitigation that rely on machine learning [21,56].

These approaches, unfortunately, fall short of expectations for battery-less IoT devices, where energy constraints are way more severe. Intermittent executions add a new dimension to the problem that requires specialized solutions.

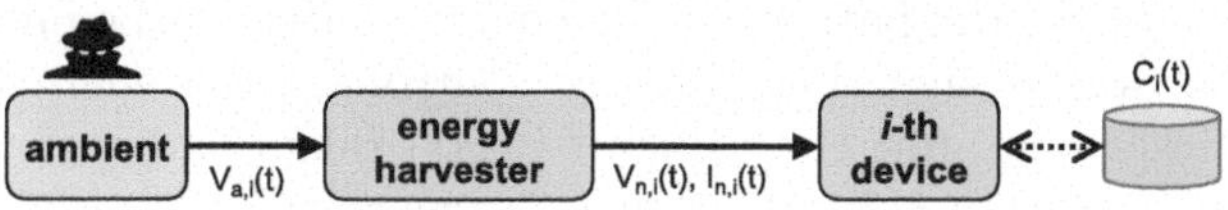

Fig. 2. System and attack model.

Security in Intermittent Computing. The prevailing intermittent computing architecture includes a mixed-volatile MCU with built-in NVM and one or multiple capacitors to tame fluctuations of energy intake [20]. This configuration is seen in available platforms [31,34] and deployments [1,18,23,33].

The few existing security solutions in intermittent computing focus on securing persistent state. As an example, Krishnan et al. [37] demonstrate that persistent state is vulnerable to sniffing, spoofing, or replay attacks. In other works, Asad et al. [7] experimentally evaluate the use of different encryption algorithms and ARM TrustZone protection. Krishnan et al. [38] build on this and propose a configurable checkpoint security setting that leverages application properties to reduce overhead. Ghodsi et al. [28] use lightweight algorithms [13] for securing checkpoints. Valea et al. [60] propose a SECure Context Saving hardware module inside the MCU. In contrast, Grisafi et al. [30] present a hypervisor to manage and protect checkpoints.

Unlike these works, we study how to detect new types of attacks realized by exerting control on ambient energy provisioning.

3 Energy Attacks

We describe first the system and attack model we adopt; next, we show evidence of example vulnerabilities.

System and Attack Model. Figure 2 illustrates the system and attack model. Energy coming from the ambient a and arriving at the energy harvester of node i is modeled as a continuous signal of voltage $V_{a,i}(t)$. This describes the energy content made available by the ambient to node i at time t. For simplicity, our description here considers a single energy source. The corresponding analysis, however, applies no matter the number of energy sources, as long as the attack model is applicable to each of them. Relying on multiple energy sources may be, nonetheless, a way to defend against energy attacks, as we discuss in Sect. 6.

The energy harvester of node i takes $V_{a,i}(t)$ as input and transforms it into an energy signal of voltage $V_{n,i}(t)$ and current $I_{n,i}(t)$. The latter is a function of $V_{n,i}(t)$ and of the equivalent resistance offered by the charging circuitry at node i. The energy signal described by $V_{n,i}(t)$ and $I_{n,i}(t)$ charges the local energy buffer, eventually discharged while sensing, computing, or communicating. We model the charge available in the energy buffer of node i as $C_i(t)$.

The attacker has no physical access to the devices and no knowledge of the relation between $V_{a,i}(t)$ and $V_{n,i}(t)$ or $I_{n,i}(t)$. She can sniff and inspect packets, as well as intervene along the path from the energy source to the energy harvester attached to the device, including directly controlling the energy source. This means the attacker can alter the value of $V_{a,i}(t)$ taken as input at node i. We model this as a function $a_i(V_{a,i}(t))$, that is, a transformation a from the voltage domain to the same domain, specific to node i.

A straightforward example of function a that causes a denial of service at node i from t' onwards is $a_i(V_{a,i}(t)) = 0, t > t'$, that is, the harvester at node i receives no energy after t'. The energy buffer at node i progressively discharges because of application processing and capacitor leakage, until the device persists the state before entering the charging phase, as shown in Fig. 1. However, because $a_i(V_{a,i}(t)) = 0, t > t'$, that is, there is no energy arriving at node i later than t', $C_i(t)$ never reaches V_{on} again, and node i never resumes.

The attacker can access to the application's source code or reverse-engineer from binaries [58]. Codebases for battery-less IoT systems, including those used in real deployments [1,18,23], are often public, including operating system layers [5] and hardware drivers [15], while compilers [26] often require the entire source code to perform full-program optimizations.

Example Attacks. Existing literature reports three specific instances of energy attacks [49]. These create situations of livelock, denial of service, and priority inversion. For illustration, we show how an existing vulnerability leads to to the former situation, using a TI MSP430FR5969 Launchpad running HarvOS [11], an existing checkpointing system for intermittent computing, and two Powercast transmitter-receiver pairs. The same situation can be achieved, for example, by controlling the incident solar radiation [12].

Existing intermittent systems recommend setting the activation threshold V_{on} by striking a balance between charging times and energy content when the system is at V_{on} [4,11,20,31,54]. The former suggests a lower V_{on}, whereas the latter pushes for a higher V_{on}. In most existing systems [4,11,54], V_{on} is statically set before deployment and does not necessarily guarantee that the energy content is sufficient to make progress in the application logic and persist the state whenever necessary. The ambient is indeed supposed to provide some energy also during the active times [12].

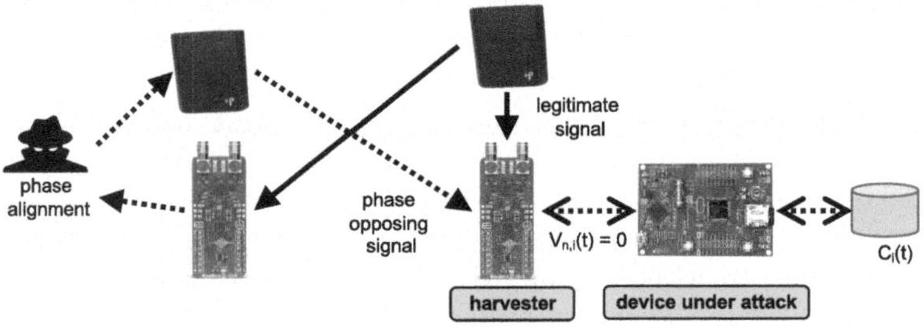

Fig. 3. Generating an opposing RF energy signal.

An attacker may systematically block the energy source at a node i while the device is computing, that is, he creates a transformation a such that $a_i(V_{a,i}(t)) = 0, t' > t > t''$, where t' and t'' are the points in time where the system reaches V_{on} and V_{off}, respectively. Concretely, while the first Powercast transmitter normally powers the device, the attacker implements function a by generating an opposing signal with a second Powercast receiver-transmitter pair, as shown in Fig. 3. This may be achieved by generating a signal in phase opposition [49] with the regular one, yielding destructive interference [43, 50]. The attacker thus cancels out the energy contribution of the legitimate Powercast transmitter.

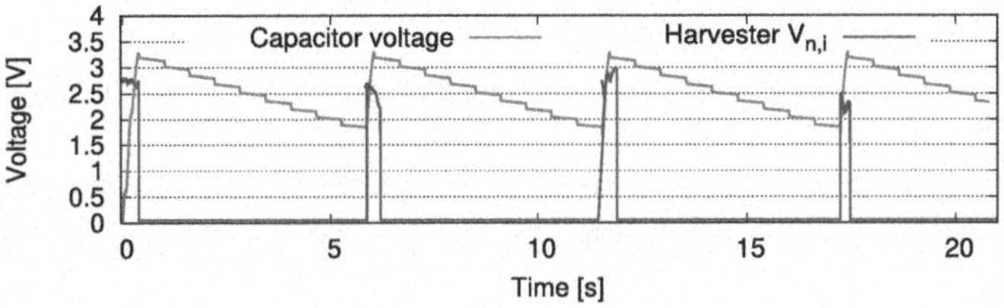

Fig. 4. Livelock situation caused by an energy attack.

Figure 4 shows an example execution once the phase alignment is achieved. Without any contribution of energy during active times and a V_{on} setting that does not account for this, the system approaches V_{off} with insufficient energy to persist state, that is, no new checkpoint is created. When the system reaches V_{on} again, HarvOS resorts to the previous checkpoint, that is, the one that does not include the progress achieved between t' and t''. The previous operations are then executed again, and with the attacker replaying the same function a once more, the system approaches V_{off} again with insufficient energy to persist the state. As long as the attacker keeps doing so, the system continues to restart from the same checkpoint, making no progress in the long run.

Note that in the case of RF energy harvesting, this attack may occur not just without physical access to the device, but also without being anywhere close to it. As long as the attacker is in the (wireless) range of both the legitimate Powercast transmitter and of the device under attack, as shown in Fig. 3, she may detect both the incoming energy wave and regular network packets.

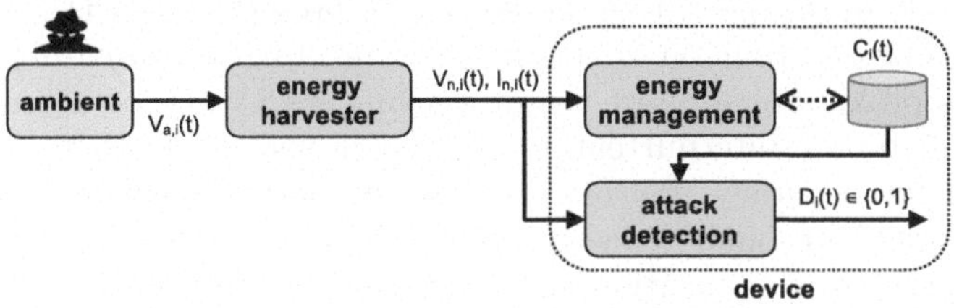

Fig. 5. Detection system architecture.

4 Attack Detection

We study the problem of *detecting* energy attacks when they are not as simple as completely and suddenly stopping the system. This means understanding when ambient energy does not follow the expected patterns, which is a case of anomaly detection [17]. Most deployments of IoT battery-less devices operate in areas with little to no opportunities for external instrumentation [1,18,23,33]; for example, to install systems to detect physical intrusion of the attacker using surveillance cameras. We are, therefore, to meet specific requirements:

R1 *be accurate*, that is, minimizing false positives and false negatives so a device can rely on factual information;
R2 *operate online with low latency*, as countermeasures may be effective only in the short term;
R3 *run locally on the IoT device* due to the excessive energy consumption and additional latency that offloading the process to a third party would incur.

4.1 Design Space

Figure 5 shows the detection system architecture. The detection process runs periodically, every T. We indicate with $D_i(t) \in \{0,1\}$ a binary indicator that corresponds to whether the attack detection system thinks that an energy attack is ongoing at time t, with $t = kT$, $k \in \mathbb{N}$.

Regardless of how to detect energy attacks, the inputs to the detection system at node i may only be voltage $V_{n,i}(t)$, current $I_{n,i}(t)$, and capacitor charge $C_i(t)$. This is because the device has no information about ambient energy at node i, indicated as $V_{a,i}(t)$ in Fig. 4, before its transformation into usable energy by the harvesting mechanism. This means that whenever an attack described as a function $a_i(V_{a,i}(t))$ occurs, the detection system cannot observe the attack directly, but it only has access to its effects after the harvesting processing.

Of the requirements above, **R1** is common [17]; **R2** excludes techniques that require the anomaly to stabilize in the long term or even to stop occurring before they can return an indication that it did happen. Most difficult, however, is **R3**. It rules out anomaly detection methods that demand large memories [24], significant processing power [39], or based on sharing information among nodes. It demands reducing energy consumption. The ideal solution would be one that does not cause additional energy failures, which may require persisting state and indirectly cause an overhead that would not be present otherwise.

We base our solution on *approximate intermittent computing* [9,59] and develop an approximate support vector machine (ASVM) for detecting energy attacks. Approximate intermittent computing provides a knob to trade energy consumption for accuracy. We elect to use support vector machines because of their accuracy for binary classification [14,53] and their optimal trade-off between accuracy of classification and resource consumption [10,22].

4.2 ASVM for Attack Detection

An ASVM is a support vector machine trained as a regular SVM, but capable of using a subset of the signal features for inference [9,59].

We train the ASVM using a total of 52 features by sampling every T the input signals $V_{n,i}(t)$, $I_{n,i}(t)$, $C_i(t)$ for a given ambient energy source, and combinations thereof. Example features include statistical parameters like averages and standard variations, up to various maximum likelihood estimators. The features are computed over different sliding windows over the past $wT, w \in \mathbb{N}$ time instants, which we tune based on the energy source. For example, in case of solar radiation, we use different windows to account for the behavior of the energy source over the last 24 h and the last 10 min. Training happens on a regular machine using the SVM library of the `ScyPy` package.

If we were to run the resulting model as a regular SVM, it may happen that running the energy attack detection step becomes the cause of an energy failure, prompting the system to dump the state on NVM to resume the work once energy is newly available. The energy required for NVM operations is significant and even if it is not directly required for detecting energy attacks, its overhead is in fact indirectly caused by that process exceeding the available energy.

To mitigate these occurrences, we profile the energy required for computing each of the 52 features, including the cost for hardware interaction, and analytically study the contribution to the overall accuracy each of them provides [3]. Next, we order the 52 features according to the ratio between their contribution to the resulting accuracy and their energy cost. This means that features that come first are those with the lowest cost per unit of contributed accuracy.

When the detection system runs, we probe the capacitor for the energy level and determine the first m features, out of the total 52 features, we can afford for classification without causing an energy failure. As probing the capacitor is required anyways, the energy cost for doing so is not considered in the energy cost profile of any of the features. We then compute the classification incrementally and return the classification determined using $m \leq 52$ features. By placing the call to the energy attack detection system as last in an application period, we ensure that the attack detection process only runs with the energy "leftovers", without ever causing an energy failure that would not be there already.

5 Evaluation

Our evaluation is entirely based on real-world energy traces and accounts for 500K+ data points. The analysis is three-pronged. In Sect. 5.2, we evaluate the accuracy and system performance of the ASVM by generating energy attacks in a synthetic manner, that is, by varying the statistical parameters representing how an attacker manipulates the energy signal. This is instrumental to assess the general behavior of our design in a multitude of conditions. In Sect. 5.3, we concentrate on three specific attacks with existing experimental evidence [49]. Sect. 5.4 measures the performance against attacks whose patterns are never seen before, testing our design's ability to tackle previously unseen scenarios.

5.1 Setting

Because of the highly non-deterministic behavior of energy sources, achieving perfect reproducibility when evaluating energy-harvesting systems is challenging using real devices [5]. We thus opt for system emulation over hardware-based experimentation. Still, in the specific case of Sect. 5.3, we manage to run experiments with a *real device and energy harvester.*

Setup. We use the custom Siren MSP430 emulator [25]. We extend the tool with a model of 64 Kbyte of FRAM NVM next to a 2 Kbyte SRAM space, corresponding to the memory layout of the MSP430-FR5969, often employed in intermittent computing [44,54,61]. We account for the energy consumption per clock cycle of various operating modes of the MSP430-FR5969, such as regular computation, non-volatile/volatile memory operations, and I/O.

We simulate a paradigmantic sense-process-transmit IoT application [5] and use HarvOS [11] for checkpointing. We do not emulate sensors and radio, but the time and energy overhead for both are synthetically accounted for at the end of every application round. Note that the application processing is orthogonal to the energy attack detection and useful only to quantify the relative overhead of the energy attack detection system. In our case, we insert a call to the energy attack detection system at the end of every application round, thus generating the highest relative overhead.

Metrics and Traces. We compute three key metrics: *i) the percentage of false negatives (positives)* measures the accuracy of the detection process as the fraction of energy attacks that are definitely missed (wrongly detected); *ii)* the *time to detection* is the number of application rounds between attack injection and when the detection system signals the attack, which measures how rapidly a given technique realizes that the signal represents an anomaly[1]; and *iii)* the relative *energy overhead* as the additional energy consumption due to the energy attack detection system, compared with the application alone.

We feed the emulator with twelve diverse energy traces, offering a mixture of energy source, harvesting technology, and setting. In the following, the terms "indoor/outdoor" coupled with "static/mobile" refer to the location and mobility of the harvester unit, respectively. The M-RF trace is from Mementos [54] and is recorded using a Powercast transmitter [55]. Four traces are from EPIC [3] and are recorded using a mono-crystalline solar cell in settings including outdoor mobile (E-SOM), indoor mobile (E-SIM), outdoor static (E-SOR), and indoor static (E-SIR). The M-VIB and M-TEG traces are obtained using a ReVibe modelD kinetic energy harvester and a Thermalforce 254-150-36 thermoelectric energy harvester [1], respectively. The remaining traces are from the development of the Bonito protocol [27] and account for scenarios involving solar cells (B-JOG and B-OFI) and piezoelectric (B-STA, B-CAR, B-WAS) harvesters.

[1] False negatives are excluded from aggregate statistics.

We use a 75/25 split between training and test data for every trace [47]. During each experiment, we inject no attack for 0.5 h of simulated time to let estimators stabilize. Experiments last between 12 h and 24 h of simulated time.

Baselines. We compare the performance of the ASVM in detecting energy attacks against an equivalent SVM that uses the same model with the regular inference step, called REGULAR SVM, as well as two additional baselines.

One baseline is the k-nearest neighbors algorithm (K-NN) [47], together with hyperparameter optimization to select k. K-NN is often used for anomaly detection of time series [17]. As in existing work [17], we obtain the classification by majority vote across the 52 features. The other baseline is called isolation forest (FOREST) and is known to provide accurate anomaly detection with a linear time complexity and very limited memory consumption [41].

5.2 Synthetic Attacks

We inject energy attacks by considering the original trace as a signal $V_{n,i}(t)$ with mean μ and variance δ and by manipulating the latter two, changing the mean as $\mu' = k\mu$ and/or the variance as $\delta' = h\delta$, with $0 \leq k, h; k < 1; h < 2; h, k \in \mathbb{Q}$. Intuitively, $h > 1$ means increasing the randomness in the signal. Attack occurrence is drawn from a Poisson distribution with arrival rate λ of one every 10 min; the duration is drawn from a Normal distribution with mean 3 min. These parameters model existing energy attacks [49], which are proven to be successful. The application period is one minute.

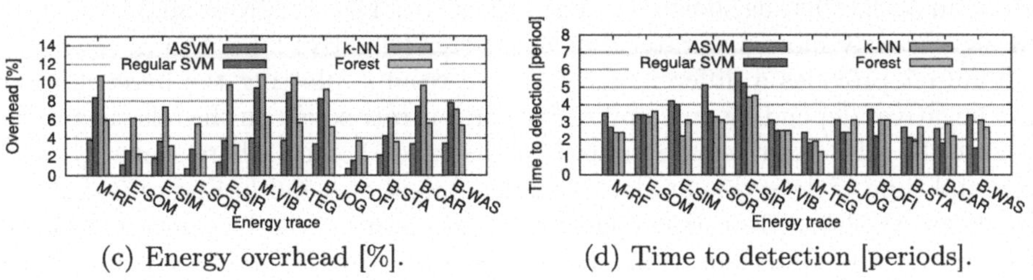

(a) False positives [%].

(b) False negatives [%].

(c) Energy overhead [%].

(d) Time to detection [periods].

Fig. 6. Performance as a function of energy trace.

Results. Figure 6 shows the results we obtain as a function of the energy trace. The percentage of false positives, shown in Fig. 6(a), is limited across all designs and energy traces, never even reaching 1% of the cases. This is reassuring: in the presence of a mitigation technique, the price to pay for counteracting an energy attack would rarely be paid unnecessarily.

Different considerations apply to the results for false negatives, show in Fig. 6(b). The performance of both SVM-based solutions is markedly better than the other two baselines for most of the energy traces. The only exceptions are the E-SOR and B-STA traces, obtained using solar cells in an indoor setting, where the performance is comparable among all designs. The chances that temporary occlusions of the solar cells occur in this setting, for example, because of people passing by, is much higher than elsewhere. It is difficult to separate these legitimate energy variations from short-lived energy attacks.

Crucially, Fig. 6(b) demonstrates that the loss of accuracy, measured in terms of false negatives, due to using fewer features in ASVM is extremely limited compared to the REGULAR SVM. In the worst case, shown by the B-OFI trace, the ASVM is only 2.4% less accurate than the REGULAR SVM. In return, the ASVM imposes between half and one third of the energy overhead of the REGULAR SVM, as shown in Fig. 6(c). Two factors concur to this result: *i)* the ASVM uses first the features that contribute the most to an accurate result; and *ii)* the ASVM is inherently adaptive: if sufficient energy is available, it uses all available features and the performance is the same as the REGULAR SVM. The energy overhead of the other baselines tends to be higher than ASVM, with FOREST generally outperforming K-NN due to the linear time complexity.

Figure 6(d) shows, on the other hand, that both SVM-based approaches take slightly longer to detect attackes compared to the other baselines. On average, ASVM (REGULAR SVM) takes roughly 12% (8%) additional time. Given the absolute numbers at hand, however, this additional time rarely corresponds to more than one application period. Provided the attack is eventually detected, this means the application spends limited time without being aware of that.

Given the accuracy and energy performance of the ASVM, the additional time to detect an attack is a fair price to pay, given that the other two baselines are slightly faster to detect an attack if they do detect one, but often miss the detection altogether, as shown earlier in Fig. 6(b). The ASVM is slightly slower, but significantly more accurate, that is, "better (slightly) late than never".

Figure 7 provides a different view on the results, plotting the percentage of false negatives depending on k and h. We concentrate solely on the false negatives because the false positives are limited, as discussed before, whereas energy overhead and time to detection are largely independent of k and h. Figure 7(a) shows that both SVM-based designs consistently outperform the baselines regardless of k and h. The increasing trend is due to attacks with smaller k being easier to detect: the smaller the k, the more different is the manipulated signal compared to the original one. The corner case is with $k = 0$, which corresponds to completely zeroing the energy signal, for example, modeling an occlusion of a solar cell, which all designs recognize accurately. The more k approaches 1, that

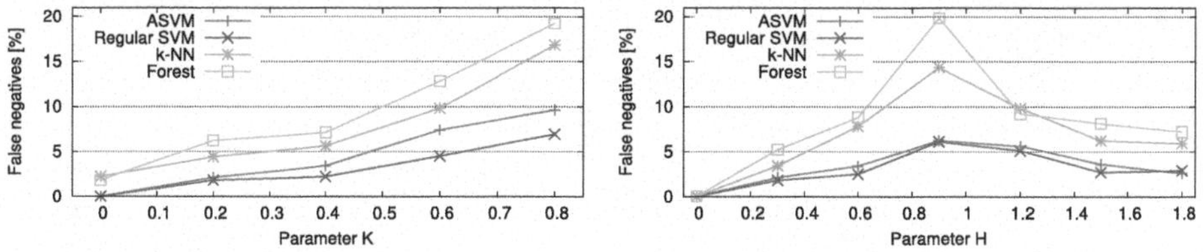

(a) False negatives with varying k, $h = 1$. (b) False negatives with varying h, $k = 1$.

Fig. 7. Percentage of false negatives as a function of k and h.

is, the closer is the manipulated signal to the original one, the wider is the gap between the SVM-based designs and the baselines.

Similar considerations apply to Fig. 7(b), plotting the percentage of false negatives as a function of h. Again, the more h approaches 1, which means the more the manipulated signal is similar to the original one, the less accurate is the detection. The gap between the ASVM and either k-NN or Forest is largest precisely around $h \approx 1$, which is the most difficult setting.

5.3 Concrete Attacks

We verify the performance of the ASVM against the three specific attacks experimentally reported in the literature [49]. We use the same configuration and real hardware as in Sect. 3 and examine 22 instances of the attack leading to a livelock. For attacks leading to denial of service and priority inversion, we generate 100 instances each using the same setup and traces of Sect. 5.1 as input.

There is no guarantee that the attacks we generate are successful. By monitoring the signal $V_n(t)$ during the experiments, we measure that 16 instances (out of 22) are successful for the livelock attack, 88 instances (out of 100) are successful in the case of denial of service attack, and 38 instances (out of 100) are successful for the priority inversion attack. This models a realistic setting where one attempts to exploit a vulnerability, but does not always succeed.

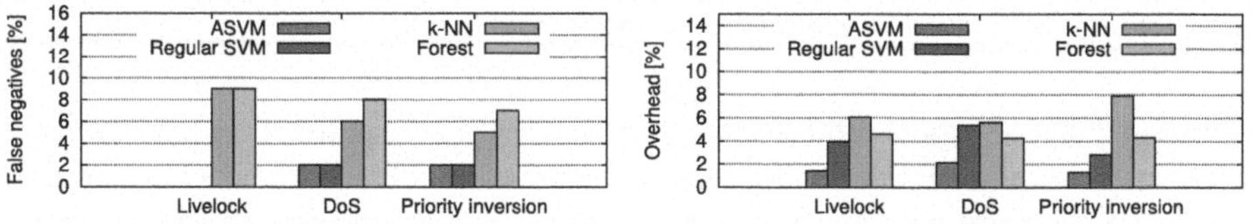

(a) False negatives [%]. (b) Energy overhead [%].

Fig. 8. Performance for three concrete attacks [49].

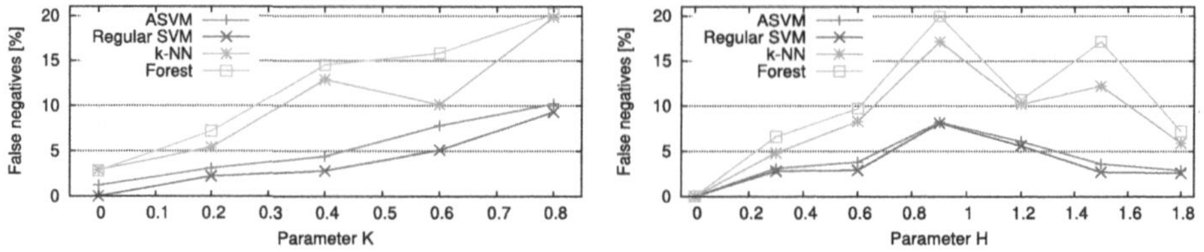

(a) False negatives with varying k, $h = 1$. (b) False negatives with varying h, $k = 1$.

Fig. 9. Percentage of false negatives as a function of parameter k and h, when using non-overlapping parameter settings for training data and test data.

Results. Figure 8 shows the results. The trends of Sect. 5.2 are confirmed. False positives, not shown for brevity, top to 3% of the cases, and yet the ASVM, despite the approximate processing, returns no false positives at all. Crucially, Fig. 8(a) shows that the ASVM has the exact same accuracy as the REGULAR SVM. We conclude that the additional features processed by the REGULAR SVM are not sufficient to sway the classification, and hence the related processing entirely represents unnecessary overhead. The impact of the unnecessary overhead shows in Fig. 8(b), where the ASVM outperforms all other designs, with FOREST being the second most efficient technique as seen in Fig. 6(c). The time to detection for the ASVM, not shown for brevity, is comparable to K-NN and FOREST, and only the REGULAR SVM performs 17% better in the case of denial of service and prority inversion, while being roughly as fast for the livelock attack.

5.4 Unknown Attacks

We evaluate what accuracy we may obtain against unknown problem instances. We repeat the experiments of Sect. 5.2 with a different split between training data and test data. We use as training set the instances with $k \in \{0.2, 0.6\}$ and $h \in \{0.6, 1.2, 1.8\}$. All other parameter setting for either k or h are only used to generate test data. This has two effects: *i)* it reduces the size of the training data, and *ii)* the designs we test are confronted with unseen patterns of the energy signal, which might be legitimate or represent attacks.

Results. Figure 9 shows the results. For the reasons explained earlier, we focus on the percentage of false negatives as a measure of accuracy. Compared to Fig. 7, the absolute values are generally larger, likely because of the reduction in the size of the training data, yet the trends remain largely the same. The observations we outline earlier, especially on the limited loss of accuracy of the ASVM compared to the REGULAR SVM, do remain.

Most importantly, the parameter settings that do not appear in the training set represent no particular outlier in Fig. 9 for either of the SVM-based designs. This is not the case for the other baselines, as seen in Fig. 9(x) when $k = 0.4$

and in Fig. 9(b) when $h = 1.5$. This provides evidence of the general robustness of our design also when facing previously unseen problem instances.

6 Inspiring Defense

Designing defense techniques is a manifold problem, whose implications possibly percolate through both software and hardware layers. We discuss next key dimensions of the design space, hopefully inspiring follow-up work in the area.

Consider a scenario where *energy* is the major concern, hence the ratio between energy consumed and useful work is to be minimized. Defense techniques may be developed in this scenario by applying mixed-criticality concepts [16], that is, by splitting code functionality or application tasks in critical and non-critical ones. During an attack, the latter may be suspended, thus shifting the reduced energy budget towards critical functionality.

Say the amount of *collected data* is crucial, regardless of how energy is spent. One may employ concepts of context-oriented programming, which also exist for low-power embedded systems [2], to dynamically change the application behavior. For instance, the system may temporarily log data locally instead of using wireless transmissions, should the latter be affected by the energy attack.

One may design techniques that mitigate particular negative effects. These require an additional step to identify the type of attack. Examples are techniques that mitigate attacks preventing a device from making progress, that is, akin to the example attack of Sect. 3. Recognizing this kind of attack may be achieved by instrumenting the code with intermittence-aware programming constructs [45]. Adapting techniques that dynamically adjust the activation threshold [8] may provide a way to resolve the livelock.

On the other hand, we argue that generally-applicable defense techniques may take inspiration from energy management in mobile devices [32]. Mobile operating systems feature sophisticated techniques to handle situations of energy scarcity, for example, when the battery is about to run out. These include tuning a number of hardware knobs, which are normally not available on resource-constrained embedded platforms, as well as software techniques such as throttling the execution of a subset of system processes. The latter effectively represent a generalization of many of the attack-specific techniques we discuss. These techniques may be adapted to intermittently-computing devices.

The defense techniques outlined above are mainly implemented in software. A natural option at the hardware level is to rely on multiple energy sources. Existing hardware platforms [31] and deployed battery-less IoT systems [1,18,33] seldom rely on multiple energy sources, yet prototypes exist [42]. Combining energy-rich sources that may be attack vectors, with energy-poor sources that are exceedingly difficult to employ as attack vectors, may provide an effective combination to sustain long-term operation in regular conditions, while mitigating the effects of energy attacks when they occur.

7 Conclusion

We presented a technique to detect energy attacks that is accurate, timely, and imposes a limited energy overhead, enabling detection on resource-constrained IoT devices. Our ASVM design combines machine learning and approximate intermittent computing concepts. Our evaluation, entirely based on real-world energy traces, shows that the ASVM detects energy attacks with 92%+ accuracy, that is, up to 37% better than the baselines, and with up to one fifth of their overhead. We concluded with directions to inspire defense techniques.

References

1. Afanasov, M., et al.: Battery-less zero-maintenance embedded sensing at the mithræum of circus maximus. In: Proceedings of the ACM Conference on Embedded Networked Sensor Systems (SENSYS) (2020)
2. Afanasov, M., Mottola, L., Ghezzi, C.: Context-oriented programming for adaptive wireless sensor network software. In: IEEE International Conference on Distributed Computing in Sensor Systems (2014)
3. Ahmed, S., et al.: The betrayal of constant power × time: finding the missing joules of transiently-powered computers. In: International Conference on Languages, Compilers, and Tools for Embedded Systems (LCTES) (2019)
4. Ahmed, S., et al.: Efficient intermittent computing with differential checkpointing. In: Proceedings of the ACM International Conference on Languages, Compilers, and Tools for Embedded Systems (LCTES) (2019)
5. Ahmed, S., et al.: The Internet of Batteryless Things. ACM, Commun (2024)
6. Alajlan, N.N., Ibrahim, D.M.: TinyML: enabling of inference deep learning models on ultra-low-power IoT edge devices for AI applications. Micromachines (2022)
7. Asad, H.A., et al.: On securing persistent state in intermittent computing. In: International Workshop on Energy Harvesting and Energy-Neutral Sensing Systems (2020)
8. Balsamo, D., et al.: Hibernus++: a self-calibrating and adaptive system for transiently-powered embedded devices. IEEE Trans. Comput. Aided Des. Integr. Circ. Syst. (2016)
9. Bambusi, F., et al.: The case for approximate intermittent computing. In: International Conference on Information Processing in Sensor Networks (IPSN) (2022)
10. Banbury, C.R., et al.: Benchmarking TinyML systems: Challenges and direction. arXiv preprint 2003.04821 (2020)
11. Bhatti, N.A., Mottola, L.: HarvOS: efficient code instrumentation for transiently-powered embedded sensing. In: International Conference on Information Processing in Sensor Networks (IPSN) (2017)
12. Bhatti, N.A., et al.: Energy harvesting and wireless transfer in sensor network applications: concepts and experiences. ACM Trans. Sens. Netw. (2016)
13. Borghoff, J., et al.: PRINCE–a low-latency block cipher for pervasive computing applications. In: International Conference on the Theory and Application of Cryptology and Information Security (2012)
14. Boser, B., Guyon, I., Vapnik, V.: A training algorithm for optimal margin classifiers. In: Proceedings of the Workshop on Computational Learning Theory (1992)
15. Branco, A., et al.: Intermittent asynchronous peripheral operations. In: International Conference on Embedded Networked Sensor Systems (SENSYS) (2019)

16. Burns, A., Davis, R.I.: A survey of research into mixed criticality systems. ACM Comput. Surv. (CSUR) **50**(6) (2017)
17. Chandola, V., Banerjee, A., Kumar, V.: Anomaly detection: a survey. ACM Comput. Surv. (CSUR) **41**(3) (2009)
18. Chen, Q., et al.: Harvest energy from the water: a self-sustained wireless water quality sensing system. ACM Trans. Embed. Comput. Syst. (2017)
19. Chen, S., et al.: Power attack and detection technology in data centers: a survey. In: International Conference on Communications, Computing, Cybersecurity, and Informatics (CCCI) (2020)
20. Colin, A., et al.: A reconfigurable energy storage architecture for energy-harvesting devices. In: International Conference on Architectural Support for Programming Languages and Operating Systems (ASPLOS) (2018)
21. da Costa, K., et al.: Internet of Things: a survey on machine learning-based intrusion detection approaches. Comput. Netw. (2019)
22. David, R., et al.: TensorFlow lite micro: embedded machine learning for TinyML systems. Proc. Mach. Learn. Syst. **3** (2021)
23. Denby, B., et al.: Kodan: addressing the computational bottleneck in space. In: International Conference on Architectural Support for Programming Languages and Operating Systems (ASPLOS) (2023)
24. Dietterich, T.G.: Ensemble methods in machine learning. In: International Workshop on Multiple Classifier Systems. Springer (2000)
25. Furlong, M., et al.: Realistic simulation for tiny batteryless sensors. In: International Workshop on Energy Harvesting and Energy-Neutral Sensing Systems (ENSSYS) (2016)
26. Gay, D., et al.: The nesC language: a holistic approach to networked embedded systems. ACM SIGPLAN Notices (2003)
27. Geissdoerfer, K., Zimmerling, M.: Learning to communicate effectively between battery-free devices. In: USENIX Symposium on Networked Systems Design and Implementation (NSDI) (2022)
28. Ghodsi, Z., et al.: Optimal checkpointing for secure intermittently-powered IoT devices. In: International Conference on Computer-Aided Design (ICCAD) (2017)
29. Greenberg, A., Hamilton, J., Maltz, D.A., Patel, P.: The cost of a cloud: research problems in data center networks (2008)
30. Grisafi, M., Ammar, M., Yildirim, K.S., Crispo, B.: MPI: memory protection for intermittent computing. IEEE Trans. Inf. Forensics Secur. (2022)
31. Hester, J., Sorber, J.: Flicker: rapid prototyping for the batteryless Internet of Things. In: International Conference on Embedded Network Sensor Systems (2017)
32. Hoque, M.A., et al.: Modeling, profiling, and debugging the energy consumption of mobile devices. ACM Comput. Surv. (CSUR) (2015)
33. Ikeda, N., et al.: Soil-monitoring sensor powered by temperature difference between air and shallow underground soil. Int. Conf. Interact., Mob., Wearable Ubiquitous Technol. (IMWUT) (2020)
34. Jackson, N., et al.: Capacity over capacitance for reliable energy harvesting sensors. In: International Conference on Information Processing in Sensor Networks (IPSN) (2019)
35. Kanwar, J., et al.: JamSense: interference and jamming classification for low-power wireless networks. In: Wireless and Mobile Networking Conference (WMNC) (2021)
36. Krentz, K.F., et al.: Countering three denial-of-sleep attacks on ContikiMAC. In: International Conference on Embedded Wireless Systems and Networks (EWSN) (2017)

37. Krishnan, A., Schaumont, P.: Exploiting security vulnerabilities in intermittent computing. In: SPACE International Conference (2018)
38. Krishnan, A.S., Schaumont, P.: Benchmarking and configuring security levels in intermittent computing. ACM Trans. Embed. Comput. Syst. (2022)
39. Langley, P., Iba, W., Thompson, K., et al.: An analysis of bayesian classifiers. In: International AAAI Conference on Artificial Intelligence (1992)
40. Li, C., et al.: Power attack defense: securing battery-backed data centers. ACM SIGARCH Comput. Archit. News (2016)
41. Liu, F.T., et al.: Isolation forest. In: International Conference on Data Mining (2008)
42. Liu, H., et al.: Hybrid energy harvesting technology: From materials, structural design, system integration to applications. Renew. Sustain. Energy (2021)
43. Liu, Q., et al.: Safe and secure wireless power transfer networks: challenges and opportunities in RF-based systems. IEEE Commun. Mag. (2016)
44. Maeng, K., et al.: Alpaca: Intermittent execution without checkpoints. In: Proceedings of the ACM Programming Languages (2017)
45. Maioli, A., Mottola, L.: Intermittence anomalies not considered harmful. In: International Workshop on Energy Harvesting and Energy-neutral Sensing Systems (2020)
46. Maioli, A., Mottola, L.: Alfred: Virtual memory for intermittent computing. In: International Conference on Embedded Networked Sensor Systems (SENSYS) (2021)
47. Mohri, M., Rostamizadeh, A., Talwalkar, A.: Foundations of machine learning. MIT press (2018)
48. Mottola, L., et al.: Enabling scope-based interactions in sensor network macroprogramming. In: International Conference on Mobile Ad-hoc Sensor Systems (MASS) (2007)
49. Mottola, L., et al.: Energy attacks in the Battery-less Internet of Things: directions for the future. In: European Workshop on Systems Security (2024)
50. Naderi, M.Y., et al.: RF-MAC: a medium access control protocol for re-chargeable sensor networks powered by wireless energy harvesting. IEEE Trans. Wirel. Commun. (2014)
51. Nguyen, V.L., Lin, P.C., Hwang, R.H.: Energy depletion attacks in low power wireless networks. IEEE Access **7** (2019)
52. Portilla, J., et al.: Adaptable security in wireless sensor networks by using reconfigurable ECC hardware coprocessors. Int. J. Distrib. Sens. Netw. (2010)
53. Pradhan, A.: Support vector machine-a survey. Int. J. Emerg. Technol. Adv. Eng. **2**(8) (2012)
54. Ransford, B., et al.: Mementos: System support for long-running computation on RFID-scale devices. ACM SIGARCH Comput. Archit. News (2011)
55. Sample, A., et al.: Design of an RFID-based battery-free programmable sensing platform. IEEE Trans. Instrum. Measur. (2008)
56. Tahsien, S.M., et al.: Machine learning based solutions for security of Internet of Things (IoT): a survey. J. Netw. Comput. Appl. (2020)
57. Thakor, V.A., et al.: Lightweight cryptography algorithms for resource-constrained IoT devices: a review, comparison and research opportunities. IEEE Access (2021)
58. Udupa, S.K., et al.: Deobfuscation: reverse engineering obfuscated code. In: Working Conference on Reverse Engineering (WCRE) (2005)
59. Umesh, S., Mittal, S.: A survey of techniques for intermittent computing. J. Syst. Archit. **112** (2021)

60. Valea, E., et al.: SI ECCS: SECure context saving for IoT devices. In: International Conference on Design & Technology of Integrated Systems In Nanoscale Era (2018)
61. Van Der Woude, J., Hicks, M.: Intermittent computation without hardware support or programmer intervention. In: International Conference on Operating Systems Design and Implementation (OSDI) (2016)
62. Yildirim, K.S., et al.: InK: reactive kernel for tiny batteryless sensors. In: International Conference on Embedded Networked Sensor Systems (SENSYS) (2018)

Is Expert-Labeled Data Worth the Cost? Exploring Active and Semi-supervised Learning Across Imbalance Scenarios in Financial Crime Detection

Bahar Emami Afshar[1(✉)], Paula Branco[1], Tolga Kurt[2], Utku Gorkem Ketenci[2], and Hikmet Mazmanoglu[2]

[1] EECS, Faculty of Engineering, University of Ottawa, Ottawa, ON, Canada
bemam006@uottawa.ca

[2] H3M Analytics Inc., Montreal, QC, Canada

Abstract. The ongoing fight against financial crime and fraudulent activities is crucial to safeguarding privacy and security. Addressing this issue is critical for protecting global financial integrity and disrupting illicit attempts. Despite the potential of machine learning, its application in fraud detection encounters unique challenges including limited labels, extremely rare fraud cases, and a vast volume of instances. This is a challenging imbalance scenario where learners must rely solely on an exceptionally small set of labeled instances. Active learning and semi-supervised learning have been proposed to handle such situations. However, their effectiveness and usefulness in these scenarios where different resampling techniques can be applied have not been compared. This paper tackles this gap by conducting a comparative analysis of active and semi-supervised learning approaches for fraud detection. We investigate how the imbalance ratio affects their effectiveness and observe their sensitivity to different resampling techniques. Our results show that both frameworks improve fraud detection, even when the imbalance increases. Highly imbalanced datasets are more affected by different settings for requesting expert labeling than the less imbalanced. In less imbalanced domains, active learning tends to outperform others while in highly imbalanced domains, the performance differences are less pronounced. Applying sampling techniques and moderately adjusting the imbalance ratio improves performance across different subsets of the dataset.

Keywords: Fraud Detection · Active Learning · Semi-Supervised Learning

1 Introduction

Credit card fraud is a primary concern for banking institutions and a global security threat, as it can facilitate a wide range of illicit behaviors, such as identity theft. In the past, credit card fraud was simpler to detect, mainly involving thieves stealing credit cards and using them at ATMs or retail outlets to

K. Adi et al. (Eds.): FPS 2024, LNCS 15533, pp. 174–186, 2025.
https://doi.org/10.1007/978-3-031-87496-3_12

make unauthorized transactions. However, with the rise of electronic commerce, fraud has become more complex and sophisticated [14]. According to the Nilson Report, which monitors the card industry, payment card fraud led to $33 billion in losses worldwide in 2022, with $13.6 billion of those losses occurring in the United States[1]. Machine learning (ML) has shown its potential in detecting credit card fraud, but these approaches are usually supervised, and the challenge arises as obtaining labeled data is time-consuming and human-intensive. Given this challenge, we focus on active and semi-supervised strategies. The primary distinction between these two approaches lies in their interaction with the user. Active learning involves a human-in-the-loop system, requiring user interaction to obtain true labels for the most uncertain samples. In contrast, semi-supervised learning generates pseudo labels for the most certain samples. In an active learning setting, a budget is usually defined, representing the number of cases that the domain experts can review and manually label. The process of manual verification and labeling of examples in the dataset is costly, time-consuming, and limited. The budget represents exactly this limit associated with that task. We aim to determine whether the costly user interactions associated with active learning consistently yield better performance compared to semi-supervised learning in the domain of credit card fraud detection. Moreover, we will also observe how different budget configurations affect the results. While we focus on credit card fraud detection, the experimental approach we present can be applied to any imbalanced domain, including areas like malware detection, attack prediction, or any scenario where rare-case detection is critical. The use of active learning and semi-supervised learning, are well-suited for cases with limited and scarce labeled data. We also focus on other challenges typically present in credit card fraud detection scenarios. In particular, we consider the severe imbalance of datasets, which turns the problem into anomaly detection. To evaluate the robustness of the different models under an imbalanced setting we tested multiple resampling strategies in combination with the active and semi-supervised strategies. This will allow us to understand the combined impact of the learning methods and the resampling strategies in a fraud detection setting. In this paper, we conduct a comparative analysis between strategies that do not depend on a huge amount of labeled data-specifically, semi-supervised learning and active learning, which can be used with a limited set of labeled data. We implemented multiple active and semi-supervised learning solutions and tested them on 24 dataset subsets with varying degrees of imbalance. Moreover, we study the complex relationships between the different learning algorithms and the usage of multiple resampling techniques.

Our main contributions are as follows. (i) We provide a literature review focused on recent efforts to tackle credit card fraud detection using active learning and semi-supervised learning. This review identifies gaps in the current research and motivates our study, clarifying how our work addresses these gaps and contributes to the field; (ii) We carry out a comprehensive set of experiments

[1] https://www.financial-world.org/news/news/financial/26036/how-banks-are-winning-the-battle-against-credit-card-fraud/.

across 24 distinct imbalance subsets of two large, highly realistic datasets, to evaluate the effectiveness of various approaches across different imbalance domains and sampling techniques, considering multiple budget configurations such as the number of iterations and queries per iteration. Our analysis aims to assess the strengths and weaknesses of active learning versus semi-supervised learning, determining whether the costs associated with active learning are justified and whether it consistently outperforms semi-supervised learning.

This paper is organized as follows. Section 2 covers the background on active and semi-supervised learning, including a review of credit card fraud detection methods. Section 3 explains our methodology and experimental configurations. In Sect. 4, we discuss the results obtained, and Sect. 5 concludes this study.

2 Background and Related Work

2.1 Background

Active learning uses a human annotator or oracle to obtain true labels for specific instances it queries. In this study, we used a pool-based scenario to simulate the role of the human annotator, where the model selects the most optimal instances to be labeled from an unlabeled pool. We focused on two active learning querying strategies: uncertainty sampling and query by committee. In binary classification, uncertainty sampling queries the most uncertain instances, with their posterior probability of being positive closest to 0.5 [19,20]. Two uncertainty sampling variants are **Marginal Uncertainty Sampling**, which considers the margin between the first and second most probable class labels, and **Entropy Uncertainty Sampling**, which uses Shannon entropy as an uncertainty measure. **Query by Committee** involves a committee of different models trained on the labeled set, with each member voting on the labeling of query candidates. The most informative query is the instance with the most disagreement among the committee members. Semi-supervised learning can label data without human intervention. Self-training and co-training, are two well-known semi-supervised wrapping methods. **Self-Training** uses a single supervised classifier trained on the labeled data, adding instances to the training set whose posterior probability exceeds a threshold with the model's predicted labels. **Co-Training** extends self-training to multiple classifiers, each trained on multi-correlated views of the data. The most confident predictions of each classifier are added to the labeled set of another. In each iteration, instances on which all classifiers agree on the label are added to the labeled set.

2.2 Related Work

Several works have addressed the problem of credit card fraud detection. However, most of these works use supervised techniques, assuming that a sufficient volume of labeled data is available. Still, this is not true with real-world credit card scenarios where transactions are available but the true labels typically are not. Some works have explored active and semi-supervised learning methods.

Carcillo et al. [6] apply active learning to streaming transaction data, where investigators label a small subset of high-risk cardholders daily. Several active learning strategies are evaluated, including Highest Risk Querying, Exploratory Active Learning, and Stochastic Semi-Supervised Learning , along with multiple instance learning techniques like Querying by Frequent Uncertainty and a Combined Function. The paper highlights the importance of the exploration/exploitation trade-off in active learning for fraud detection, noting that unsupervised outlier detection performs poorly in scenarios with limited manual review. Druck et al. [13] focuses on labeling input features instead of instances by selecting features that offer significant feedback to reduce model uncertainty. Using generalized expectation criteria and a feature-based active learning algorithm, their approach outperforms several baselines.

In financial fraud detection, Lablanca et al. [17] introduce Amaretto, a hybrid active learning framework that combines unsupervised anomaly detection with supervised models using expert feedback. It addresses the cold-start problem and class imbalance, significantly improving detection performance. Barata et al. [3] present ODAL, an Outlier-based Discriminative Active Learning system for imbalanced datasets, achieving up to 80% better results than random sampling. Tang et al. [23] propose an ensemble-based deep active learning framework that integrates unsupervised and semi-supervised models, reducing false positives and outperforming benchmarks across multiple domains, including credit card fraud. ALLIE [12] is a framework for improving active learning on large-scale imbalanced graphs in financial fraud detection. It uses a reinforcement learning agent with an imbalance-aware reward function to efficiently sample from major and minor classes. It incorporates focal loss to boost accuracy for rare classes and uses graph coarsening to cut computational time by up to 38%. Niu et al. [21] found that supervised techniques for credit card fraud detection outperformed unsupervised ones, though the difference was not large. However, only one dataset and AUC scores were considered. Building on the idea that both methods can be useful, Carcillo et al. [7] proposed a hybrid approach, using unsupervised outlier scores to enhance a fraud classifier's features. This still requires a labeled dataset for supervised learning. Semi-supervised techniques are more commonly explored than active learning in credit card fraud detection. Several works (e.g., [18,24]) use graph-based methods, transforming transaction data into graphs for graph neural networks. Other studies explore semi-supervised methods combined with data augmentation [22], and in online gambling fraud detection, Generative Adversarial Networks have been applied [8].

Researchers have focused on supervised learning techniques for credit card fraud detection making use of the few existing public and labeled datasets on this domain. Semi-supervised and active learning are less explored even though they are more realistic from a practical point of view. Although comparisons between active and semi-supervised learning have been made (e.g., [1]), these works do not target the particular context of credit card fraud detection. Our work examines the strengths and weaknesses of semi-supervised and active learning, assessing their performance across various imbalanced scenarios.

3 Methodology

3.1 Learning Algorithms

To ensure a fair comparison we implemented similar algorithms for active and semi-supervised learning. For active learning, we used entropy-based uncertainty sampling, marginal uncertainty sampling, and Query by Committee (QBC). The QBC consisted of five models: Gaussian Naïve Bayes (NB) [4], Random Forest (RF) Classifier [5], Logistic Regression [11], Support Vector Classifier (SVC) [10], and Multilayer Perceptron (MLP) Classifier [15]. We measured the disagreement between the models' predictions using vote entropy (VE), defined as follows: $x^*_{VE} = \arg\max_x \left(-\sum_i \frac{V(y_i)}{C} \log \frac{V(y_i)}{C}\right)$, where y_i spans all possible labels, $V(y_i)$ denotes the number of "votes" received by a label among the committee members' predictions, and C represents the committee size. This method extends entropy-based uncertainty sampling to the QBC framework.

For semi-supervised learning, we implemented self-training and co-training. Given that active learning strategies are iterative, we incorporated this aspect in the semi-supervised algorithms. In self-training, at each iteration, we selected the most uncertain samples within our budget limit and generated their pseudo-labels. For co-training, we used the same set of five models: Gaussian NB, RF Classifier, Logistic Regression, SVC, and MLP Classifier. We created two random views of the data with an equal number of features. The first three models were trained on the first view, and the last two models were trained on the second view. We identified the most certain predictions where the total probabilities predicted by the five models exceeded 4.8, and we used the most frequent labels for these predictions as pseudo-labels.

We selected Random Forest (RF) and XGBoost (XGB) [9] as baselines because they are widely recognized tree-based ensemble models, known for their robustness and adaptability in various ML tasks. To further prioritize the minority group, we used the class weight parameter, helping the models emphasize the importance of the underrepresented class in fraud detection. To address the imbalance problem in each dataset and analyze the performance of our frameworks across various imbalance ratios, we employed random oversampling to double the number of fraud cases and random undersampling to halve the number of non-fraud cases. It is important to note that while we selected these two models and resampling techniques for consistency across our experiments, our approach can be extended to other ML models and resampling methods. Techniques like synthetic case generation, including the use of GANs and VAEs, can also be applied in such scenarios to further enhance the handling of class imbalance.

3.2 Dataset

We used two datasets designed for credit card fraud detection: the Card Transactions (CCT) [2] Dataset and the Bank Account Fraud (BAF) Dataset [16]. CCT contains around 24 million transactions from 2,000 synthetic U.S. customers over several decades, including about 33,000 fraudulent cases. Despite being synthetic, the dataset closely resembles real-world data in fraud rates, purchase amounts, and Merchant Category Codes (MCCs). To preprocess the data, we split it into training (25%), pool (50%), and test sets (25%) in a stratified manner. We dropped the 'Errors?' column due to missing values, imputed the rest, and encoded categorical columns using hashing. Each partition was normalized to have a mean of 0 and a standard deviation of 1. For feature selection, we removed noisy, redundant, or uninformative features based on correlation with the target and excluded personal details like card numbers and addresses, as they are irrelevant to fraud detection. This ensured the model could focus on meaningful relationships in the data, improving both performance and interpretability. This careful selection process plays a crucial role in reducing noise, speeding up model training, and ultimately enhancing the quality of the predictions. We engineered new features, including total purchase amount and transaction count per merchant, and the number of cards used by each user. The final dataset has 34 features, with 14 categorical features encoded numerically.

The BAF dataset, consisting of six synthetic bank account fraud datasets, provides a realistic and reliable test bed for evaluating ML algorithms and is built on a contemporary, real-world dataset. We used the base dataset, with 1 million records and 11,029 fraud cases. The data was split into train, pool, and test sets using the same stratified percentages. With no NaN values, categorical columns were hashed into numerical representations and normalized to a mean of 0 and standard deviation of 1. We used XGBoost to identify and remove features with zero importance, retaining only impactful ones. Unlike the CCT dataset, no extra aggregated features were created, due to the differences in available information. The final BAF dataset includes 30 features, 5 of which are categorical and numerically encoded. The predictive task for both datasets is binary, indicating whether a transaction is fraudulent. To simulate real-world conditions, we used imbalance ratios provided by our industry partner H3M: low (0.21), medium (0.077), and extremely high (0.000048), along with the original ratio of each dataset. We created four random subsets without replacement and tested how Random Under Sampling (US) and Random Over Sampling (OS) impacted results. We undersampled by halving non-fraudulent cases and oversampled by doubling fraudulent ones. Table 1 shows key characteristics of our training datasets.

3.3 Evaluation Methodology

We observed a set of performance metrics including accuracy, F1 score, precision, and recall, and focused on F1 score and recall, as failing to detect false negatives can be costly. We addressed two sets of hyperparameters: the internal hyperparameters of the baseline models and the external hyperparameters of our frameworks. For baseline hyperparameter tuning, we used 5-fold cross-validation with grid search. The hyperparameters explored during the tuning phase are detailed in the GitHub repository that can be accessed through Sect. 4. Once fine-tuned,

Table 1. Main characteristics of the training datasets used.

CCT Dataset	Size	IR	Fraud Cases	BAF Dataset	Size	IR	Fraud Cases
Low	28300	0.21	5943	Low	12100	0.21	2542
Low - US	17121	0.34	5943	Low - US	7322	0.34	2542
Low - OS	34243	0.34	11886	Low - OS	14643	0.34	5084
Med	28300	0.077	2180	Med	12100	0.077	932
Med - US	15241	0.14	2180	Med - US	6516	0.14	932
Med - OS	30480	0.14	4360	Med - OS	13032	0.14	1864
XHigh	28300	0.000048	2	XHigh	12100	0.000048	1
XHigh - US	14151	0.00014	2	XHigh - US	6050	0.00016	1
XHigh - OS	28302	0.00014	4	XHigh - OS	12101	0.00016	2
ORG	40239	0.0014	55	ORG	12100	0.01102	134
ORG - US	20148	0.0027	55	ORG - US	6117	0.021	134
ORG - OS	40294	0.0027	110	ORG - OS	12234	0.021	268

these models were integrated into our active learning and semi-supervised learning frameworks. The external hyperparameters for active learning and semi-supervised learning included the number of iterations and the number of queries per iteration. To simulate real-world situations where labeled data is costly, we limited our labeling budget to 1,500 instances, using it in five sets of different experiments as follows: (1) 300 queries per iteration over 5 iterations; (2) 150 queries per iteration over 10 iterations; (3) 100 queries per iteration over 15 iterations; (4) 75 queries per iteration over 20 iterations; (5) 60 queries per iteration over 25 iterations. This allowed us to evaluate the performance of our models under various query and iteration conditions, reflecting practical constraints on data labeling.

4 Result and Discussion

We used 2 baseline models across 24 generated datasets with varying imbalances, applying 5 active and semi-supervised learning algorithms with 5 budget configurations. Due to space constraints, the full results can be found in the GitHub repository https://github.com/beafshar/AL_vs_SSL_Extreme_Imbalance.

4.1 Experimental Results

Our main experimental results for F1 score and recall across different imbalance domains are presented in Figs. 1 to 4. Figure 1 shows the average F1 score over different budget configurations within their intervals for the five implemented algorithms compared to the fine-tuning model on undersampled, oversampled, and normal datasets with no sampling across various imbalance ratios. Due to space constraints, we have included figures for the BAF dataset only. Results for

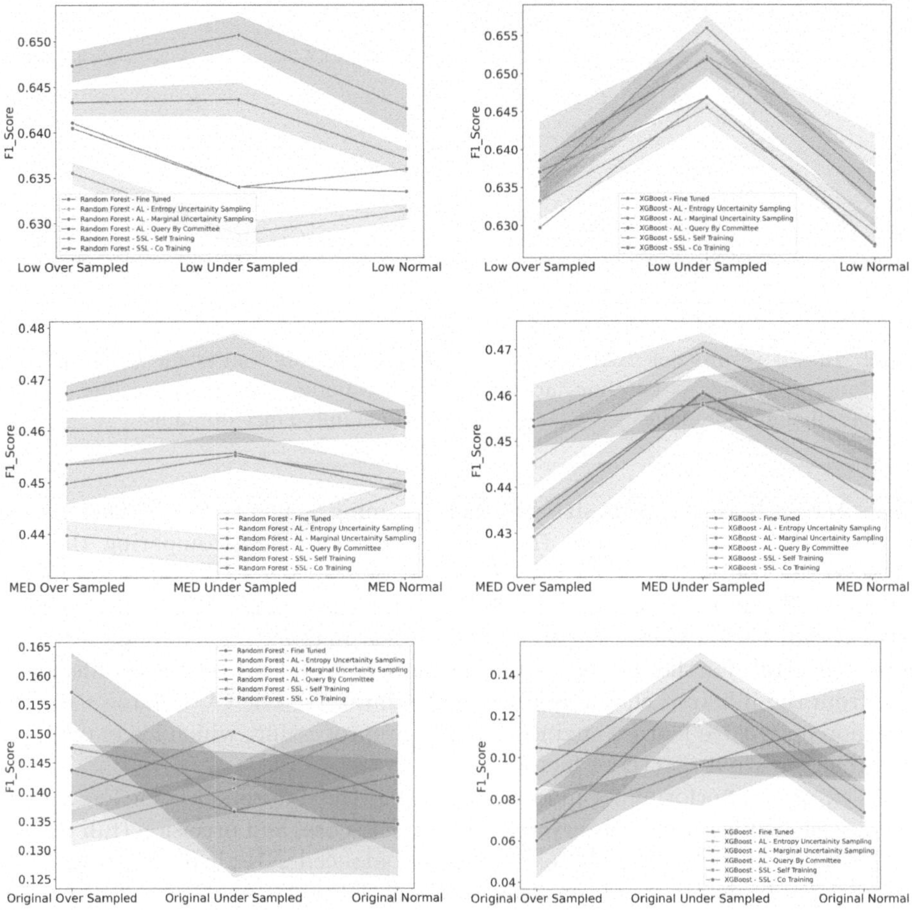

Fig. 1. Experimental results for BAF dataset across different imbalance ratios.

the CCT dataset are available on our GitHub repository. For the less imbalanced scenarios (Low and Med), active learning methods outperform semi-supervised approaches in F1_score, while the latter fails to surpass baselines. However, in more imbalanced datasets, the trend reverses. On the BAF dataset with RF as the baseline, SSL-Co-Training performs best on the undersampled data, improving the F1 score by 1%. For the CCT dataset, all five algorithms perform similarly on low-imbalanced data, but XGBoost-AL-Marginal Uncertainty stands out with an 88% F1_score, 10% higher than the fine-tuned model.

Figures 2 and 3 show recall changes across different imbalance ratios for five algorithms with various budgets, using RF as the baseline for BAF and CCT datasets. When prioritizing recall to reduce false negatives in imbalanced domains, semi-supervised methods outperform active learning, especially in low to medium imbalance scenarios. The improvements are greater with undersam-

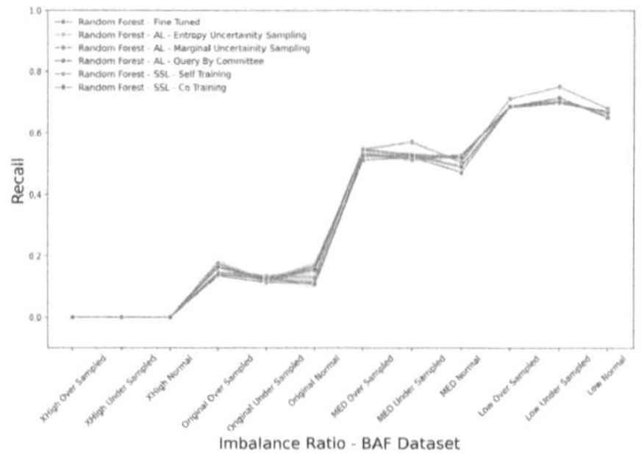

Fig. 2. Recall results for BAF dataset and Random Forest as baseline, across various imbalance domains.

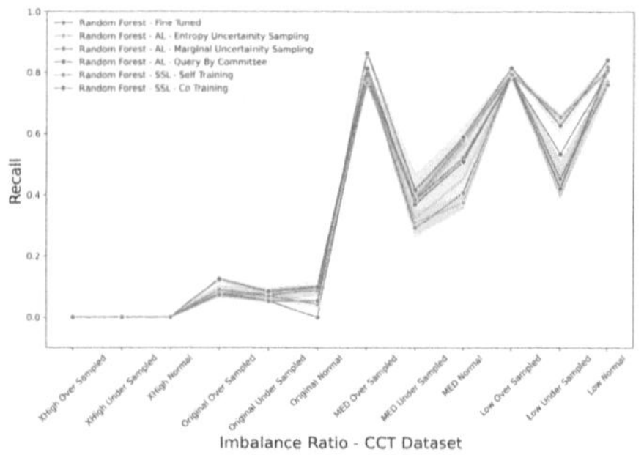

Fig. 3. Recall results for CCT dataset and Random Forest as baseline, across various imbalance domains.

pling. Across both datasets, RF-SSL-Self Training achieves the highest recall, improving by 5% to 10% over the RF-Finetuned model. Comparing the two datasets, the tradeoff between iterations and queries per iteration is more crucial for CCT, as its range of changes is wider than BAF. While BAF shows stable recall, CCT exhibits greater fluctuations, making the sampling strategy more impactful. Further analysis of other models revealed that these differences arise from the inherent characteristics of the datasets. The CCT dataset undergoes more extensive feature engineering and preprocessing, which likely explains its higher sensitivity to these factors.

As expected, performance metrics improve as the datasets become less imbalanced, with similar trends observed for recall, F1 score, and precision (full results available on GitHub). For the extremely imbalanced XHigh dataset, all algorithms failed to detect fraud, resulting in recall, F1, and precision of 0. With the BAF original imbalance, recall averages around 14%, 50% for medium imbalance, and 75% for low imbalance. For recall, oversampling performed best on the CCT dataset, despite introducing duplicates, while undersampling was optimal for the BAF dataset in low and medium imbalance domains. For RF as the datasets became less imbalanced, recall fluctuations across algorithms increased. This trend is consistent across both datasets.

Improvements were more significant on the CCT dataset, likely due to its more extensive preprocessing, additional features, and larger labeled data. Despite the CCT original dataset being 8 times more imbalanced than BAF, it showed a 7% F1 score improvement, while BAF saw only a 2% improvement. In the low imbalance scenario, CCT's oversampled dataset achieved an average F1 score of 77%, while BAF's best-performing algorithm, AL-Query by Committee, reached 64%. As datasets become more imbalanced, the range of F1 score changes across budget configurations widens, indicating that for less imbalanced datasets, configurations yield similar results, while for more imbalanced datasets, the choice of iterations and queries per iteration is crucial for efficient budget use. This behavior can be seen in Figs. 2 and 3. As shown in Fig. 4 the results are consistent across iterations for the Low and Medium imbalance datasets, but the Original dataset, being more imbalanced, shows greater fluctuations. In this dataset, optimal performance is typically achieved with medium iterations (15–20), rather than extreme values (5 or 25).

Active learning and semi-supervised learning effectively detect credit card fraud with limited labeled data. Sampling techniques, such as random oversampling and undersampling, improved F1 score by 2% to 15%. Semi-supervised learning, in particular, enhanced recall, suggesting it may be a better alternative to the resource-intensive and time-consuming active learning in some cases.

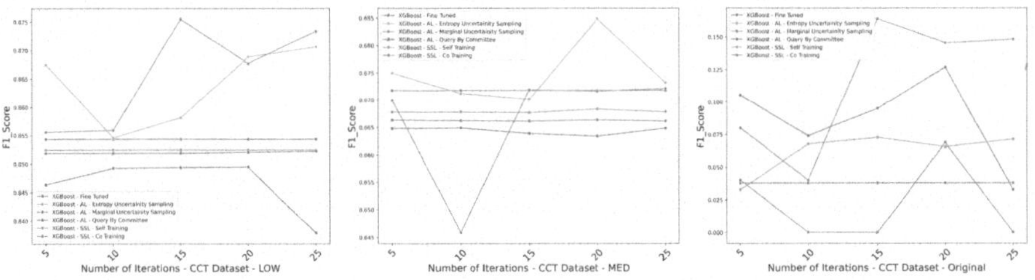

Fig. 4. Results per number of iterations used in each algorithm for CCT dataset across different imbalance ratios with no resampling (baseline: XGBoost).

4.2 Limitation and Guidelines

Limitations: This study focused on two sampling strategies; exploring more techniques and imbalance ratios could yield deeper insights. While we used two synthetic datasets and 24 subsets, incorporating more diverse datasets would help validate the framework. We only tested Random Forest and XGBoost, representing a bagging and a boosting ensemble; including more models would provide a better assessment of active learning and semi-supervised strategies. This study compared active learning and semi-supervised learning using the most comparable algorithms, such as uncertainty sampling vs. self-training, and QBC vs. co-training. Future work will explore advanced, computationally intensive semi-supervised methods like Graph-based Semi-Supervised Learning (GSSL) and Generative Adversarial Networks (GANs).

Guidelines and Lessons Learned: The impact of different budget configurations on the F1 score becomes more pronounced as the datasets become more imbalanced (Fig. 4). For highly imbalanced datasets optimal performance appears to occur at medium iterations. Given the increased sensitivity of these imbalanced domains to the budget settings, it is crucial to analyze various configurations to determine the optimal setup. For the BAF dataset and RF model, both AL-Entropy and AL-Marginal Uncertainty Sampling selected the same indices in each iteration, resulting in similar performance. This was not observed with other models or datasets, suggesting that the most uncertain samples were identical. To differentiate these approaches, additional feature engineering and preprocessing with aggregate features may be helpful. For the extremely imbalanced dataset, none of the algorithms detected fraud, resulting in zero performance. In such cases, unsupervised anomaly detection methods are typically more effective than active or semi-supervised learning, which rely on limited labeled data. Traditional methods like undersampling and oversampling have limited effectiveness. A more promising solution for these scenarios is to employ synthetic data generation and data augmentation techniques, such as GANs and Variational Autoencoders (VAEs). These methods can produce large volumes of high-dimensional data, but they are computationally expensive.

5 Conclusion

This paper compares active and semi-supervised learning effectiveness across different imbalance ratios using various sampling techniques. Our results indicate that the effectiveness of these approaches depends on the imbalance ratio. In less imbalanced domains, active learning strategies achieved the highest F1 scores, demonstrating their overall effectiveness. However, semi-supervised approaches excelled in recall, which is a crucial metric for imbalanced datasets, as it focuses on minimizing false negatives and ensuring better detection of rare instances. In highly imbalanced domains, the differences between these approaches were less significant, with semi-supervised approaches occasionally outperforming the others. This suggests that active learning, being resource-intensive and time-consuming, should be chosen carefully, as semi-supervised learning can often offer a more efficient and equally effective alternative. As expected, as the datasets became more imbalanced, both F1 score and recall dropped. We found that using sampling techniques and modestly increasing the imbalance ratio could improve performance on any subset of the dataset. Nevertheless, detecting fraudulent cases in extremely high imbalance datasets remains a challenge that requires unsupervised anomaly detection techniques. The budget configuration must be carefully selected, especially for highly imbalanced datasets, where the impact of budget utilization becomes more significant.

In the future, we aim to combine these two frameworks with a dynamic threshold to leverage the strengths of both. We also plan to address highly imbalanced scenarios using advanced data augmentation techniques, such as GANs, and explore more sophisticated, graph-based algorithms within both semi-supervised and active learning strategies.

References

1. Afshar, B.E., Branco, P., Kurt, T., Ketenci, U.G., Mazmanoglu, H.: To label or to pseudo label? Active learning vs semi-supervised learning for windows malware prediction. Proc. Can. Conf. Artif. Intell. (2024)
2. Altman, E., Nitsure, A., Mroueh, Y.: Credit card transactions fraud detection and other analyses (2019). https://www.kaggle.com/datasets/ealtman2019/credit-card-transactions. Accessed 20 Jun 2024
3. Barata, R., Leite, M., Pacheco, R., Sampaio, M.O., Ascensão, J.T., Bizarro, P.: Active learning for imbalanced data under cold start. In: Proceedings of the Second ACM International Conference on AI in Finance, pp. 1–9 (2021)
4. Bishop, C.M., Nasrabadi, N.M.: Pattern recognition and machine learning, vol. 4. Springer (2006)
5. Breiman, L.: Random forests. Mach. Learn. **45**, 5–32 (2001)
6. Carcillo, F., Le Borgne, Y.A., Caelen, O., Bontempi, G.: Streaming active learning strategies for real-life credit card fraud detection: assessment and visualization. Int. J. Data Sci. Anal. **5**, 285–300 (2018)
7. Carcillo, F., Le Borgne, Y.A., Caelen, O., Kessaci, Y., Oblé, F., Bontempi, G.: Combining unsupervised and supervised learning in credit card fraud detection. Inf. Sci. **557**, 317–331 (2021)
8. Charitou, C., Garcez, A.d., Dragicevic, S.: Semi-supervised GANs for fraud detection. In: 2020 IJCNN, pp. 1–8. IEEE (2020)
9. Chen, T., Guestrin, C.: XGBoost: a scalable tree boosting system. In: Proceedings of the 22nd ACM SIGKDD International Conference on Knowledge Discovery and Data Mining, pp. 785–794 (2016)
10. Cortes, C., Vapnik, V.: Support-vector networks. Mach. Learn. **20**(3), 273–297 (1995)
11. Cox, D.R.: The regression analysis of binary sequences. J. Roy. Stat. Soc.: Ser. B (Methodol.) **20**(2), 215–232 (1958)
12. Cui, L., et al.: ALLIE: active learning on large-scale imbalanced graphs. In: Proceedings of the ACM Web Conference 2022, pp. 690–698 (2022)
13. Druck, G., Settles, B., McCallum, A.: Active learning by labeling features. In: Proceedings of the 2009 Conference on Empirical Methods in Natural Language Processing, pp. 81–90 (2009)
14. Hartstein, A.: What is credit card fraud detection? (2023). https://www.nerdwallet.com/au/credit-cards/credit-card-fraud-detection. Accessed 25 Jun 2024
15. Haykin, S.: Neural networks: a comprehensive foundation. Prentice Hall PTR (1994)
16. Jesus, S., et al.: Turning the tables: biased, imbalanced, dynamic tabular datasets for ML evaluation. Adv. Neural Inf. Process. Syst. (2022)
17. Labanca, D., Primerano, L., Markland-Montgomery, M., Polino, M., Carminati, M., Zanero, S.: Amaretto: an active learning framework for money laundering detection. IEEE Access **10**, 41720–41739 (2022)
18. Lebichot, B., Braun, F., Caelen, O., Saerens, M.: A graph-based, semi-supervised, credit card fraud detection system. In: International Workshop on Complex Networks and their Applications, pp. 721–733. Springer (2016)
19. Lewis, D.D.: A sequential algorithm for training text classifiers: corrigendum and additional data. In: ACM SIGIR Forum. vol. 29, pp. 13–19. ACM New York, NY, USA (1995)

20. Lewis, D.D., Catlett, J.: Heterogeneous uncertainty sampling for supervised learning. In: Machine Learning Proceedings 1994, pp. 148–156. Elsevier (1994)
21. Niu, X., Wang, L., Yang, X.: A comparison study of credit card fraud detection: Supervised versus unsupervised. arXiv preprint arXiv:1904.10604 (2019)
22. Salazar, A., Safont, G., Vergara, L.: Semi-supervised learning for imbalanced classification of credit card transaction. In: 2018 International Joint Conference on Neural Networks (IJCNN), pp. 1–7. IEEE (2018)
23. Tang, X., Astle, Y.S., Freeman, C.: Deep anomaly detection with ensemble-based active learning. In: 2020 IEEE International Conference on Big Data (Big Data), pp. 1663–1670 (2020). https://doi.org/10.1109/BigData50022.2020.9378315
24. Xiang, S., et al.: Semi-supervised credit card fraud detection via attribute-driven graph representation. In: Proceedings of the AAAI Conference on Artificial Intelligence. vol. 37, pp. 14557–14565 (2023)

ExploitabilityBirthMark: An Early Predictor of the Likelihood of Exploitation

Kobra Khanmohammadi[1], Zakeya Namrud[2], François Labrèche[3], and Raphaël Khoury[2(✉)]

[1] Sheridan College, Toronto, Ontario, Canada
kobra.khanmohammadi@sheridancollege.ca
[2] Université du Quebec en Outaouais, Gatineau, Quebec, Canada
raphael.khoury@uqo.ca, zknamrud@gmail.com
[3] Sophos, Montreal, Quebec, Canada
Francois.Labreche@sophos.com

Abstract. In recent years, there has been a steady increase in the number of reported vulnerabilities (CVEs), increasing the workload of organizations trying to update their systems promptly. This underscores the need to prioritize specific critical vulnerabilities over others to effectively prevent cyberattacks. Unfortunately, the current methods available for assessing the exploitability of vulnerabilities have substantial shortcomings. In particular, they often consist in prediction models that encode data that may not be immediately available at the time a vulnerability is first reported. In this paper, we introduce an innovative exploitability prediction method that exclusively uses information accessible at the time of a CVE's initial publication. Our approach outperforms the most widely used vulnerability exploit prediction algorithms in scenarios where data is subject to the aforementioned limitations.

1 Introduction

The National Vulnerability Database (NVD)[1] stands as a reliable and free resource, dedicated to compiling and publishing a comprehensive list of vulnerabilities, with a commitment to refreshing the data every two hours. Numerous products leverage this resource as a data provider for managing vulnerabilities. Companies, in turn, utilize these products to safeguard their systems, addressing risks and applying necessary patches.

In line with their commitment to safeguarding customer data against cyberthreats, companies are obliged to address vulnerabilities in accordance with their Service Level Agreements (SLAs) with customers. They rely heavily on reports from the NVD and other similar tools to gauge the severity of vulnerabilities. However, the large number of vulnerabilities that are discovered and published each day (an average of 176.5 in 2023), imposes an obligation on organisations to prioritize some vulnerabilities over others. Thus, they must

[1] https://nvd.nist.gov/.

K. Adi et al. (Eds.): FPS 2024, LNCS 15533, pp. 187–199, 2025.
https://doi.org/10.1007/978-3-031-87496-3_13

have a mechanism to identify the vulnerabilities most critical to fix. Additionally, a newly published vulnerability might be present on tens or even hundreds of systems in a company, significantly increasing the number of patches to apply.

A number of solutions have thus been suggested to rank vulnerabilities according to their *exploitability*, i.e., according to the probability that the vulnerability will be actively exploited by malicious agents. Indeed, recent research shows that less than 2% of vulnerabilities are ever actively exploited [3,10].

Most of these solutions are ML-based approaches that assign an exploitability score to each vulnerability according to different features extracted from the CVE report, such as the vulnerability's CVSS score or its Common Platform Enumerations (CPE) which lists the affected software.

However, recent research by Khanmohammadi et al. [7] shows that this data is often unavailable on the day a vulnerability is published, and is only aggregated into the report in the day or weeks that follow. For example, about 60% of CVE are initially published without a CVSS score, while 97% initially lack a CPE list. Several days often elapse before this information is incorporated in the CVE report. Other data used for predictions, such as links to known exploit code or activity on the dark web, become available even later, at a time when adversaries have already taken interest in the vulnerability.

The predictors naturally underperform if they are deprived of the information upon which they rely. Such models show great performance when applied to historical data, but perform poorly on new samples when used in a live context.

To address this gap, we propose ExploitabilityBirthMark, a novel vulnerability exploitability prediction algorithm that relies exclusively on information that is certain to be available on the initial day of publication of a CVE report. This score can provide an initial assessment of the likelihood of exploitation of a vulnerability, even if the CVE report is missing key information.

The need for a solution that bypasses metadata from CVE records is made even more pressing by the fact that in February and March 2024, the suspended reporting of CVSS scores, CPEs and CWEs temporarily, citing "working to establish a consortium to address challenges in the NVD program and develop improved tools and methods" as the reason [9]. Although this is a temporary situation, the fact that lapses in the availability of this type of data may occur further highlights the need for the solution we advocate in this paper.

To facilitate this task, we have expanded the existing dataset of daily vulnerability reports downloaded from the National Vulnerability Database (NVD) provided by Khanmohammadi et al. [7], now encompassing data from November 2022 to November 2023.

The contributions of our work are outlined as follows:

- We propose a data-driven methodology to forecast the exploitability of vulnerabilities using only the information available on the initial day of publication. This includes data reported by NVD and additional data sourced from both public and commercial resources.
- We propose a methodology to extract the vendor and product from a vulnerability summary, thus palliating the absence of a CPE in a vulnerability report for any application where vendors and products are needed.

The remainder of this paper is organized as follows: Sect. 2 surveys prior research on this topic. Section 3 describes the two datasets that serve as the basis for this study. An analysis of these datasets, which highlights the limitations of existing vulnerability predictors, is presented in Sect. 4. Section 5 presents our exploitability prediction method. Concluding remarks are given in Sect. 6.

2 Related Works

The most widely used exploitability predictability metric is EPSS, a collaborative metric developed by resources from the Cyena institute, the Rand corporations, amongst others. EPSS v.2, published in 2022 [5], is computed from 16 features, including 7 names of vendors, taken from the CPE field of the CVE report, 6 tags that capture the presence of keywords in the CVE report's description section or in the associated links, and the log of the number of links in the references section of the report. The other two features indicate whether or not there exists a Proof of concept for the exploitation of this vulnerability, and whether exploit code already exists.

An improved version, EPSS v.3 was released in 2023 [6]. EPSS v.3 is computed from 1,477 features, of which the most impactful ones are whether or not there already exists an exploit proof of concept or attack code. Other features include the vulnerability's CVSS score, CWE categorizations, 146 keywords from the vulnerability's description and over 1000 vendors, extracted from the CPE. The EPSS v.3 score also considers the presence of chatter about this vulnerability on social media, as well as whether or not the vulnerability is being used by offensive vulnerability pentesting tools.

Naturally, much of this information is likely to be unavailable on the initial day a vulnerability is discovered, and only accrues slowly in the days and even months after the initial publication of the discovery. Our research shows that EPSS underperforms if the information it relies upon is unavailable.

Unlike the solution proposed in this paper, EPSS is meant to provide a dynamic rating of exploitability, which evolves as new information is made available. The EPSS rating takes into account the age of the vulnerability, and reflects the probability that a vulnerability will be exploited in the next 90 days. As new information that makes this more likely becomes available, the EPSS rating of the vulnerability increases. By contrast, we propose a static metric, available on its release date, that predicts if a vulnerability will eventually be exploited.

A number of researchers have sought to provide alternatives to EPSS. Younis et al. [12] suggest bypassing the CVE report entirely, and propose a vulnerability exploitation metric called Structural Severity, which is derived from an analysis of the underlying code. Their analysis takes into account factors such as dangerous system calls and readability analysis.

Bhatt et al. [2] predict the likelihood of exploitability of vulnerabilities using a classification method that depends exclusively upon information contained in the CVE reports. Using three repositories as ground truth of exploitation: (Exploit Database, Zero Day Initiative, and Dark Web), they obtain 85% accuracy of classification.

Similarly, Labrèche et al. [8] predict if an exploit will be published for a vulnerability, or if a vulnerability will be used in malware. They train an LDA model on vulnerability descriptions and achieve high recall and accuracy.

In a 2015 thesis, Edkrantz [4] applies a variety of machine learning algorithms to this task, again employing data present in the CVE report as the basis for classification, and data from three public databases (exploitDB, milw0rm and metasploit) as ground truth. They obtained 83% accuracy of classification, and observed minimal differences between the different algorithms. u

Alperin et al. [1] obtained similar accuracy when performing classification based upon a feature set derived from different parts of the CVE report, including its description, CVSS score and vector and CPE, and again using the vulnerability's presence in exploit-DB as ground truth. Noting that a vulnerability's presence in exploit-DB may not be proof of exploitation, they improve their model by incorporating threat reports from a specific adversary into their model.

In order to circumvent potential false negatives in the ground truth data, Suciu et al. [11] developed the Expected Exploitability, a metric indicating how likely it is that attack code will be developed for a given vulnerability. As discussed above, this feature is the single most determining factor in EPSS's own determination or whether or not a vulnerability will be exploited. Their classification is based both on data gathered from the CVE reports, as well as data gathered from an analysis of published exploits.

There are two main takeaways from the analysis of previous work in this section. First, existing works overwhelmingly base their analysis on information that is often unavailable at the initial time of vulnerability disclosure. Second, there is no agreement on what constitutes "ground truth" w.r.t. whether or not a vulnerability is exploited. In particular, a number of studies view the existence of attack code in public sources as evidence that the vulnerability is actively exploited, while EPSS uses this fact as a feature that predicts possible future exploitation. Table 1 summarizes existing methods for exploitability prediction, and compares them to the method proposed in this paper.

3 Datasets

Throughout this paper, our analysis is grounded in two distinct datasets of vulnerabilities.

Day-1 Vulnerability Dataset: The primary dataset encompasses the initial daily vulnerability reports issued by the National Vulnerability Database (NVD). We systematically compiled this dataset by downloading the NVD's modified vulnerability list at midnight every day, for a period of 1 year, spanning from November 2022 to November 2023. An empirical study has been done by Khanmohammadi et al. [7] based on three months of data from June to August 2021. The findings from that study indicate that on the day they are published, vulnerability reports often lack crucial information, such as the CVSS score.

This observation motivates us to devise a methodology to predict a vulnerability's exploitability, even when limited information is available.

Table 1. Comparing our work to existing Methods for Vulnerabilities Exploitability Prediction.

Study	Summary	Vendors & Products	CVSS score	References	Exploit Code of PoC	CWE	Other	Ground Truth
Availability day-1	100%	3%	36%	100%	6.2%	1%	—	NVD
EPSS v.2 [5]	●	●	○	●	●	○		Fortinet, AlienVault, Shadowserver, GreyNoise
EPSS v.3 [6]	●	●	●	●	●	●	Chatter on SS, detection via security tools, age	Fortinet, AlienVault, Shadowserver, GreyNoise
Yourniss et al. [12]	○	○	○	○	○	●	code analysis	NVD, Apache HTTP server bug repository
Bhatt et al. [2]	○	○	●	○	○	●	Software class	Exploit Database, Zero Day Initiative, and Dark Web
Labreche et al. [8]	●	●	●	●	◑[1]	○		Exploit Database, Packetstorm, Github POCs, ClamAV, Secureworks
Edkratz [4]	●	●	●	●	●	●[2]		Exploit Database
Alperin et al. [1]	●	●	●	○	○	○		Exploit Database
Suciu et al. [11]	●	●	○	○	○	○		Exploit Database, Bugtraq, and Vulners
Proposed approach	●	●[3]	○	○	○	○	Wikipedia, Open Source	Greynoise, ClamAV, Secureworks, and CISA

[1] Only used for predicting malware
[2] CWE derived in part from CAPEC.
[3] Vendor and product extracted from the summary.

To ensure the quality of our dataset, we implemented a cleaning process to remove reports for which the summary indicated that the CVE had been rejected, or was invalid or disputed. Out of the 440,140 CVE reports in the Day-1 vulnerability dataset, 16,233 reports were identified as needing removal because they were rejected, disputed, unsupported, or invalid.

2020 NVD Vulnerability Dataset: Additionally, we conducted an analysis on a dataset of vulnerabilities reported by the NVD in 2020. The reason for focusing on a slightly older dataset is that it often takes time for attackers to exploit a given vulnerability. Furthermore, there is a delay before such exploitation attempts are detected and reported by cybersecurity tools, such as Greynoise. Consequently, it is still uncertain which of the vulnerabilities published in 2022 or 2023 will eventually be exploited, meaning that recent data lacks a trustworthy ground truth of exploitability. By focusing our study on the 2020 NVD vulnerability dataset, we ensure that we have access to at least three years' worth of reports on the exploitation of these vulnerabilities, grounding our analysis on a robust foundation.

We also sought to determine whether the vulnerabilities have been actively exploited in the wild, as merely uncovering the existence of an exploit script for a vulnerability does not suffice as ground truth for exploitability. Confirming the actual exploitation of a vulnerability by attackers is crucial. To this end, we used four resources: Greynoise, ClamAV, Secureworks, and CISA, to identify the vulnerabilities from the NVD 2020 dataset that have been exploited.

In total, 705 out of the 20,160 vulnerabilities (3.4%) reported in 2020 have been exploited, showcasing the extent of active exploitation across the cyber landscape.

An analysis of this data yields a few insights. Notably, the CVSS scores alone, even if they were consistently present in CVE reports, are not sufficient to predict the exploitability of vulnerabilities. Indeed, only fixing vulnerabilities with a high severity score or a high exploitability score would not address all exploited vulnerabilities and may also lead to a number of unexploited vulnerabilities being prioritized for patching. Other CVSS metrics exhibit the same pattern of high similarity between exploited and non-exploited vulnerabilities.

4 Analysis of the Dataset

We extended the previous study by Khanmohammadi et al. [7], applying the same methodologies to the Day-1 Vulnerability dataset, but considering a full year's worth of data. The results indicate that, on average, a CVE report will be updated 11 times after its initial publication. Out of the 466,807 vulnerability reports examined, 99,049 reports (21%) have identical published and last modified dates, leading us to categorize them as the *initial reports* for their respective vulnerabilities. Within this subset of initial reports, a staggering 89,076 ($\sim$ 90%) were published without an accompanying CVSS score. Furthermore, less than 1% of these initial reports (902 out of 99,049) contained CPEs, which are crucial for identifying the products affected by the reported vulnerabilities. Every report did contain a summary description and a source. The summary is a concise description of the vulnerability, detailing its nature, potential impact, and any other pertinent information that can provide insights into the vulnerability's characteristics and potential exploitability. The source identifies the entity which reported the vulnerability.

Each CVE report also includes a "References" section which lists hyperlinks to resources that discuss the vulnerability in more detail. Each hyperlink is assigned a *resource tags* describing the content of the link (e.g., source code, exploit, etc.). Prior research has leveraged the reference links and data extracted from them as features in machine learning algorithms 2, as part of exploitability prediction. However, our analysis shows that on the initial day of publication, CVE reports usually include a single reference, often a third party advisory, and only 1,507 out of 23,971 reports (6.2%) include a resource tag.

In order to measure the impact of this paucity of information on exploit prediction, we replicated the EPSS v.2 methodology, as described in [5], applying it to all vulnerabilities reported in 2020. However, we excluded from the analysis information that is usually absent on the initial day of publication of a vulnerability, such as CPE, references, and reference tags. We refer to this metric as the Day-1 EPSS score.

Strikingly, our findings present a stark contrast with those depicted in Fig. 4 of the EPSS v.2 paper [5]. Indeed, the model is deprived of too much information and cannot accurately predict exploitation. Consequently, the distinction between the two classes is not as pronounced. This discrepancy highlights the challenges and potential inaccuracies that may arise when predicting exploitability scores based on limited initial data.

Figure 1 plots the cumulative number of exploited CVEs (according to our label), and allows us to measure the effectiveness of Day-1 EPSS as a function of effort—the percentage of CVEs that are patched, vs coverage— the percentage of exploited CVEs that are patched. With this, patching the top 15% vulnerabilities with the highest Day-1 EPSS score (effort = 15%) would result in only about 28% of exploited vulnerabilities being treated. The corresponding figure for EPSS (with complete data) is 69.9% [6]. Even an effort of 40% only achieves a coverage of 50%, instead of the expected 84.7%. These results clearly motivate the need for an exploitability predictor that is more resilient to limited data.

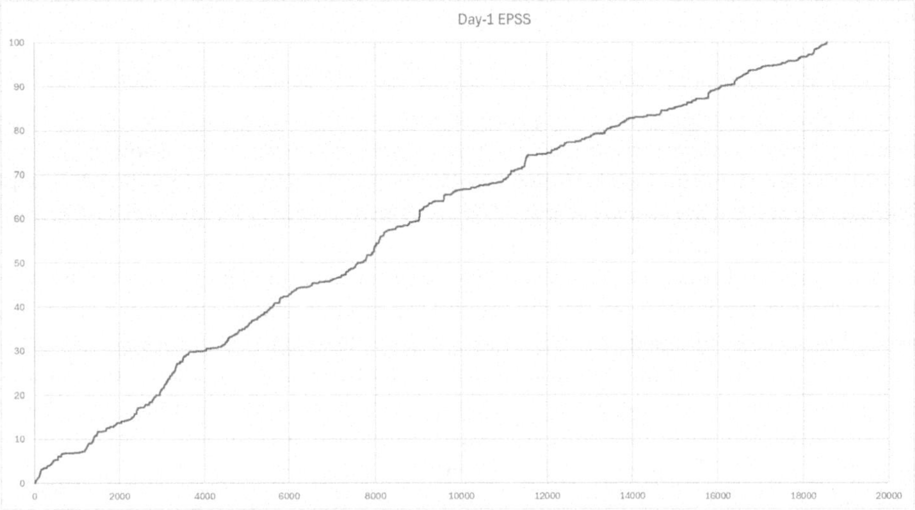

Fig. 1. Cumulative Effort Efficiency of Day-1 EPSS.

5 Prediction of Exploitability with Partial Data

In this section, we introduce ExploitabilityBirthMark, a novel method to predict the exploitability of a vulnerability that relies exclusively upon data that is likely to be available on the day of publication of a CVE report. More specifically, our classification extracts information from the source and the summary of the vulnerabilities, which are always present in the CVE report. Additional features are then constructed from public sources of information using data in the summary, as detailed below. More specifically, our classification is made according to the features listed in the next section.

5.1 Classification Features

CVE Source - Every NVD CVE report includes a Source, which identifies the entity that initially published the vulnerability report. While normally ignored in the context of exploitability prediction, we found it useful to incorporate this datum as a feature since it is always present in new reports.

Number of Attack Reports for Vendors and Products - The products and vendors associated with CVEs can be identified via the CPEs mapped to them, in the CVE reports. However, CPE information is often missing in the initial reporting of a CVE. To circumvent this limitation, we have developed an algorithm to extract the product and the vendor from the summary.

We extracted a list of all vendors from the NVD's CPE dictionary and searched for the presence of any listed vendors in the CVE summary. Applying a similar method to identify product names is impractical for several reasons. Firstly, the product list in the CPE feed is not consistently updated. Additionally, certain product names (such as 'core', 'firmware', or 'service') are common and may appear as part of a sentence in the summary without actually referring to a specific product.

Therefore, in order to identify product names in the summary, we follow these steps: Firstly, we locate the vendor's name in the summary. Subsequently, any capitalized word immediately following the vendor's name is considered as the product name, with the exception of a precompiled list of common keywords, including 'version' and 'aka'. The majority of summaries contains a phrase similar to 'a vulnerability has been reported in [Vendor]'s [product]'. Consequently, the method described above is sufficient to pinpoint the product in nearly all cases. This was confirmed through a manual verification of a sample of reports.

Using every vendor and product names as features in the classification model would lead to the curse of dimensionality due to the large number of products and vendors. Moreover, we aim to map the vendor and product's relation to the exploitability of vulnerabilities. To address this, we conducted a search for both product and vendor names in Greynoise's dataset, aiming to ascertain the number of attack incidents reported for each vendor and product. Subsequently, we employ the DBSCAN algorithm to categorize vendors and products based on the frequency of attack reports found in Greynoise, resulting in the formation of 18 distinct clusters. We assign each CVE to a cluster based on the highest number of reports associated with either the vendor or the product. We included this cluster as another feature for our classification model.

It's important to note that Greynoise reports may explicitly mention either the product or the vendor name. Therefore, it is essential to search both product and vendor names in Greynoise's dataset.

TF-IDF of Keywords from the CVEs' Summaries - We further extract keywords from CVE summaries to use as features in our classification model. This task is performed by applying the TF-IDF algorithm on the summary text.

The text is first preprocessed to eliminate stop words. Words are reduced to their roots via stemming. We then perform synonym replacement, in order to treat synonymous words as identical within the TF-IDF framework. For example, we consider the words 'buffer overflow' and 'buffer overrun' as synonyms, and treat them as common occurrences of the same word for the purposes of classification.

Then, in order to extract keywords from the cleaned text, we apply n-gram with $n = 1$ and $n = 2$ along with TF-IDF. Note that we tested TF-IDF with larger n-gram lengths, but $n = 1$ and $n = 2$ provided us with the best results. Among the TF-IDF keywords, we used the top 100 keywords with the highest percentage of appearance in exploited CVEs and low percentage of appearance in non-exploited CVEs, as well as the top 100 keywords with the highest appearance in non-exploited CVEs with low presence in exploited CVEs. This list of keywords and their percentage and difference are reported in our Github repository[2].

Word Count of the Summary. In addition to keywords, we also use the word count of the summary as a feature. This datum was frequently used in previous approaches from the literature.

Commonly Used Software. EPSS v.2 includes the names of 7 vendors as discriminating features, while EPSS v.3 considers 1000 different vendor names. In total, the Platform Enumeration (CPE) Dictionary includes over 17,630 vendors. We wished to incorporate information about the vendor (reconstructed from the summary as described above) without unduly multiplying the number of features. To this end, we created three additional features that indicate (1) If the vendor is commonly known; (2) the size (number of employees) of the vendor; and (3) if the code is open-source.

We asserted that a vendor or product is *commonly known* if there is a Wikipedia dedicated it. This task was performed using an automated script, but we manually verified a random sample of the results to ensure that we did not mistakenly include unrelated pages to topics that share the same name as a software product or vendor.

In addition, we created a script that extracts the number of employees from the Wikipedia page of the vendor (if it exists). The different numbers of employees are then grouped into 14 clusters using the DBSCAN algorithm, with epsilon value 1000, and the cluster is used as a classification feature.

We ascertain that a software is open-source if any one of the following 3 elements holds: (1) there exists a Wikipedia page for the product which identifies it as open-source; (2) the product is listed in the Open-Source Directory[3] or (3) if the CVE report includes a link to a Github or Gitlab repository. We note in passing that even though links to external resources are usually added in the days after a vulnerability is published, links to the source code (if available) are normally present at the onset. Taken together, these three features allow us to take into account information about the vendor and the product, without including an explicit list of vendors and products as is the case with EPSS and other methods.

Figure 2 illustrates the process of feature extraction in our methodology.

[2] https://github.com/kkhanmohammadi/ExploitabilityBirthMark.

[3] https://opensourcesoftwaredirectory.com/.

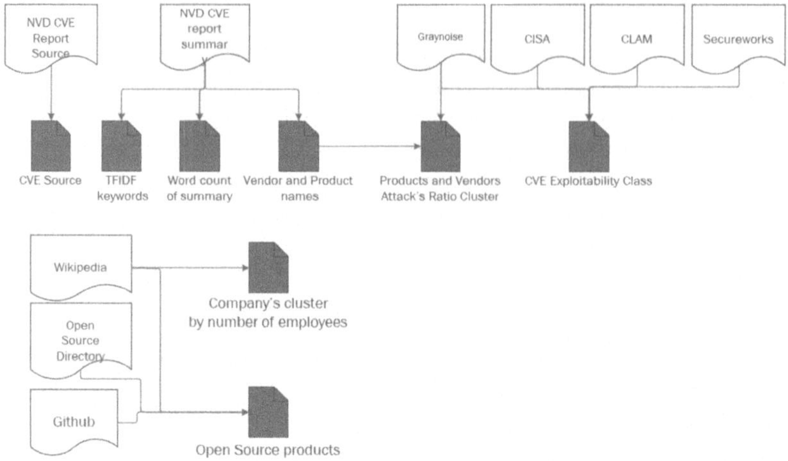

Fig. 2. Overview of the methodology to obtain ExploitabilityBirthMark features.

Finally, the complete list of features used in our classification is available in Table 2.

Table 2. Features used by ExploitabilityBirthMark for predicting Exploitability.

Features	Type	#
CVE source	String	1
Cluster of attack ratio for Vendors and Products	Category	18
TF-IDF of keywords from CVE report summary	String	200
Total word count of the vulnerability summary	Integer	1
Is the product open source	Binary	1
Is the product well known	Binary	1
Cluster of vendors' number of employees	Category	14

5.2 Modeling

Having identified a set of relevant features to perform exploitability prediction, we proceed to select the optimal machine learning algorithm for this task. This selection requires consideration of several characteristics of our dataset;

Firstly, our dataset is highly imbalanced, with the number of CVEs exploited in the wild being 25 times fewer than the number of unexploited CVEs. Secondly, most of the features within our dataset are binary, and we are dealing with sparse features. For example, certain keywords identified through TF-IDF analysis are predominantly associated with exploited CVEs, whereas they are absent in others. Given these considerations, XGBoost emerged as a suitable choice for our dataset. To validate our choice of machine learning algorithm, we also evaluated

RandomForest and Bernoulli, two well-regarded supervised learning algorithms. The experiments conducted and the modeling results confirmed the effectiveness of the approach selected.

We used `GridSearch` to identify the optimal parameters for our dataset. The parameter values obtained from `GridSearch` are detailed in Table 3. To address the class imbalance, we applied a class weight when training, where the weight is set to the class' number of instances divided by the total number of instances.

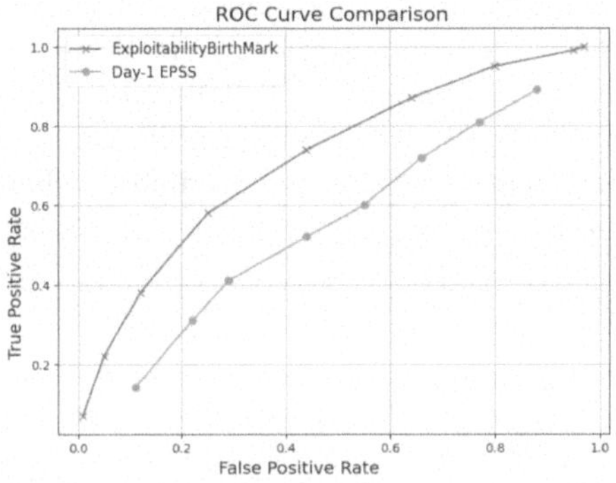

Fig. 3. Comparison between ExploitabilityBirthMark and Day-1 EPSS for Effort.

Table 3. XGBoost Model Parameters.

Parameter	Value
colsample_bytree	0.7
gamma	0
learning_rate	0.1
max_depth	6
min_child_weight	1
n_estimators	200
reg_alpha	0.01
reg_lambda	0.1
subsample	0.9
scale_pos_weight	$\frac{\sum(y==1)}{\sum(y==0)} = 25$

5.3 Results and Evaluation

Following Jacobs et al. [6], we evaluate the effectiveness of using XGBoost using the notion of *Effort* which quantifies the number of all CVEs classified as exploited and accordingly processed, including those inaccurately classified as exploited, out of the total number of CVEs. This metric consists of the receiver operating characteristic (ROC) curve, and is named *Effort* because it encapsulates the potential workload faced by security analysts tasked with patching any vulnerability deemed likely to be exploited. Specifically, when a CVE unlikely to be exploited in the wild is mistakenly identified as exploited by the model, it may lead to an unnecessary allocation of resources towards these vulnerabilities.

To evaluate the performance of our methodology, we calculated the mean of the specified metrics across a 5-fold evaluation on our XGBoost model. Given the small dataset, a time series split is not used for either approach. We computed the Effort obtained by using ExploitabilityBirthMark as a predictor of exploitability, and compare the result to a reimplemented EPSS v2, which only takes into account data available on the day a vulnerability is published. Figure 3 illustrates the Effort in both cases.

As can be seen in the Figure, an analyst who patches the top 30% of CVEs identified as most likely to be exploited according to our model would address nearly 70% of the CVEs that are actually exploited. In contrast, the percentage of exploited vulnerabilities that are patched drops to approximately 40% if the analyst patches the top 30% vulnerabilities with the highest EPSS v2 score.

It's important to stress that our method might underperform relative to EPSS if a vulnerability is initially published with extensive data. However, this limitation is acceptable, as our approach is specifically designed to address situations where data is sparse.

6 Conclusion

In this paper, we present a novel method to assess the likelihood of vulnerabilities being exploited, which relies exclusively on information that is always available on the day a CVE report is initially published. The availability of an early signal of exploitability can significantly reduce costs for companies by allowing them to prioritize efforts in mitigating the threats posed by these vulnerabilities. Our method performs favorably compared to a replication of existing predictors when operating in a context of limited information.

References

1. Alperin, K., Wollaber, A.B., Ross, D.M., Trepagnier, P.C., Leonard, L.: Risk prioritization by leveraging latent vulnerability features in a contested environment. In: 12th ACM Workshop on Artificial Intelligence and Security (2019)
2. Bhatt, N., Anand, A., Yadavalli, V.: Exploitability prediction of software vulnerabilities. Qual. Reliab. Eng. **37** (2020)
3. Brilhante, M.d.F., Pestana, D., Pestana, P., Rocha, M.L.: Measuring the risk of vulnerabilities exploitation. Appl. Math **4**(1), 20–54 (2023)
4. Edkrantz, M.: Predicting Exploit Likelihood for Cyber Vulnerabilities with Machine Learning. Master's thesis, Chalmers University (2015)
5. Jacobs, J., Romanosky, S., Edwards, B., Adjerid, I., Roytman, M.: Exploit prediction scoring system (EPSS). Digital Threats **2**(3) (2021)
6. Jacobs, J., Romanosky, S., Suciu, O., Edwards, B., Sarabi, A.: Enhancing vulnerability prioritization: Data-driven exploit predictions with community-driven insights. In: 2023 IEEE European Symposium on Security and Privacy Workshops, pp. 194–206 (2023)
7. Khanmohammadi, K., Khoury, R.: Half-day vulnerabilities: a study of the first days of CVE entries. In: Conference on Applied Machine Learning in Information Security CAMLIS (November 2023)
8. Labrèche, F., Paquette, S.O.: Threat class predictor: an explainable framework for predicting vulnerability threat using topic and trend modeling. In: Proceedings of the 5th Conference on Applied Machine Learning for Information Security (2022)
9. Poireault, K.: NIST NVD disruption sees CVE enrichment on hold (2024). https://www.infosecurity-magazine.com/news/nist-vulnerability-database/
10. Sabottke, C., Suciu, O., Dumitras, T.: Vulnerability disclosure in the age of social media: exploiting twitter for predicting real-world exploits. In: 24th USENIX Security Symposium (USENIX Security 15), pp. 1041–1056 (2015)
11. Suciu, O., Nelson, C., Lyu, Z., Bao, T., Dumitras, T.: Expected exploitability: predicting the development of functional vulnerability exploits. In: 31st USENIX Security Symposium, pp. 377–394. Boston, MA (2022)
12. Younis, A., Malaiya, Y.K., Ray, I.: Assessing vulnerability exploitability risk using software properties. Softw. Qual. J. **24**(1), 159-202 (2016)

Author Index

K. Adi et al. (Eds.): FPS 2024, LNCS 15533, pp. 201–202, 2025.
https://doi.org/10.1007/978-3-031-87496-3

The manufacturer's authorised representative in the EU is Springer Nature Customer Service Centre GmbH, Europaplatz 3, 69115 Heidelberg, Germany. If you have any concerns regarding our products, please contact ProductSafety@springernature.com

Printed and bound by CPI Group (UK) Ltd, Croydon, CR0 4YY
30/09/2026
02225585-0001